YELLOWSTONE
AND THE GREAT WEST

EDITED BY MARLENE DEAHL MERRILL

YELLOWSTONE
AND THE GREAT WEST

Journals, Letters, and Images from
the 1871 Hayden Expedition

University of Nebraska Press, Lincoln and London

© 1999 by the University of Nebraska Press. All rights reserved.
Manufactured in the United
States of America. ⊚ Library of
Congress Cataloging-in-Publica-
tion Data. Yellowstone and the
Great West : journals, letters, and
images from the 1871 Hayden
Expedition / edited by Marlene
Deahl Merrill. p. cm. In-
cludes bibliographical references
and index. ISBN 0-8032-3148-2
(cl. : alk. paper) 1. Yellowstone
National Park – Discovery and
exploration – Sources. 2. West
(U.S.) – Discovery and exploration – Sources. 3. Yellowstone
National Park – Description and
travel. 4. West (U.S.) – Description and travel. 5. Hayden,
F. V. (Ferdinand Vandeveer),
1829–1887. 6. Geological and
Geographical Survey of the Territories (U.S.) I. Merrill, Marlene. F722.Y33 1999
978.7'5202 – dc21 99-12068 CIP
ISBN 978-0-8032-8289-6 (pa. : alk. paper)

IN MEMORY OF MY PARENTS,
ORLO AND JESSIE DEAHL,
WHO, IN THE 1940S,
INTRODUCED ME TO
THEIR TREASURED YELLOWSTONE
AND TO WHAT IS NOW
GRAND TETON NATIONAL PARK
AND
FOR MY CHILDREN,
STEPHEN DEAHL MERRILL AND
KAREN RUTH MERRILL,
AND MY GRANDSON,
THEO JACKSON UMPHREY MERRILL,
WHO ARE BUILDING THEIR OWN
MEMORIES OF AND VISIONS FOR
"THIS GREAT WEST"

If these explorations in the far West shall
tend to the honor of our country or to
the increase of human knowledge, the
main object will be attained.

FERDINAND HAYDEN

Preliminary Report
of the United States
Geological Survey
of Montana and Portions
of Adjacent Territories

Contents

Illustrations

Preface

This book presents the first daily account of the historic 1871 Yellowstone Survey. Led by geologist Ferdinand Hayden, the survey explored Utah, Idaho, Montana, and Wyoming Territories, providing a vast amount of new scientific and practical information about these areas. This work, in turn, led to the formulation and successful passage of a congressional bill that in 1872 set aside a large part of the Upper Valley of the Yellowstone as the world's first, and probably best-known, national park.

As if this were not enough, the survey will long be remembered for the work of its official photographer, William Henry Jackson, and its guest artist, Thomas Moran. Jackson's startling photographs and Moran's luminous watercolor and oil paintings created the earliest on-site images of the area—images that have shaped the public perception of Yellowstone and the American West to this day.

Secondary descriptions of this survey abound in books and articles published over the past one hundred years. Many, if not most, of these accounts are deeply flawed because of their heavy reliance on Hayden's and Jackson's published writings about the expedition. These writings include Jackson's two misremembered recollections, both written (with the assistance and intervention of coauthors) decades after the survey, and Hayden's detailed official report as well as his popular and scientific articles, prepared soon after the survey. The fact that Jackson and Hayden remain the survey's two most famous members lends credence to the belief that their expedition accounts are both reliable and complete. This, however, is not the case. Just as their publications omit important facts, they contain errors and misleading claims concerning the survey's discoveries and accomplishments.

There is much more to the survey's story than the accounts of Jackson and Hayden. Until now, only scattered unpublished letters and newspaper articles written at the time of the survey have been readily available to western history scholars and enthusiasts. The daily narrative presented here is drawn primarily from the unpublished journals kept by two survey members, supplemented by additional primary documents. This narrative is fully annotated, based on a careful reading of related reports, correspondence, and articles of the period.

Jackson's two autobiographies, *Pioneer Photographer* (1929) and *Time Exposure* (1940), include his recollections of the 1871 Yellowstone expedition. For instance, in *Time Exposure* Jackson asserts that the Hayden party was the first group of white men — on record — to visit Mammoth Hot Springs. Inasmuch as the party was greeted there by squatters who had staked out a claim to the area, as well as another group of men who were enjoying the benefits of bathing in the hot springs, Jackson's claim is more than merely misleading. This is not surprising. Jackson waited more than fifty years to write his 1929 account, and *Time Exposure* was written still later, when he was in his late nineties. By this time he had embellished stories and confused his work on the 1871 expedition with his participation in Hayden's second Yellowstone survey a year later.

Although Jackson claimed to have consulted his field journals in preparing both autobiographies, no diary of the 1871 survey exists in either of the two repositories that now hold his journal collections — the New York Public Library Manuscript Collection and the Colorado Historical Society in Denver. Also in the New York Public Library there are some of Jackson's typescript recollections of his participation in the Hayden surveys, including the 1871 survey. It remains unclear whether Jackson's typescript of the 1871 expedition was based on a diary that has now disappeared or whether it was based only on his recollections. Late in his life Jackson and his son, Clarence, reportedly destroyed a great deal of his personal material, perhaps including his 1871 diary (see Hales 1988, 285–86).

Similarly, Hayden, who was a prolific writer and publicist, apparently disposed of his 1871 field journal, as well as journals or notes from all his other surveys. His once immensely popular, but now seldom read, annual reports (published by the Government Printing Office) remain the most complete scientific account of his surveys. Hayden described them as "a somewhat crude . . . mass of observations" detailing what he observed along the survey route. He wanted them published quickly so the survey's findings could be used by the public, by people considering emigrating to new western territories, for instance. We know, however, that he relied on field journals after his first (1867) and second (1868) western surveys, when he forwarded them directly from the field to Washington DC, where they were published without his editing or supervision (see Hayden's introduction to his *First* [1867], *Second* [1868], *and Third* [1869] *Annual Reports*, published in 1873).

By 1871, however, Hayden realized the value of editing his journals in order to publish a coherent and positive account of the survey's work. These reports were, after all, becoming increasingly important, for they helped Hayden ensure continued government funding for his western surveys and fed his growing reputation as the most popular interpreter of western lands and resources.

Hayden's 1871 survey report was published in 1872 as a "preliminary report" (hereafter cited as Hayden 1872a or Fifth Report). He did not immediately follow it with a final report but later incorporated some of the survey's more important findings in a massive general résumé of the geology of the West, written in 1878 (but not published until 1883) as his Twelfth (and final) Report.

No matter how "preliminary" Hayden intended his Fifth Report to be, it remains an indispensable source of detailed observations about the geology and natural history of the areas visited by the party. There is a great deal more to relate about the human story of this expedition, however. Hayden makes scant reference to the negative aspects of the experience — the times the party was lost, and the blunders, hardships, and disappointments that also were an integral part of the survey's history. He also fails to identify most of the survey's support party (the cooks, packers, hunters, and guides) or to acknowledge many of the scientific contributions made by individual members of the survey.

Fortunately, two unpublished personal journals and a series of letters survive. Written from the field, they chronicle in detail both the scientific and the human story of the 1871 Yellowstone expedition. The journals — the only known extant journals of this expedition — were written by two members of the survey: the geologist George Allen and the mineralogist Albert Peale. They contain a lively record of Allen's and Peale's daily work and personal experiences, as the party trekked through the territories of Wyoming, Utah, Idaho, and Montana. Aside from a brief gap in late September, the journal entries cover the full period of the survey from May 25 to October 6, 1871.

Because Allen was unable to withstand the rigors of the trip, he left the party just as it was preparing to enter Yellowstone. Nevertheless, his accounts provide articulate descriptions of the party's early route and of the operation of the survey. They also describe Allen's personal reactions to camp life and the changing western landscape with its developing or dying settlements and towns.

Albert Peale was also keeping a written record of his observations, but unlike Allen, he wrote only sparse and factual accounts during the early part of the expedition. As the party approached the Yellowstone area, however, Peale's accounts became more detailed and personal, and by the time George Allen left, Peale was providing engaging accounts of his and the party's experiences.

This fortunate meshing of Allen's and Peale's journals dictated how I have presented the expedition narrative for this book. Allen's journal provides the beginning and early narrative. This is followed by a brief section containing both Allen's and Peale's entries; and finally, after Allen's departure, Peale's journal supplies the remaining narrative. For readers who are interested in Peale's complete journal account, I have included his early portions (those not in the expedition narrative) in appendix 2.

I have also included in the journal narrative a series of ten letters written by Hayden during the expedition to his mentor and friend, Spencer Fullerton Baird, then assistant secretary of the Smithsonian Institution. Baird arranged for excerpts of these letters to be published in *Harper's Weekly* during the course of the survey, but he first made sure the published version did not include any of Hayden's personal comments or opinions. With the chronological incorporation of Hayden's original letters into the expedition narrative, readers have an opportunity to learn what Hayden wished to accomplish in the survey, how he evaluated the work of individual party members, and how he reacted to Yellowstone's dramatic features and diverse natural history.

In order to provide a still richer and more detailed text, I have woven portions of two other documents, also written by Allen and Peale during the expedition, into this survey narrative. They are from George Allen's field notebook and from Peale's field "letters," which were written to and later published by the *Philadelphia Press*.

Peale's *Press* "letters" originated from campsites that were established for at least two days in order to rest the party and their horses. Although Peale based these letters primarily on his journal accounts, they are not verbatim copies. Because he had more time for writing during these layovers, he was able to take earlier, hastily written entries and elaborate on them in a more thoughtful manner. He also added occasional new information that he undoubtedly later recalled or learned about from other party members. Until now, members of the survey's support party have remained unidentified. Fortunately, at the back of George Allen's journal is his invaluable list of the name and the primary job of each man in the party. For the first time, their names and the duties they performed appear here along with the names of the official survey members.

I have frequently consulted another Yellowstone official report, also written in the summer of 1871. Its primary author, Captain John W. Barlow, led a small army survey team through Yellowstone at the same time as the Hayden Survey. Barlow and his men joined the Hayden party in southern Montana Territory just as Hayden's group prepared to enter the Yellowstone area. Although the two parties did not work in tandem, they frequently explored the same areas at or about the same time, and they shared information as well as similar experiences. Furthermore, Barlow and Hayden occasionally took side trips together. Barlow's published account is extremely valuable, not only for its own sake but also for what it tells us about the Hayden party. I have included relevant information from Barlow's journal in notes at the back of this volume.

The publication of this book also provides an opportunity to present rarely seen drawings and photographs, also created on the scene. Guest artist Thomas Moran's watercolor sketches and his later finished paintings of Yellowstone so captured the public's attention in the years immediately following the survey that the work of the survey's official artist, Henry Wood Elliott, was largely ignored. Unlike Moran, Elliott was self-taught, and his early natural talent for realistic drawing led to his appointment at the Smithsonian Institution at age sixteen. There he illustrated fossil specimens and studied natural history. His skills were enhanced when he learned to draw carefully detailed landscape panoramas, a field assignment he began on Hayden's 1869 survey of the Colorado and New Mexico Territories.

By 1871 Elliott had noticeably sharpened his artistic and topographical talents, and he created field panoramas that, if laid end to end, would measure some twenty-seven feet and would illustrate the party's route from Ogden, Utah, to Bozeman, Montana. Each panorama usually included such details as the identification of campsites, small ranches along the route, stage stops, and developing settlements. Elliott also identified canyons, geological formations, lakes, streams, and rivers. These panoramas are among the Elliott drawings deposited at the National Archives, the Yellowstone Museum, and the USGS Library in Denver.

Once the party reached Yellowstone, Elliott also made smaller, more informal sketches of special features, such as geysers, waterfalls, and mud-pots. These sketches, along with a few landscape sections, were used as illustrations for Hayden's Fifth Report. Also during the expedition Elliott tried his hand at painting, although only one watercolor (a scene of Yellowstone Lake that he presented to survey manager James Stevenson) has been located.

Hayden recognized the value of Elliott's work both during and after the expedition. In addition to using some of Elliott's drawings to illustrate his official report, in 1872 he arranged for a limited edition of one hundred copies of selected panoramas and drawings by Elliott (done during the 1869, 1870, and 1871 surveys) to be reproduced by photolithography and published under the title *Profiles, Sections, and Other Illustrations*. The subtitle of this now-rare volume suggests the importance of Elliott's work to Hayden, for it reads, "Designed to Accompany the Final Report of the Chief Geologist of the Survey and Sketched under His Direction."

It was not to be, however. Elliott left the survey soon after returning from Yellowstone, and the panoramas of his replacement, artist-topographer William Henry Holmes, appeared in Hayden's twelfth and final report, published in 1883. Despite the rightful claim that Holmes "was perhaps the greatest artist-topographer . . . that the West ever produced" (Goetzmann 1966, 512), I have included portions of an 1871 Elliott panorama (from his *Profiles, Sketches, and Other Illustrations*) as an illustrative heading for each of the ten chapters. Perhaps they will allow readers to "see" some of the panoramas that the party saw as it made its away across an ever-changing West—panoramas that were too vast to be captured by any nineteenth-century camera lens.

Many of William Henry Jackson's photographs that illustrate this book feature camp scenes or candid portraits of members of the survey team. Unlike his now-familiar landscape photographs, which were quickly made available to the public through his published catalogs, few of Jackson's more informal photographs have been published. Because Jackson developed his photographs soon after taking them, he often presented them to fellow members of the survey or to people the party met along the way. Many of these remain unidentified or are in private hands. The photographs used here are from the following repositories: the National Archives, Washington DC; the National Gallery, Washington DC; the Photographic Library at the USGS Field Records Library, Federal Center, Denver; the Swann Gallery, Inc., New York City; and the Yellowstone Research Library, Park Headquarters, Mammoth WY.

Four appendices follow the text. The first provides biographical sketches of some survey members. The second, as already noted, is a transcription of the early portion of Peale's journal that is not included in the expedition narrative. The third is Allen's brief description of a portion of the survey route that he wrote especially for a then-absent fellow survey member. The fourth is a synopsis of Hayden's draft report to the Committee on the Public Lands, which states his reasons for supporting the official Yellowstone Park Bill, and the park bill itself, passed by Congress and signed by President Grant on March 1, 1872. Finally, a glossary of geological terms is followed by the References.

Acknowledgments

Without the acquisition by the Oberlin College Archives of Professor George Allen's field notebook and his personal journal — both written while Allen served on the 1871 Hayden expedition — this book would not have been possible. Both documents were part of a large, well-cared-for collection of family papers which from 1936 to 1996 were sent periodically to the college. I was first alerted to the acquisition of Allen's field notebook in the early 1980s by the former college archivist, William Bigglestone. Several years later the remaining and largest share of the collection began arriving, including Allen's personal journal, as the gift of two sisters, Ellen Spears and the late Carolyn Miller. I gratefully acknowledge not only the Spears-Miller gifts but also the effort of College Archivist Roland Baumann, who was instrumental in expediting the acquisition process and provided me with comfortable space for the tedious transcription process of the Allen documents. He and the archival staff, Ken Grossi and Tammy Martin, assisted me in many valuable ways. Bill Bigglestone has shared his considerable knowledge of George Allen with me, and over the years has contributed the kind of support, interest, and advice so needed in preparing this kind of documentary book. I also wish to thank Clayton Koppes, dean of the College of Arts and Sciences at Oberlin College, who showed an interest in my work from its inception and helped provide college funds for the publication of additional photographs by William Henry Jackson.

Wyoming geologist David Love took an early interest in my work and provided me with a master's thesis on Ferdinand Hayden written in 1978 at the University of Wyoming by Sandra Oliver. Oliver's thesis alerted me to the existence of Albert Peale's 1871 Yellowstone journals, which, when combined with Allen's half-finished account of the Yellowstone Survey, made it possible to provide a complete narrative of the survey. Later Dr.

Love and historian Richard Bartlett endorsed my ideas for this volume when I applied for (and received) a research travel grant in 1990 from the Wyoming Council for the Humanities.

The archive and museum staff at Yellowstone's Research Library in Mammoth Hot Springs provided uniformly gracious and enthusiastic assistance from my earliest research visits there in the late 1980s, when Beth Blacker served as museum curator and Tom Tankersley as park historian. Lee Whittlesey, the present park archivist and a Yellowstone historian, has helped me in more ways than I could ever enumerate. A partial list includes sharing with me his thorough knowledge of Yellowstone history and his immense firsthand knowledge of the park itself based on his earlier service as a ranger-naturalist. He served as a careful reader of my manuscript at different stages of its completion and offered valuable suggestions for changes and additions.

Aubrey Haines, retired Yellowstone Park historian, has also contributed greatly to this work. His two-volume history, *The Yellowstone Story*, remains the definitive history of the park, and I drew from it again and again in editing the survey narrative and preparing the many notes. Mr. Haines also carefully read the final draft of my manuscript, corrected a number of errors, and called into question some place-name identifications as well as the dating of one Jackson photograph. His detailed and gracious responses to the manuscript and to my inquiries have made this a better book.

I am also indebted to historian Mike Foster, who in 1991 published the first book-length biography of Ferdinand Hayden, *Strange Genius*. An early and enthusiastic supporter of my research, he helped me determine the scope and content of this work and contributed important factual information as a reader of the manuscript. Another Hayden scholar, James Cassidy, who is completing his own biography of Hayden, also critiqued a semifinal form of the manuscript and contributed many valuable suggestions, especially for filling out the introduction and afterword.

I have turned to other historians and scientists for assistance in preparing some of the more complex or technical notes, the geological glossary, and editorial explanations in the introduction and afterword. I am especially grateful to Cliff Nelson, United States Geological Survey historian and geologist, who read portions of the manuscript and provided me with suggested readings, especially on the subject of Hayden's early paleographic work with Fielding Bradford Meek. I also thank two members of the Department of Geology at Oberlin College, William Skinner and Keith Meldahl, who reviewed my geological glossary for accuracy and were helpful consultants on several other geological questions.

Historians Robert Righter and Sherry Smith provided me with the kind of deeply appreciated professional and personal friendship that enriched my work immeasurably. Dr. Righter was also an astute reader of my manuscript. Thomas Offutt, director of the Yellowstone Foundation, has been an enthusiastic supporter of this project ever since he read an early draft of the manuscript. I've greatly appreciated his encouragement and thoughtful advice.

My indebtedness to the published writings of historians is reflected in my notes. I am especially grateful for the work of Richard Bartlett, Mike Foster, William H. Goetzmann, Aubrey Haines, Joni Kinsey, and Lee Whittlesey. I also thank all those who have commented on my manuscript, even when I have disagreed with them on certain points. Collectively, they have saved me from many errors, but I take full responsibility for those that remain.

When I began this project, information about the survey topographer, Anton Schönborn, was quite meager. B. J. Earle at the BLM office in Buffalo, Wyoming, had recently begun researching Schönborn's life and was acquiring new information about him. Ms. Earle generously shared her findings with me as well as her ideas for further research. Rick Stewart, currently the director of the Amon Carter Museum, also provided me with information on Schönborn, including a catalog from an earlier watercolor exhibition of Schönborn's western forts, held at the museum.

Many people at both large and small libraries, historical societies, and museums provided me with helpful assistance, whether I visited them personally or wrote for information. I especially thank Carol Edwards at the United States Geological Survey Field Records Library in Denver for undertaking the preservation of the Peale journal deposited there and for making my research visits there productive and enjoyable. I wish it were possible to thank the late Fritiof Fryxell and J. V. Howell for the many years they researched the Hayden surveys. Their work resulted in the superb Fritiof M. Fryxell Collection (#1638) now on deposit at the American Heritage Center in Laramie. Emmet Chissum, former research historian, assisted me while the collection was still housed in the University of Wyoming library. After it moved to its new quarters, Rick Ewig, the current archivist, and the center's former director, Gene Gressly, assisted me with my work and contributed to making my time in Laramie most pleasant.

Ralph Ehrenberg, director of the map division at the Library of Congress, patiently helped me search for an elusive mountain identified on maps and in the Peale and Allen journals as "Mt. Madison." So did Bill Resor, a Jackson Hole rancher and historian, whose outstanding private collection of maps plus his own familiarity with the country surrounding both Yellowstone and Grand Teton parks makes him a valuable resource on all questions relating to early maps and local geography. My great thanks especially go to Rod Drewien, from the Hornacher Wildlife Institute at the University of Idaho, who over a period of several months sought to locate, by car and airplane, the "Mt. Madison" that was described in 1871 by Allen, Hayden, and Peale and that appeared on maps of the time. Dr. Drewien was able to narrow down the mountain's actual location and present name to one of two adjoining mountains in southwestern Montana.

In July 1990, during a visit to the Beaverhead County Museum in Dillon, Montana, Everett Johnson, president of the museum society, graciously provided me with information on the geography and history of the shortcut route taken by the Hayden party from present-day Monida to Virginia City.

My thanks also go to Mark Frazier Lloyd, director of archives at the University of Pennsylvania, who explained Hayden's arrangement (as adjunct professor) with the medical school there. He also provided me with biographical information on Albert Peale, Robert Adams, and Charles Turnbull — all graduates of the university.

Leslie Reinhardt, editorial assistant at the Peale Family Papers in Washington DC, located several letters by and to Albert Peale in the collection, although she was unable to locate any documents relating to Peale's work on the 1871 Hayden Survey.

I'm also grateful to Bill Deiss, Bruce Kirby, and Bill Cox at the Smithsonian Institution Archives, who assisted me in numerous ways. Similarly, Bob Clark, Brian Shovers, and Dave Walter — all on the staff of the Montana Historical Society — promptly answered my questions about place-names and settlers in early Montana Territory. Linda Thatcher, reference librarian at the Utah Historical Society, located in old city directories the addresses of several Salt Lake City establishments referred to in the diaries. In attempting to discover more information about Albert Peale's little-known father, Charles Willson Peale II, I was helped by Linda Stanley at the Historical Society of Pennsylvania, Judith A. Meier at the Historical Society of Montgomery County, and several reference librarians at the Norristown Public Library. Staff at the Library of the American Philosophical Society, especially Jan Ballard, provided prompt responses to my questions. John M. Pfeffer Jr., newspaper researcher at the Philadelphia Public Library, carefully checked through six months' worth of *Philadelphia Press* issues to locate A. C. Peale's published letters for me.

Oberlin College Library's valuable collection of U.S. Geological Survey reports and other related documents is due in no small measure to the many personal contributions made to the college by Ferdinand Hayden, class of 1850. Ready access to all this historical material made my work much easier. For material that was not available at the library, I am most grateful for the assistance of the library's reference and interlibrary loan staff, Diane Lee and Michael Palazzolo. I especially thank Ray English, director of the Oberlin College Libraries; Allison Gould, head of circulation; Cynthia Comer, head of the Reference Department; Marjorie Henderson, library technician; Sharon Miller, stack supervisor; and the staff at the Irvin E. Houck Computing Center, especially Kevin Weidenbaum, Reg Lyman, and Shelby Warrens.

Identifying, locating, and arranging for publication the images used to illustrate this book required assistance from a number of people. I am grateful to the staffs at the National Archives for facilitating my inspection of their collection of Henry Elliott's panoramic drawings and their valuable nineteenth-century western maps. I also thank Martha Sandweiss of Amherst College for her helpful advice on questions relating to the book's illustrations. Early on, I was fortunate to make contact with Carl Droppers of Berea, Ohio, whose wife, Ruth Elliott Droppers, is the granddaughter of the survey artist Henry Wood Elliott. She possessed a sizable collection of her grandfather's papers, as well as slides of his drawings and panoramas, which her husband has organized and catalogued. He shared much of this collection with me and also provided me with valuable information about Elliott's Alaskan career. Mr. Droppers also put me in touch with another Elliott grandchild in Gunnison, Colorado, the late Marsha Julio. Mrs. Julio and her husband, Pat, corresponded with me for several years, sent me a number of photographs and documents related to Henry Elliott's life and career, and even provided me with a route they had prepared of the 1871 Hayden Survey on contemporary road maps. This map was a valuable aid in preparing a similar map for this book.

Hallam Webber, a collector and scholar of nineteenth-century photographs, generously shared with me his discoveries of several little-known Jackson photographs taken on the 1871 Hayden Survey. Another Jackson scholar, Bob Blair, used his vast knowledge of Jackson's photographs to help me date several illustrations used in this book. I especially thank Joe McGregor, head of the photographic library at the USGS Field Records Library in Denver, who spent many hours sorting through the library's collection of Jackson photographs to assist me in identifying those photos mentioned in the journal narratives. Bob Grove, in the photographic department at the National Gallery, helped me select a number of Jackson's 1871 photographs from the Yellowstone collection that the gallery had recently made available in digitized form. My thanks also go to Steve Jackson, curator of art and photography at the Museum of the Rockies at Montana State University, who graciously shared his knowledge of the photographer Joshua Crissman with me. Leslie Laufler of Swann Galleries, Inc., in New York City, arranged a photo reproduction of a rare Jackson photograph for this book after it had been purchased at a Swann auction. I am most appreciative for an entire afternoon spent with Mary Frances Iammarino, curator of fine arts at the Cleveland Museum of Natural History, who showed and described to me the museum's large collection of Henry Elliott's magnificent watercolors of Alaskan seals.

I am grateful to several people connected with Oberlin College who advised me or produced the digitized images of the Henry Elliott drawings used for chapter headings in this book, especially Fred Zwegat, director of the audio-visual department; John Appley, project director of the college communications office; Whitney Pape, special collections curator; Michelle Landau, electronics intern; and Stefan Yost, assistant curator of western art at the Allen Art Museum. Far from Oberlin, John Olsen at Blissnet Computer Services in Jackson, Wyoming, prepared a Jackson photograph for me in digitized form.

I am also indebted to Martha Merrill Pickrell and Karan Cutler, who, while engaged in their own writing projects, read my manuscript and provided me with valuable stylistic advice.

Family members, friends, and colleagues also helped me with a great variety of tasks related to this book. Some served as readers at different stages of the manuscript, others helped with proofreading, while others provided me with advice, information, or contacts with other Yellowstone scholars. I am very grateful to David Delo, Alfred MacKay, Geoffrey Blodgett, Norman and Barbara Care, Ricky Clark, Sid Comings, Barbara Eastman and Tom Kimbrough, Dorothy Holbrook, Nancy Day Merrill, the late Jackson Hole scholar Lee Ortenberger, Lynette Palmer, Laurel and Rhys Price Jones, Jean and Walt Reeves, John Schwartz, Martha Umphrey, Joanna Walters, and my Oldsquaw friends Molly Anderson, Louise Dunn, Judy Sheldon, and Betty Weinstock.

My copyeditor, Kim Vivier, contributed careful additions and important corrections. Her patience and expertise mean a lot to me personally and add a great deal to the quality of this book.

Finally, I thank my family. My son, Stephen Merrill, has taken an active interest in this project from its inception and helped me clarify several important portions of the text. My daughter, Karen Merrill, a historian, served as a frequent and always-willing consultant and adviser. She not only shared with me her considerable knowledge of the West but also put me in touch with several scholar-colleagues who assisted me with particular research problems. Most of all, I wish to thank my husband, Dan Merrill, who has enthusiastically and patiently helped me with all aspects of this entire project.

YELLOWSTONE
AND THE GREAT WEST

Editorial Method

The initial transcriptions of George Allen's journal and field notebook (both deposited in the Oberlin College Archives), as well as Albert Peale's journal, on deposit at Yellowstone's Research Library at Mammoth Hot Springs, were done from their original notebooks. Peale, however, kept *two* journal notebooks and seemed to switch randomly between them every few weeks or so. His other journal is deposited with the United States Geological Survey Field Records Library in Denver, where its damaged condition called for preservation before handling for transcription. Its pages were removed, deacidified, and individually encapsulated in Mylar. Photocopies of each encapsulated page were sent to me, and I used them for the initial transcription. When the transcription was complete, I checked it against the original document in Denver.

The process of transcribing the Allen and Peale journals was complicated by the nature of the documents themselves. Each leather-bound notebook, when closed, is not much larger than a medium-sized hand and obviously received hard use. Many pages are torn and spotted, and the cramped handwriting is often barely legible because of the use of blunt, worn pencil points.

Hayden's letters to Baird (deposited at the Smithsonian Institution Archives) were transcribed from unusually clear photocopies. Any transcription difficulties were due to Hayden's notoriously poor handwriting.

Because the journals were often hurriedly written and not intended as literary documents, I have taken some editorial liberties in order to present them in a more readable form. I have broken overlong journal entries into several paragraphs. I have formatted datelines uniformly for all three writers and integrated interlineations into the text by following page markings or contextual clues. I have spelled out ampersands and most abbreviations and supplied missing punctuation. I have retained capitalizations (although they are often haphazard) in accordance with the writing style of the time. I have retained most misspelled words, as well as words with an earlier English spelling (examples: "ranche" and "sulphur") or whose spelling was then undergoing a change in the United States (examples: "Wahsatch" instead of today's "Wasatch," and "travelled/travelling" with two *l*s) and words often appearing in two parts and later spelled as one word (examples: "Fire Hole" and "Beaver Head," which became "Firehole" and "Beaverhead"). Letters and words appearing within brackets signify that a transcription judgment has been made because of a problem with legibility. Italicized words and numerals appearing in brackets are editorial insertions.

The haphazard spellings of names presented a problem. To avoid confusion, the first time a misspelled name appears in the text, it is spelled as it is written but with the correctly spelled name italicized and set within brackets beside it: for example, "Hughes [*Huse*]." Thereafter the name is silently spelled correctly.

Deletions are rare and include only Allen's mentions of repairs being done on his Oberlin house, a brief reference in a Hayden letter to a controversy with another geologist, and several redundant passages in both Allen's and Peale's journals. Peale's long lists of temperatures for groups of hot springs have been omitted from the text; information about them is supplied in corresponding notes. Ellipses indicate where any of these textual deletions occur. Repeated words, however, are silently deleted.

I have also silently altered some awkward word order within sentences to make the text more readable: for example, "It has been cool quite . . ." has been changed to "It has been quite cool. . . ." Because both Allen and Peale had tendencies not to write about the day's events in chronological order, I have silently reordered some portions of their entries where the chronology is particularly confusing. Peale's habit of beginning his entries with "This morning" becomes a tiresome leitmotif throughout his journal, so I have periodically silently deleted these two words or integrated them within the remainder of his first sentence.

Those portions of Allen's field notes and Peale's *Press* letters that are integrated within the text appear enclosed in braces, for example: "After making up bundle, as above, went with Mr. Adams up into cañon nearby {collecting whatever came in my way, but looked in vain for shells}."

Allen's and Peale's location at the end of the day (usually a campsite) appears at the conclusion of their journal entries and is set in italics. These appear only for the first night at a particular location. Except for campsites at the Geyser Basins, which are based on a reading of Peale's journal and Hayden's Fifth Report, all campsite identifications from Ogden to the conclusion of the expedition are modernized spellings of campsites found in the meteorological tables from Hayden's Fifth Report, pages 503–17. I have occasionally supplemented or corrected them, adding information in brackets. Because Allen and Peale often did not know mileage figures from one campsite to another, I have provided them when necessary, based on mileages in the same meteorological tables. Blank brackets indicate the writer omitted relevant information.

Finally, when Peale is close to or in what is today's Yellowstone Park, I have added the official placenames beside his descriptions of well-known features. These names appear in italics and are set within brackets. If the placename was bestowed in 1871 by Hayden, an H appears by the name; if Barlow created the name, a B appears. Excellent histories of Yellowstone placenames are provided by Whittlesey 1988 and Haines 1996.

1. Ferdinand Hayden in 1873. Courtesy of the National Academy of Sciences

2. Professor George Nelson Allen, c. 1870. Courtesy of the Oberlin College Archives

3. Albert C. Peale, c. 1870. Courtesy of the American Heritage Center, University of Wyoming

Introduction

On May 17, 1871, white-bearded George Allen, a fifty-eight-year-old professor of geology, boarded a passenger train in northeast Ohio and headed for the Far West. Several days later Albert Peale, a twenty-two-year-old with a brand-new medical degree, boarded a Philadelphia train also heading west. Both men were traveling to Cheyenne, Wyoming Territory, where they would join some thirty men to form the 1871 Yellowstone expedition. Led by the pioneering geologist Ferdinand Vandeveer Hayden, head of the United States Geological and Geographical Survey of the Territories, this group would become the first scientific party to explore and study the area known today as Yellowstone National Park.

Hayden, forty-two years old in 1871, was already a master of reconnaissance in the Upper Missouri country. Since his first pioneering western geological investigations in 1853, he had explored huge areas in the western territories. Until the Civil War his work had been privately sponsored (primarily by the American Fur Company) or funded by the U.S. Corps of Topographical Engineers. In 1867 Hayden was appointed geologist-in-charge of the geological survey of Nebraska (one of four government surveys under the auspices of the Department of the Interior). These federal surveys became the country's leading scientific bureau in the post–Civil War era and its most productive research organization as well.[1]

By 1871, while serving as an adjunct professor of geology at the University of Pennsylvania, Hayden had expanded his summer surveys into the most ambitious scientific undertaking in the American West. He was revealing the geological structure of western landforms and establishing himself as the foremost collector of rocks, fossils, and natural history specimens in America. One of the best-known scientists of his time, Hayden headed one of the most successful and generously funded government geological surveys in the Western world.[2]

Hayden believed that because his expeditions were made at public expense, their practical purpose should be kept at the forefront. The object of such scientific knowledge, he felt, was to develop the material resources of the territories in a way that would be of use to the public.[3] His annual survey reports were snatched up by ordinary Americans, especially those considering moving west to farm, mine, ranch, or start new businesses. Consulting them provided the kind of information about particular western areas that many people needed to know before pulling up their eastern stakes. It was certainly no accident, for instance, that Hayden frequently invited agriculturist Cyrus Thomas on his surveys. In the Fifth Report, for instance, Hayden included Thomas's fascinating assessments of existing or potential agricultural resources along the survey's route through Utah, Idaho, and Montana Territories. Thus, at the same time Hayden's surveys contributed new scientific information to the scientific community, the government, and the public, they emphasized opportunities for western development and state building.

On the 1871 expedition three scientific generations were represented by Hayden, Allen, and Peale, and all three men shared a passion for geology. Allen had been Hayden's geology professor at Oberlin College in the late 1840s; Peale, some twenty years later, studied geology under Hayden while he was a medical student at the University of Pennsylvania. Like Hayden and other nineteenth-century American scientists, Peale used his medical degree as a stepping-stone to a professional career in geology and the natural sciences.

At the time of the Yellowstone survey neither Allen nor Peale had visited what Hayden often described as "this great west."[4] For them, joining Hayden's survey was an extraordinary opportunity to investigate scientifically the little-known Yellowstone region, as well as to observe a rapidly developing West.

THE WEST IN 1871

Hayden's Yellowstone expedition began just two years after the tracks of the Central Pacific and Union Pacific railroads were joined at Promontory Point, Utah. This first transcontinental linkage was already stimulating rapid development of the Far West, while making eastern access to it quicker, easier, and technologically exciting.

The railroads taking George Allen, Albert Peale, and Ferdinand Hayden to Cheyenne had already begun to transform the American West. Between

1862 and 1871 Congress made land grants of more than one hundred seventy-four million acres of public land for the construction of four transcontinental railroads. As major land-administrating agencies in the West, railroad companies became powerful empire builders. In addition to seeking passenger business, their land and colonization departments promoted farming, mining, and ranching so that they could also profit as shipping companies.[5] Railroads and western exploration had been linked since the winter of 1848–49, when John C. Frémont's party failed in its attempt to determine a railroad route between St. Louis and San Francisco along the thirty-eighth parallel.[6]

Sectional infighting soon followed between northern and southern railroad interests. In response, Congress passed the Pacific Railroad Survey bill in 1853 for the purpose of determining the most practical and economical trans-Mississippi railroad route to the Pacific. Three parties, made up of topographical engineers and civilian scientists, were authorized that summer to make surveys across the northern, southern, and middle sections of the trans-Mississippi West. Marking the beginning of teamwork and specialization in the study of the natural sciences, each team was led by a topographical engineer and included astronomers, meteorologists, botanists, naturalists, geologists, cartographers, and artists as well as military escorts, interpreters, guides, hunters, blacksmiths, and muleteers. Although the Pacific railroad surveys did not lead to a transcontinental rail route in the 1850s, their work greatly benefited the nation's scientific community in the form of thirteen lavishly illustrated volumes of the *Pacific Railroad Reports*, issued between 1855 and 1860. "A veritable encyclopedia of the west," these reports provided detailed descriptions of western geology, botany, animals, birds, and fish, as well as ethnographic reports of Indian tribes. In 1857 these surveys also produced the first scientifically accurate, detailed, and comprehensive map of the trans-Mississippi West.[7]

The Pacific railroad surveys, with their combination of practical benefits and scientific knowledge, served as a model for the four independent western surveys undertaken during the decade following the Civil War. They were called the "Great Surveys" because of their federal sponsorship, the huge areas they explored, the wide range of their scientific investigations, and the large number of personnel they employed. Their leaders – Ferdinand Hayden, Clarence King, John Wesley Powell, and George Wheeler – all saw the West as a scientific laboratory. They and their survey teams ranged across vast areas, exploring, mapping, studying the geology, collecting specimens, and gathering ethnological data. During 1871 all four surveys were at work in western territories, but they followed no standard or coordinated method of operation.[8]

As these survey teams worked their way across a seemingly limitless territory, eastern immigrants traveled by train to new western settlements. These expanding populations created new demands for the transportation of eastern goods, mail, and manufactured products to the West, just as increasing amounts of western farm produce, livestock, gold, and other valuable minerals required transportation from western territories to the East and other parts of the country. By the late 1860s western stage and wagon roads had mushroomed, along with commercial freighting businesses, mail, and passenger lines, all linking the prosperous and populated northern Utah Territory with a Montana Territory rich in minerals but still isolated from railroads.

No group of immigrants so dominated a particular area as did the Mormons in Utah Territory. Under the leadership of Brigham Young, members of the Church of Jesus Christ of Latter-day Saints had traveled from Nauvoo, Illinois, to the Great Salt Lake Valley in two massive wagon-train migrations during the late 1840s, picking up converts along the way. Still more Mormons emigrated from Great Britain to Utah to become farmers, and by 1848 there were some fifty-six hundred Mormons living in the valley. In 1871 the Hayden party observed many Mormon settlements along the Cache Valley in northern Utah, where farmers took advantage of melting snow from the Wasatch Mountains, damming streams and building lines of irrigation canals and ditches. Formerly dry valleys were rapidly becoming productive farmland.

Salt Lake City, founded in 1847 as the capital of the Mormon theocracy, was an impressive city in 1871. It was well regulated and clean, and its shops were well stocked. Thanks to its elaborate irrigation system, the city was full of colorful gardens and verdant shade trees. After the arrival of the railroad in 1869 many Salt Lake City merchants became prosperous providers of both merchandise and freighting services to developing settlements in Idaho and Montana Territories.

Some Civil War veterans also came West hoping to undertake homesteading as a new way of life. Moreover, the army had thousands of experienced soldiers still on its rolls who were free to serve in the West. They were assigned to western forts, where they were to protect new white settlements from increasingly hostile Indians whose hunting grounds and food sources were quickly disappearing. At the same time, soldiers were supposed to protect Indians from avaricious white settlers. For this protection, the army relied on technically sophisticated weaponry that had been developed during the Civil War. Well-known Civil War heroes commanded the western troops, heroes such as William Tecumseh Sherman, who was appointed commander of the U.S. Army in 1869, and Philip Henry Sheridan, who began commanding the Division of the Missouri in 1867. Both Sheridan and Sherman made it clear that they favored armed retaliation against any resisting Indians.[9]

Other groups besides displaced Mormons and soldiers also sought roles in the American West. Chinese and Mexican immigrants, as well as African Americans, often became the West's laborers, cowboys, miners, and railroad builders. On the other hand, western Native Americans found themselves with virtually no roles at all in this developing West. Pushed off their lands by new white settlements and transportation systems, large numbers of Indians were placed on unproductive reservations where they were carefully watched and contained by soldiers based at nearby army forts. Not surprisingly, by the late 1860s numerous conflicts had occurred between hostile tribes and white settlers. The area around Bozeman, Montana, was especially vulnerable to Indian attacks in the early 1870s, when Northern Pacific surveyors worked close to, and even on, what had been undisturbed, treaty-protected Indian land.[10] Although Hayden seemed convinced that his survey party was large enough to intimidate hostile Indians, he safeguarded it by taking along a large military escort for the Yellowstone portion of the expedition.

Just as Native Americans were becoming displaced and fragmented, so were the buffalo herds on which the Indians depended for food and hides. Between 1870 and 1883 eager hunters swarmed over the western plains to supply eastern tanners with millions of hides.[11] Buffalo were also killed merely for the sake of killing, as George Allen later observed as he traveled by train through Kansas on his way back to Ohio. Passengers with rifles in the forward cars shot at a small herd of about twenty animals, including calves, that were near the tracks. Allen accurately noted that "this herd of Buffalo in Colorado and Kansas is permanently separated from the greater herds farther north and will soon doubtless become extinct."[12]

Rapid western development also encouraged lawlessness and damaged the environment. Perhaps nowhere was this more evident than in overcrowded mining areas, such as Alder Gulch, Montana. After the discovery of gold there in 1863, the boom town of Virginia City serviced an estimated ten thousand miners. By the time the Hayden party visited there in 1871, the area was largely mined out. Huge piles of gravel and dirt blighted the area, and Virginia City seemed on its way to becoming yet another ghost town. This West-in-transition is addressed both directly and indirectly by George Allen and Albert Peale in their journals. Their primary focus, however, was on the ever-changing western landscape and its geological implications – from Idaho's desertlike Snake River plain to the snow-capped Rockies. Nonetheless, as interesting as this landscape was and still is, the 1871 expedition has always been best known for its work in Yellowstone.

YELLOWSTONE BEFORE 1871

Native people had been familiar with the Yellowstone Basin for thousands of years, and they "knew the area in a way no modern people ever will."[13] Recent discoveries of tools made from Yellowstone's Obsidian Cliff can now be dated as early as ten thousand years ago. Paul Schullery, Yellowstone historian and naturalist, writes that even limited archaeological data suggest "that Yellowstone was a busy place at times . . . [peopled by] hunters, gatherers, fishermen, miners and assorted other travelers who came and went over the millennia before white [people] came along and tacked a couple of centuries of 'history' on to the story."[14] For most white Americans in 1871, however, the Yellowstone Basin was regarded as nearly the last remaining unknown area in the country.[15]

The first white intrusions began as early as the winter of 1807–8, when John Colter, a Virginian frontiersman, made his solitary trek through at least part of the Yellowstone wilderness. Colter apparently entered Yellowstone from the south (having first visited Jackson Lake and the Tetons). He continued north to near the southern extremity of Yellowstone Lake. He probably then trekked through Two Ocean Pass and onto the upper Yellowstone River, where an ancient Indian trail took him around the west side of Yellowstone Lake and the west bank of the Yellowstone River to a crossing at Hot Spring Brimstone (the Bannock Trail ford at the mouth of Tower Creek). There is no map or written evidence that Colter saw any geyser basins. Although Colter saw only a portion of what is today's park, he is usually acknowledged as Yellowstone's first white discoverer.[16]

Following Colter, commercial explorations of the Yellowstone area began, lasting until fur trading ceased in the northern Rocky Mountains. Park historian Aubrey Haines believes that the Yellowstone plateau was probably visited by American trappers every year from 1826 through 1845.[17]

Between 1840 and 1845 those trappers who remained in the Yellowstone area had to find other ways of earning a living. Many became scouts for the army or served as guides to notables who wished to hunt in the area. Jim Bridger, for instance, built a way station (later Fort Bridger) on the Oregon Trail, from which he guided emigrants to the West and also prominent visitors to the Yellowstone country.[18] These trappers-turned-guides contributed valuable firsthand geographical knowledge of the area to its later explorers. Unfortunately, they have been more often portrayed as spinners of yarns about Yellowstone's amazing and sometimes frightening thermal phenomena rather than as very real contributors to the knowledge about this region. Robert Meldrum, Joe Meek, Johnson Gardner, Osborne Russell, Jim Bridger, and Jesuit missionary Father Pierre Jean DeSmet are some of the legendary names associated with this era.

Ferdinand Hayden first heard "wonderful tales" about the Yellowstone Basin from Jim Bridger in 1856, when they both served on a survey that explored northeast of what is today's park under the command of Lieutenant Gouverneur Kemble Warren.[19] In 1859–60 Hayden and Bridger served on another survey, led this time by Captain William F. Raynolds. The Raynolds party was the first organized group to attempt an exploration of the Yellowstone Basin itself, including "the head waters of the Yellowstone and Missouri rivers, and of the mountains in which they arise."[20] Unfortunately, heavy snows in June 1860 prevented the party from penetrating the mountain barrier leading into the Yellowstone Basin from the southeast. This failure, along with Hayden's fascination with Bridger's Yellowstone accounts, strengthened his resolve to return to the area and finally see Yellowstone's wonders for himself.

In the eleven-year interim before Hayden returned, several prospecting groups found their way into various sections of the Yellowstone Basin. Perhaps the best known was a group from Bannack, Montana, led by a civil engineer by the name of Walter Washington DeLacy. In the late summer of 1863 DeLacy entered what is today's park from Jackson Hole and passed through the Shoshone and Firehole geyser basins. The party returned without finding any of the gold they sought. Instead, they brought back important new geographical information that became incorporated in DeLacy's valuable Map of the Territory of Montana, published in 1865.[21]

In 1867 several prospecting parties investigated areas that were in or close to today's park. A party of Montana prospectors, including A. Bart Henderson, explored along the east shore of Yellowstone Lake and down the Yellowstone River to the Montana settlements. Henderson came back again with a party in 1870 and discovered mines in the Beartooth Mountains on

Clarke's Fork (the present Cooke City area). New discoveries of gold in the mountains north and northeast of this area drew subsequent miners away, however, and prospecting activity there virtually ceased.[22]

By this time the Yellowstone region was becoming well enough known for one frontier publication to prophesy the area's future. In July 1867 a story appeared in the *Frontier Index* in which an informant described portions of Yellowstone country and predicted that "[a] few years more and the U.P. Railroad will bring thousands of pleasure-seekers, sight-seers, and invalids from every part of the globe to see this land of surpassing wonders."[23]

A few years later, aided by DeLacy's map, two private parties, composed primarily of Montana businessmen, undertook the first organized investigations of the Yellowstone Basin: the three-man Cook-Folsom-Peterson party in 1869 and the nineteen-man Washburn expedition in 1870.[24] Both parties contributed new names to the area's landscape and its thermal phenomena, among them Old Faithful, Tower Falls, and Mt. Washburn. They also made important but unsubstantiated observations about the area in published accounts, a few rough sketches, and improved maps. Attempts by the 1869 party to publish its story were turned down by editors of the *New York Tribune*, as well as *Scribner's* and *Harper's* magazines, who were reluctant to risk their reputations on such "unreliable material." Instead, editors of the less prestigious Chicago publication, *Western Monthly Magazine*, published the story in the July 1870 issue.[25]

That same summer the Washburn expedition (named after its leader, Henry Washburn, then surveyor general of Montana Territory) fared much better. By this time, although there is still little record of any formal association, the interests of the expedition and the Northern Pacific Railroad were closely linked. Jay Cooke, the primary financial backer of the Northern Pacific, was eager to encourage other investors in the future western line of the railroad being built from Chicago to the West Coast. Once the 1869 explorers confirmed that the Yellowstone Basin was, indeed, a place of spectacular landscapes and hydrothermal wonders, Cooke seized on the idea of publicizing the area as "America's Switzerland." American tourists, he prophesied, would no longer have to travel abroad to see sublime scenery. Instead, they could travel by train to see the wonders of the great American Northwest.[26]

With Cooke's backing, Montanan Nathaniel Langford not only helped organize the expedition but afterward presented popular lectures about Yellowstone in Helena, Virginia City, Philadelphia, Washington, and New York on behalf of the Northern Pacific Railroad.[27] He also published two installments of an article in *Scribner's Monthly* entitled "The Wonders of Yellowstone." Readers could infer that railroad interests played a large part in Langford's Yellowstone promotion, for it concluded, "By means of the Northern Pacific Railroad, which will doubtless be completed within the next three years, the traveler will be able to make the trip to Montana from the Atlantic seaboard in three days, and thousands of tourists will be attracted to both Montana and Wyoming in order to behold with their own eyes the wonders here described."[28]

Scribner's engraver Thomas Moran illustrated Langford's article with stylized woodcuts based on Langford's descriptions and a few rough sketches done at the scene. These illustrations not only enhanced Moran's artistic reputation but inspired him to see Yellowstone's wonders for himself. Not surprisingly, it was Jay Cooke who arranged for Moran to join Hayden's Yellowstone expedition as a visiting artist several months later.[29]

Langford's Yellowstone accounts may have partially inspired Hayden, who heard Langford lecture in Washington in January 1871 and undoubtedly later read his *Scribner's* articles. Hayden was also familiar with the published report (1871) of Lieutenant Gustavus Doane, who commanded the military escort that accompanied the Washburn expedition into Yellowstone country. Hayden referred to this report as "a modest pamphlet of forty pages . . . that for graphic description and thrilling interest . . . has not been surpassed by any official report made to our government since the times of Lewis and Clark."[30]

Scientifically knowledgeable and intrigued by survey work, Doane also had quite a reputation as an Indian fighter and was known for his role in leading his fellow soldiers from Fort Ellis in a brutal attack against an unsuspecting and tragically misidentified Piegan campground in north-central Montana in January 1870.[31] Although Hayden may have been impressed by Doane's military expertise, it was his firsthand knowledge of the Yellowstone Basin that prompted Hayden's request that Doane lead the army escort (also from Fort Ellis) that would accompany his own party into the Yellowstone territory.

By 1871 the time was ripe for an organized scientific survey of the Yellowstone area, one that would collect paleontological, botanical, zoological, and geological specimens, take photographs, systematically record temperatures and weather, and make other accurate readings. Although Hayden was influenced by the Northern Pacific Railroad to study the Yellowstone area, it was probably his long interest in determining the sources of the Missouri and Yellowstone Rivers that provided the greatest impetus to take his survey there.[32] Whatever Hayden's motivations, the U.S. government was certainly eager to determine whether the Yellowstone Basin was valuable other than as a tourist mecca. To this end, it agreed to underwrite the Hayden Survey.

THE 1871 HAYDEN SURVEY

In March 1871 Congress appropriated forty thousand dollars for Hayden's fifth survey season. This amount covered costs and salaries, including four thousand dollars for Hayden's year-long salary as the geologist in charge. In all likelihood, Hayden drafted most of his own objectives for the expedition – objectives that later became incorporated into his official instructions from Columbus Delano, secretary of the interior. These instructions, dated May 1, 1871, curiously ignored references to what was already known about the Yellowstone area. For instance, the survey party's explorations were to be confined "mostly to the Territories of Idaho and Montana," a strange specification, since most of the Yellowstone area to be explored was known to lie in Wyoming Territory, and the survey would spend a good third of its time there. One can only conclude that Hayden either had not yet finally determined whether to include the Yellowstone Basin or, for some unknown reason, did not wish to communicate his plans.[33]

The stated object of the survey has the familiar ring of other geological surveys: to "secure as much information as possible, both scientific and practical," and to "give attention to the geological, mineralogical, zoological, botanical, and agricultural resources of the country." If the party found itself in the vicinity of any Indian tribes, it was "to secure such information in regard to them as will be useful to this department or the country." Hayden was also instructed to prepare a geological map (in color) based on the areas visited and to send the collected specimens "to the Smithsonian Institution to be arranged according to law." Probably the most important stated object was to "collect as ample material as possible for the illustration of your final reports, such as sketches, sections, photographs, etc." Hayden would soon be able to verify what others had only related in words.[34]

Besides his survey obligations to the government, Hayden had some kind of personal understanding with Jay Cooke to survey areas along the party's route (especially in Montana and Wyoming Territories) for the location of possible Northern Pacific railbeds. Whether in personal terms or not, Northern Pacific officials had already arranged with the U.S. General Land Office to have access to information collected by the geological surveys. Even though Hayden's 1871 survey was administered by the Department of the Interior, the same arrangement undoubtedly applied, and Hayden was probably instructed to share his information with the Northern Pacific. Cooke would have been interested in locating the rail route close to actual or potential coal sources for locomotive fuel. He also hoped Hayden would discover a way of connecting the Union Pacific in southern Wyoming Territory to areas near the Yellowstone Basin and thence to the Northern Pacific line.[35]

Well aware of the potential for tourism, Cooke (through his office manager and promoter, General Alvred Nettleton) arranged for Thomas Moran, a fellow Philadelphian and an artist of "rare genius," to join Hayden's party in Montana as guest artist. Hayden was further alerted to a possibility that did not occur: that landscape artist Albert Bierstadt might also join the party for the Yellowstone portion of the trip.[36]

Hayden was happy to oblige Cooke on all these matters. Cultivating favor with railroad executives paid dividends to Hayden and his surveys. During the 1871 survey, for instance, executives from both the Central Pacific and Union Pacific railroads provided passes for Hayden's large party as well as cheap rates for transporting horses, equipment, and supplies. Because Hayden intended to continue exploring Montana Territory, he undoubtedly wished to sustain the gratitude of Cooke and Northern Pacific executives.

Choosing a Survey Team

After Hayden's official appointment, one of his first tasks was to recruit members for his survey team. There was no dearth of candidates. Ultimately, he would wind up with thirty-two men in all. Hayden later called the group "a small village." Indeed, it was, for the party included a military escort, forty-eight animals (twenty-seven horses and twenty-one mules), five four-mule wagons, and two two-horse ambulances (used for carrying both supplies and sick or injured party members). At least size had one advantage, he claimed: the party was "big enough . . . to fight off the Indians." In April, however, he confessed that the party was so large that "I am now overwhelmed and fearful, lest I cannot pull through with what I have."[37]

Hayden made sure, early on, that seven loyal and experienced survey regulars would be part of the team. They included agriculturist Cyrus Thomas and survey artist Henry Elliott, whose landscape profiles, sections, and other drawings made during his 1869 and 1870 surveys had pleased Hayden with their realistic geological detail. Hayden also quickly recruited the photographer from his 1870 survey, William Henry Jackson, recognizing that Jackson's photographs would become indispensable as the first visual records of this reported "wonderland."

4. Henry Wood Elliott (c. 1870). U.S. Geological Survey, W. H. Jackson 588

Two other survey veterans (both of whom had participated with Hayden on the 1859–60 Raynolds Survey) came on board. They were zoologist E. Campbell Carrington and James Stevenson, Hayden's indispensable survey manager (1869–78). Stevenson reportedly brought along a dog on the surveys, probably the nameless dog pictured in several of Jackson's camp photographs.

Hayden had also previously worked alongside the meteorologist and artist for the Raynolds Survey, German-born Anton Schönborn. Impressed with his surveying and cartographic skills, Hayden appointed Schönborn topog-

5. William Henry Jackson. U.S. Geological Survey, W. H. Jackson 595

rapher. The meteorologist on Hayden's 1870 survey, John Beaman, was assigned to the same position in 1871.

As he did for his 1870 survey, Hayden also obtained the services of eminent eastern botanists, zoologists, and paleontologists who would examine the specimens sent to them by the survey team (relayed through the Smithsonian Institution) and then write accounts of their findings for Hayden's published report.[38]

Four recent graduates of the University of Pennsylvania, all of whom had studied geology under Hayden, were also recruited. Three of these young men, George Dixon, Charles Turnbull, and the diarist Albert Peale, had received medical degrees from the university shortly before the survey began in the spring of 1871. The fourth, Robert Adams, Jr., had studied with Hayden in the late 1860s and graduated with a classics degree from the university in 1869. During the fall, winter, and spring he studied and eventually practiced law in Philadelphia, but during the summers from 1871 to 1875, apparently to improve his health, Adams participated in Hayden's surveys. Philadelphians were well informed about the 1871 expedition, for besides Peale's letters to the *Philadelphia Press*, Adams contributed regular articles to the *Philadelphia Inquirer* during the survey.[39]

Hayden's first-time appointments to the survey of two experienced scientists, Frederick Huse and George Allen, did not work out well. Huse, assistant secretary of the Academy of Natural Sciences in Chicago, was recommended by Spencer Baird and asked to serve as the survey's ornithologist. Allen, who had been Hayden's professor of geology at Oberlin College in the late 1840s, was asked to serve as botanist. Huse apparently turned out to be lazy, and Allen proved physically unable to carry out his work.

Deluged with applications and recommendations, Hayden acknowledged that he chose some survey members because they had politically influential fathers or relatives. He had no problems justifying these appointments, for the good feelings of congressmen helped him secure appropriations for his surveys, and the influence of top army personnel helped him obtain horses, mules, and equipment at cost.

Hayden's concern about his "formidable" party had increased even more by the time the group reached Ogden. There he learned that a small army party, under orders from General Philip Sheridan, would meet his survey in Montana and explore Yellowstone while sharing Hayden's military escort. This team of eleven, headed by Captain John Barlow (chief engineer of the U.S. Army's Division of Missouri) and his able topographer, Captain David Heap, eventually joined Hayden at Fort Ellis, where their combined parties and shared escort totaled eighty-three men. Hayden was correct in referring to this collection as "an army on the March."[40]

SURVEY OPERATIONS

As the first scientific survey to investigate the Yellowstone Basin, Hayden's party was equipped with an array of scientific instruments for determining elevations, depths, and distances; taking temperatures; analyzing the chemical components of hot springs and geysers; and excavating and testing rocks and various mineral deposits. In 1871 Hayden had not yet introduced a system of primary triangulation to measure elevations. Instead, measurements were based mainly on barometric readings, and because barometers were highly unstable and prone to breakage during rough travel, their readings were often inaccurate. Surveying was done along the immediate line of march, with the courses measured by compass and distances by an odometer, and the whole was checked in latitude by the sextant.

From the survey's published report, we know that the party carried with it wet and dry bulb thermometers, small aneroid barometers for taking elevations on the road and in mountains, and siphon (mercury) barometers (necessary to use as a check on aneroid readings). Hayden undoubtedly had other instruments at his disposal, probably not unlike those the army furnished the Barlow party for its Yellowstone work. According to Captain Barlow, these instruments were "two sextants, one artificial horizon, one sidereal chronometer, one mean solar pocket chronometer, two mercurial cistern barometers, one thermo-barometer, two aneroids, two prismatic compasses, three pocket compasses, one clinometer, two odometers, one pair odometer wheels, and a box of tools."[41]

Having packed all this scientific equipment in wagons, along with the survey's other necessary supplies, the Hayden party began its northern trek by horseback from Ogden to the Valley of the Upper Yellowstone. They traveled on rough, dusty stage and wagon roads through northern Utah and western Idaho and Montana Territories, often revisiting sites the survey visited in 1870. Like that expedition, the party surveyed a belt of land fifty to one hundred miles wide, using the "meander method." In practice, this "method" was a very informal investigation of whatever appeared along the way to be a geologically interesting site. The party also often connected its topographical and geological work with the proposed line of the Northern Pacific Railroad.

As the survey made its way north, it observed ever-changing western landscapes and such diverse human settlements as lonely stage stops, small and isolated ranches, newly irrigated Mormon farming communities, bustling military forts, arid Indian reservations, booming railroad and mining towns, as well as abandoned towns situated too far from rail centers or already mined out.

The day-to-day routing and operation of the survey was determined by its manager, Jim Stevenson, and its wagon master, Steve Hovey. This work included making advance arrangements for picking up supplies and equipment from army forts; obtaining rail transportation for both party members and supplies; allocating rations; organizing the feeding, care, and packing of horses and mules; and determining campsites in advance. Sometimes the party stopped early in the day where there was sure water and forage.

Three hunters tried to provide enough elk and deer meat for the large party, but there were times when large game was so scarce that smaller game, such as grouse, duck, and rabbit, had to be relied on. Three cooks and two waiters prepared and served meals, often with the largest meal at midday.

John Raymond ("Potato John"), from Cheyenne City, Wyoming Territory, often served on Hayden's surveys as head cook. He came by his nickname from undercooking potatoes in boiling water, not realizing that water boils at lower temperatures at high altitudes. Raymond eventually resorted to preparing potatoes by frying them instead.[42]

Not until the party reached Fort Ellis did Hayden hire a guide. He was referred to in the journals only as "José." Efforts to recover his full name have failed thus far. José seemed familiar with at least some of the Yellowstone area and may have been responsible for guiding the party to Mammoth Hot Springs, a place not visited by either the 1869 or 1870 expedition. These hot springs were becoming known to the region's hunters and prospectors, who used them to relieve arthritis and heal skin diseases, including syphilis. José served as a guide on two occasions when Hayden and a small party became lost: in the geyser basins and between Shoshone and Yellowstone Lakes.

Once the party arrived at Bottler's Ranch (in today's Paradise Valley), thirty-three miles north of Mammoth Hot Springs, Hayden established a permanent camp and divided the group. Those he assigned to the ranch would keep daily meteorological records and occasionally relay mail and supplies to the main party, which would investigate the "wonders" of Yellowstone. Hayden selected his most valued men for his exploring team, and among those he left at the permanent camp were his underperforming ornithologist, Fred Huse, and two of his politically motivated appointees.

Earlier Yellowstone visitors warned Hayden to leave the party's wagons at Bottler's. There were miles and miles, he was told, around Yellowstone Lake and among the mountains bordering it, where pines grew so closely together that it was nearly impossible for pack animals to pass through. Many areas were heavily strewn with once-towering pine trees, felled by autumnal fires and later blowdowns. Networks of these fallen pines could cover thirty or more miles at a height of three to six feet. Hayden wisely decided that his exploring team would rely on mules and horses to transport its supplies, equipment, and specimens. This was a special hardship for Jackson, for it meant he would have to carefully pack and repack his large and fragile photographic outfit, which had been so accessible in the wagons.[43]

After leaving the ranch, the exploring party often worked in small, independent groups. For instance, Moran, Jackson, and George Dixon (Jackson's assistant) usually worked as a threesome, taking their own side trips to photograph or sketch Yellowstone's dramatic scenery and thermal features. Seemingly, they worked without directions or suggestions from Hayden.

Other groups collected and prepared botanical and zoological specimens to be sent to the Smithsonian from post offices along the route. Before the survey began, Spencer Baird wrote Hayden that the Smithsonian was eager to receive "a large collection of all kinds of skulls and skeletons: many of each, at least skulls; antelope and mountain sheep especially, 20 of each! Also any perfect bison head."[44]

One or two members of the army escort usually accompanied (and often worked alongside) these smaller groups; even packers and cooks sometimes assisted with other tasks. An egalitarian and informal atmosphere prevailed. Occasionally, members of the party even suggested placenames that later became official.[45]

Several base camps were set up around Yellowstone Lake. At these camps the party would stop for a day or two to rest. Peale and Adams used these times to write accounts of the expedition for their Philadelphia newspapers. Henry Elliott also wrote a few single articles for several newspapers. In addition, his boss at the Smithsonian, Secretary Joseph Henry, sent some of Elliott's letters he had received to various newspapers for publication. Although Hayden instigated the publication of Elliott's letters to Henry, it is unclear whether he arranged for Peale's or Adams's journalistic endeavors.[46]

Hayden also used camp layovers as a time to correspond with personal friends, fellow scientists, and government officials. A restless, energetic man, Hayden much preferred geologizing to the sedentary job of writing letters, with the result that he hastily dashed off barely decipherable messages to his friends. His official letters, however, are written in a clear, legible hand and were undoubtedly inscribed by someone else in the party.

Hayden's restlessness and curiosity can be inferred from Peale's journal, for Peale often writes of accompanying Hayden on excursions away from camp to investigate geologically interesting areas, especially road cuts and mines, railroad and river beds, and other places where rock strata could be easily identified and fossils discovered. Once in the Yellowstone Basin, Hayden climbed buttes and mountains (sometimes in the company of Barlow) to determine the party's location and future routes. In superb physical condition, Hayden even outdistanced the younger Peale and Elliott when the three climbed to the summit of Mt. Washburn.

These climbing feats were partly dictated by the party's lack of accurate maps and thus its need to determine the lay of the land from high elevations. Although Hayden officially acknowledged the Army Engineer Bureau for the use of its "valuable maps," he admitted in a July letter to Secretary Delano, "We found all the maps, official and otherwise, utterly inadequate to travel by." Even the earlier Raynolds survey map was wildly inaccurate by 15° to 20° longitude and also entirely omitted the Jefferson River.[47]

The Hayden party spent the greatest amount of its time in Yellowstone investigating Yellowstone Lake and the area surrounding it. Hayden's special enthusiasm for this lake study probably derived from the fact that the 1869 and 1870 expeditions had obtained virtually no information on either the lake or its islands. The Washburn party had built a raft, hoping to investigate several islands, but it had been "dashed to pieces in an hour by the strong waves." Nor had the Washburn party been able to establish a significant baseline along the lake for measuring distances.[48]

In preparation for this study of Yellowstone Lake, some of Hayden's party made sections of a boat frame (measuring about 11 × 4.5 feet) at Fort Ellis and hauled them by mule to the lake. There they secured the frame, covered it with a double tarpaulin coated with tar, and topped it with a sail rigged from horse blankets. Once the boat proved seaworthy on such a large and volatile lake, Hayden gave orders for a map to be made of the entire lake. This map, executed primarily by Henry Elliott, became for Hayden one of the most significant achievements of his survey.

Hayden had long wished to visit the Upper Yellowstone country, as much, if not more, to solve its geographical puzzles as to see its wonders. Because one of his primary objectives for the survey was to explore and map the area's river systems and origins, it is not surprising that Peale's journal reveals that Hayden was much more interested in following streams and rivers, while others investigated Yellowstone's more dramatic features.

The highly detailed geological descriptions Hayden wrote in his published report suggest he was his own reconnaissance man. Not only did he do an enormous amount of rock and fossil hunting, but he studied a wide variety of land formations and speculated on their origins. Hayden had long been speculating on the geological evolution of the Rocky Mountains and the high plains. Earlier he had demonstrated that the Rocky Mountains were covered with freshwater lakes during Tertiary times. He recognized, as early as 1862, that the elevation of the Rockies began in the late Cretaceous period, continued throughout the Tertiary, and would continue for the eons to come.

By 1871 Hayden and his early field partner, paleontologist Fielding Bradford Meek, had collected enough fossil evidence to show that the extinction of much vertebrate life at the end of the Cretaceous period did not extend to invertebrates. Hayden's surveys continued to discover that numerous invertebrates survived into the Tertiary period and shifted "from marine (salt water) to estuary (mixed salt and freshwater) to freshwater types, as a receding Cretaceous ocean gave way under pressure of a rising continent, to freshwater lakes and streams typical of the Tertiary."[49] It is not surprising, then, that during the 1871 survey much attention was given to determining whether the fossils collected by the party came from Cretaceous or Tertiary times.

It is in his role as popularizer and promoter that Hayden has been characterized (by some scientists and historians) as a businessman's geologist and a scientific entrepreneur.[50] Hayden undoubtedly was both, but he was also much more. Because there has been such a paucity of primary evidence regarding his actual day-to-day survey fieldwork, it has been relatively easy to write him off as only a superficial scientist. The journals and letters that follow point to his active involvement in all scientific aspects of the survey, from collecting huge amounts of detailed empirical data to speculating on broad theoretical issues. These same documents also reveal how three articulate scientists responded to the dramatic western landscapes along their expedition route and within the country's soon-to-be first national park.

The Diarists

GEORGE ALLEN

After graduating from Oberlin College in 1850, Ferdinand Hayden stayed in touch with Professor George Allen, sending him the latest publications on geological subjects as well as western fossil and rock specimens for Allen's natural history collection (then called a "cabinet"). When Allen indicated his desire to join the 1870 expedition, Hayden encouraged him to participate. Allen was, after all, a respected geologist with broad field experience. Unhappily, Hayden had little inkling of just how physically and psychologically unprepared Allen was for such an expedition.

As a geologist, George Allen had endured the physical demands of arduous fieldwork in the East and Midwest, but they were nothing like what he would encounter during the 1871 survey. Moreover, he suffered from what was then called "nervous disease," a combination of anxiety and depression.

Deeply devout, Allen had long conformed to the practice of reserving Sunday as a day of worship and rest – a practice Hayden had resented while serving on the Raynolds Expedition more than a decade before. A longtime Congregationalist, Allen believed in the efficacy of personal prayer during difficult times, especially as an underpaid and underappreciated professor at Oberlin College. Yet, despite his deeply held religious beliefs, Allen enthusiastically embraced new geological theories. He celebrated scientific knowledge even when it conflicted with biblical history, saying that such knowledge "gives us the present structure and past history of this our planetary abode . . . [and is] a striking proof of the power, wisdom & goodness of the Great Creator."[1]

In contrast to his openness to new scientific ideas, Allen viewed Native Americans with a closed mind. Undoubtedly, part of this attitude was due to the missionary zeal that had permeated Oberlin from its founding forty years earlier. By 1871 Oberlin missionaries had worked with African Americans and Native Americans in the United States as well as with indigenous people in such faraway places as today's Thailand, Liberia, and the West Indies.

Allen had stereotyped western American Indians long before he joined the survey team and, like many Euro-Americans then, believed they were a primitive and pagan people much in need of Christian conversion. Moreover, Allen knew enough about past bloody conflicts between Indians and whites to be anxious about possible threats to himself and the survey team. Hayden, on the other hand, had long been fascinated with Indian languages and customs and appeared to respect Indians' differences from white people. Some Indians seemed to regard him with awe and bemused wonderment and on at least one occasion called him "the man who picks up stones running."[2]

ALBERT PEALE

Albert Peale, like George Allen, was a western neophyte when he joined Hayden's 1871 survey. Unlike Allen, he was a physically fit young man. A quiet, observant, and self-contained twenty-two-year-old, he was more than ready to learn new fieldwork techniques. In this, he differed from the rowdier members of the party who were his own age, including his good friend Charles ("Charlie") Turnbull, who sometimes seemed to regard the expedition as something of a lark.

Peale took his work as the survey mineralogist very seriously and was, in fact, the first mineralogist to study Yellowstone's many thermal features, taking the temperatures and chemically analyzing hundreds of geysers and hot springs in the Firehole Basin alone. He was also eager to describe his experiences periodically for his hometown newspaper, the *Philadelphia Press*.

As was relatively common in the nineteenth century, Peale's scientific career grew out of his training in medical school; like Hayden, Peale apparently never intended to become a doctor. What sparked his interest in science is unclear, but earlier generations of his illustrious family produced dedicated naturalists. This legacy must have played an important part in the development of Peale's scientific career. His great-grandfather, Charles Willson Peale (1741–1827), the well-known portrait painter of the Revolutionary War period, established the country's first natural history museum, the Peale Museum, in Philadelphia. Albert's grandfather, Rubens Peale (1784–1865), later served as manager of the museum in Philadelphia, and his great-uncle, Titian R. Peale (1800–1885), was a painter, explorer, and naturalist who participated in the historic Long Expedition (1819–20) to the Rocky Mountains as well as expeditions to the South Pacific and South America. Albert Peale's immediate family, however, lived far more routine lives. Little is known about his father, named after Albert's great-grandfather, except that in 1856 he was a partner in a coal mine in the village of Shamokin, near Schuylkill Haven, Pennsylvania, and that from 1864 until his death in 1871 he worked as a bookkeeper, cashier, and accountant in Philadelphia.

Whatever enthusiasm for science and exploration Peale may have picked up from his forebears, it was from Ferdinand Hayden that he obtained the scientific knowledge and technical skills that qualified him to serve as the survey mineralogist. By working in the field alongside his former professor (whom he refers to in his journal as "the Doctor"), Peale embarked on his own lifelong career.

The expedition narrative begins with several letters from Hayden to George Allen, encouraging Allen to join his western survey team. Allen had initiated the question whether he might join Hayden for geological fieldwork during Hayden's 1870 survey of southern Wyoming and adjacent territories. Eventually, Allen decided not to join this particular survey, opting instead to participate in the Yellowstone Survey the following year. Hayden's letters to Allen accurately describe the physical demands of his western surveys, just as they also reveal Hayden's affection and concern for his now retired college geology professor.

Prologue

Letters from Ferdinand Hayden to
George Allen, 1870–1871

PHILADELPHIA, MAY 11TH, 1870

My Dear Professor Allen:

Your kind letter came to me today and I reply sooner than before. . . . I [have] left the way open for you to accompany my party. I hope I shall go out every year, should you desire to go out west another year. I have no doubt that the way would open clearly. I will always make room for you in such a way that it will suit you. As to your physical ability to endure such a trip, you are, and must be the best judge. It is quite possible you would go out and enjoy a tour of the kind very much and come back wonderfully delighted and wish to continue them. A Lutheran minister, Mr. Cyrus Thomas of Illinois, accompanied me last season, and he is now far more anxious to go this summer than ever before, although he leaves a wife and two small children behind.[1]

I did not mean to imply that you could not endure the hardships of such a campaign, for to me the hardships are not great. Whatever hardships there are, the younger members of my party gladly take upon themselves, as, standing guard at night etc. I was merely saying a few words to prepare your mind for rather rough times and rough people. Still, you might find in that part your greatest benefit, so far as health is concerned, [another] greatest pleasure. I am accustomed to look back upon your life at O[berlin] as a *nice, regular, eminently proper* one, while we roam over the limitless plains with a wild joyous freedom from restraint; that is, we cannot take our home-life with us. If I could see you for one hour, I could make myself better understood – but perhaps you catch the idea. Rev. Thomas H. Robinson of Hanesbury, a classmate, is very anxious to go on the trip.[2] I am afraid I shall be so late in getting into the field that I cannot stop at Oberlin on my way west. Should you conclude to go, I will inform you so that you can meet me at Omaha. I therefore leave the matter entirely with yourself, only stating this, that I shall be glad to have your company and that the door will be kept wide open for you to enter on any terms that may best suit you. I shall be in Philadelphia until sometime in June and will be glad to know your wishes. If I can I will stop at Oberlin – either going or returning.

Yours very sincerely,

F. V. Hayden

[*Ten months later*]

WASHINGTON, DC, MARCH 17TH, 1871

Dear Professor Allen:

. . . A place was left open – It is now open. Whether you can endure such a trip must be left for you to decide. I will do all I can to make your position easy and agreeable. The work I would prefer you to do is mineralogical and metallurgical, as testing ores, minerals, rocks, also saline waters, and as much geology as possible. Can you use the blowpipe to advantage? I would like to know. If I recollect rightly, you commenced study long ago in rocks and minerals. Much of this work could be done in camp. Can you ride on Horseback?

I expect to start from Salt Lake City and go northward to Helena, Montana, explore the Missouri and Yellow Stone from their sources down. Will be absent from May 1st to Nov. 1st – six months. Idaho and Montana will be the area of my principal labors. Most of my outfit will be made at Salt Lake City.

You can take an ordinary amount of luggage as a good sized valise, two or three suits, pants and shirts etc. Blankets can be obtained in the west to better advantage – A shotgun will be good: other guns can be obtained west. You will not need a very extensive outfit.

Please let me know as soon as possible how you can work in rock and mineral studies, especially with the Blowpipe.

When I hear from you I will write further,

Yours very sincerely,

F. V. Hayden

PHILADELPHIA, APRIL 13TH, 1871

My Dear Professor:

Mr. Bartlette is here with me now. He showed me a letter from you. So far as young Wheat is concerned, I cannot possibly take another soul into my party under any circumstances.[3] I have refused more than 50 persons, and am refusing everyday. I see no reason why you should not do all the work that is needed. It would be well for you to provide yourself with such materials as you may need. You know the minerals met with in such an expedition are few and common. Those that are rare can be collected and determined afterwards. I would prefer that you give your entire attention to subjects of that kind, mines, minerals, rocks, springs – soda, warm – etc., with some geology. All the other departments are most abundantly provided for. Prof. Baird felt as though he should have one appointment.[4] A young ornithologist from Chicago goes out [*Fred Huse*]. My party now numbers 18. Politicians have had about six appointments. Gen'l Logan has two. Gen'l Negley's son goes, possibly a son of Mr. Dawes' of Massachusetts and others.[5]

All field work must necessarily be of the crudest kind. It is designed to throw some light on matters that are not obvious at once to the eye. There will be no one along but you and myself who make any pretensions to a knowledge of these subjects. It may be necessary now and then to divide the party temporarily.

I will inform you of the time to meet me in Omaha, perhaps not before the 10th or 12th of May. A portion of my party will leave in a few days for Cheyenne and other points getting things in readiness.

You do not need a large outfit, such one as you would use in field work in the state of Ohio. Transportation is always an important item in the far west. Guns, pistols, ammunition etc. will be obtained best out west unless you have them on hand. If you have a good gun of any kind, also a Pistol, you should take them with you.

In your letter to Mr. Bartlett[e] you speak of having waited for a letter from me. I think I replied to the last letter I received from you. I lose a good many letters by my Bohemian life.

I am sorry there is no place for Mr. Wheat. He is evidently qualified but I am now overwhelmed and fearful, lest I cannot pull through with what I have.

I may possibly stop at Oberlin as I go west, and you may be ready to go at that time. I think all things will work well. Should any unforeseen event occur to prevent you from going with me, please let me know in time. You should be already to start by the 12th of May or even before, say, from 5th to 12th. My address in Philadelphia will be care of "University of Pennsylvania." Hoping all things will work well with you.

I remain yours sincerely,

F. V. Hayden

I shall be glad to hear from you at any time.

NEW YORK, MAY 15TH, 1871

My Dear Prof. Allen:

Please start for Omaha Wednesday 17th and wait until I come. I shall be there soon. Perhaps as soon as you do. Call on the firm of Wilcox and Stephens and inquire for me and you will hear if I am in town.[6] Do not delay after Wednesday 17th. I cannot stop in Oberlin. I am sorry.

Your Friend,

F. V. Hayden

1871 Yellowstone Survey Members

Robert Adams, assistant botanist
George Allen, botanist
John W. Beaman, meteorologist
Bob Bushnell, second ambulance driver
E. Campbell ("Cam") Carrington, zoologist
Joe Clark, hunter
Chester M. Dawes, general assistant
George B. Dixon, assistant to the photographer
J. Wilson Duncan, general assistant
Henry Elliott, artist
Ed Flint, second mule team
John Geiselman, first waiter
Dan Gibson, cook
F. L. Goodfellow, first ambulance driver; in charge of odometer
Henry Greve, second waiter
Stephen D. Hovey, wagonmaster
Fred J. Huse, ornithologist
William Henry Jackson, photographer
José, hunter and guide
George E. Kelley, second ambulance driver
George Loucks, first mule team
William B. Logan, secretary
Clifford De V. Negley, general assistant
Albert C. Peale, mineralogist

Survey members whose names appear in italics receive brief biographies in appendix 1.

John Raymond ("Potato John"), first cook
Dick Richards, third mule team
Anton Schönborn, chief topographer
Bob Sherman, second cook
Alec Sibley, fourth mule team
Alfred J. Smith, assistant to the topographer
Joseph E. Smith, hunter
James Stevenson, manager and director
Cyrus Thomas, agricultural statistician and entomologist
Charles ("Charlie") Turnbull, physician and general assistant

Thomas Moran, guest artist

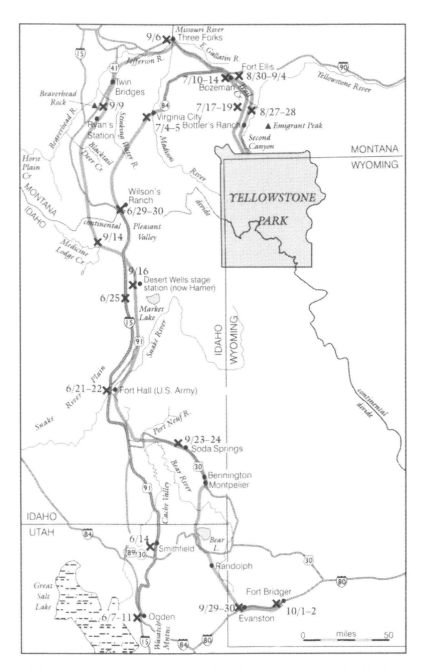

1. The survey route to and from Yellowstone. Numbers by campsites (e.g. 6/7–11) indicate month and date the survey team stayed there.

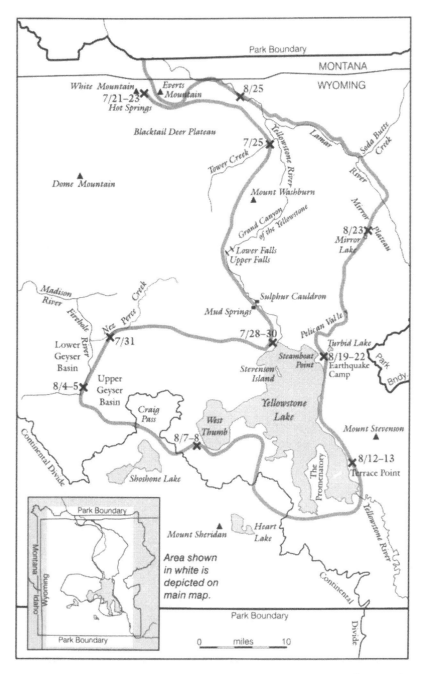

2. The survey route through Yellowstone. Numbers by campsites (e.g. 7/21–23) indicate month and date the survey team stayed there.

THE YELLOWSTONE
NARRATIVE

PART ONE

GEORGE ALLEN'S JOURNAL

I

From Omaha to
Cheyenne and Ogden

Traveling by Train

THURSDAY, MAY 25

Left Omaha at 12 Noon.

For many miles passed through country quite hilly, though with sides sufficiently sloping to allow of cultivation. The soil is very rich – a yellowish marl – the "Gheff deposit" or loess.[1]

Dined at a "smart" town called Fremont. At half past three o'clk passed Columbus, Geo. Francis Train's future capitol of the U.S.[2] It is said to be about midway between the Atlantic and Pacific. Earlier we passed the Elk-horn river where the sandstones of Cretaceous #1 appears on the bluffs. Near Columbus we passed by a bridge the Soap river which flows from the north in to the Platte. It abounds in sand bars. All the rivers in this vicinity are noted for sandbars and shifting channels.

The valley of the Platte in the eastern part of Nebraska is from 5 to 10 miles wide, and is very rapidly settling. Towns are springing up everywhere as if by magic. I noticed that the majority of the farms seemed to have been chosen from lands situated from 1 to 5 miles back from the Rail Road. The difference in the prices of lands thus situated may and probably has been the cause. Now and then a church or schoolhouse was passed indicating clearly that the attendants of civilized and established society were being transplanted to this beautiful prairie land.

Supper at Grand Island station. Our party got cups of sweet milk from a milkman near by. Grand Island is 175 miles west of Omaha. Sunset was splendid.

At Fremont saw three Indians at Depot begging of passengers, two women and one man. They belonged to some of the Reservations nearby and were decently but grotesquely clad.

Panorama 1. Red beds of Echo Canyon, May 30–31.

At Columbus, too, we saw a small camp of Indians with their ponies, just outside of the village.

Along the Platte water is obtained at the depth of 20 to 30 feet of good quality. Towards evening saw an antilope – *Antilocapen americana*, near the Rail Road.

Passenger on the Union Pacific Railroad, on way to Cheyenne

FRIDAY, MAY 26

Beautiful morning – clear and refreshing. Rose early and went outside for observation. Saw large numbers of antilopes sometimes singly and often in groups of from 6 to 10. They became less abundant as we neared the mountains. Probably the pasturage was less inviting.

Saw also one prairie wolf (coyote) and any quantity of Prairie dogs, *cynomys*. Their towns or favorite haunts were constantly occurring, and now and then as we rode along a bold fellow would stand up near its retreat and stare at us.

The valley of the Platte becomes more and more contracted, and in time we left the Platte at Julesburg and passed up the valley of the Lodge Pole Creek. The soil is greatly changed, is light colored, mo[re] sandy and gravelly, an old tertiary fresh water basin.

At Pine Bluff Station we saw the beautiful atmospheric phenomenon of *mirage*. In the distance, apparently a mile or two off, we saw what appeared to be a blue sheet of water, with a bluff beyond, but we were fully assured that no water was there. The phenomenon was wholly due to reflection of the light rays owing to an unequal heating of the air near the surface. We read of the *mirage* in the great deserts of Africa, but certainly nothing could be more eminently deceptive than this – a perfect imitation of water.

Along the Road were seen the bleached skulls and skeletons of horses and cattle – often of the Buffalo.

Pine bluff Station is so named from the fact that formerly the bluffs were covered with a growth of pine. Except a few scattering trees seen here and there, all the timber has been cut off from the vicinity of the Rail Road.

At that station the Rail Road leaves the Lodge pole creek valley and passes across the higher hills to Cheyenne with a grade of 18 or 20 feet to a mile. Saw scattered abundantly among these hills the long stiff leaved plant called the "Spanish bayonet," *Yucca augustifolia*.

For some time before reaching Cheyenne we were permitted to behold a most glorious sight – our first view of the Rocky Mountains! In the Northwest were distinctly seen the Laramie range of mountains – often called here the Black Hills – standing out with the utmost distinctiveness and presenting the deepest shade of blue in contrast with the lighter azure of the sky. They looked near, though they were forty or fifty miles distant at least.

But the most glorious vision that greeted us was presented from a different quarter – from the south west. Far in the distance towering skyward were very plainly though less distinctly seen, the snow covered summits of the main Rocky Range with "Long's Peak" in the South.[3] It was a magnificent sight and I felt fully repaid for coming so far. The northern slopes of all the mountains were shaded off into white or bluish white, hardly distinguishable from the sky – a reflection from the snow which remains, especially on the northern side, all the year round.

We reached Cheyenne at one o'clock and got down into camp about 2 o'clock, when we found dinner waiting. The Camp is a corner of the Military grounds at Fort A. D. Russel [*Fort D. A. Russell*], nearly two miles from Cheyenne.[4]

The Camp is on the north side of Crow creek, and is quite convenient, except its lack of rationacy. Made an acquaintance with the remainder of the company.

Toward evening walked out into the hills near camp where were abundance of Prairie dogs. Here I heard their peculiar cry of warning which is somewhat like the bark of a small dog – and hence the common name. They would allow me to pass within a few rods of their hiding places, while some watchman – probably male – stood sentinel and reiterated its short cry until the intruder had approached to a dangerous proximity, when suddenly in a twinkling it would descend from sight. At every bark, the tail and whole body of the little animal is thrown into violent vibration. While barking, the body is in a horizontal position, or the head perhaps a little depressed. But when making careless observation of objects at a distance, they stand nearly erect with the forelegs dropped downward – *a la grecian bend*.

Found on the sides of the hills, beds of light-colored almost white marly limestone of tertiary age, covered more or less deeply with Drift formed mostly from the debris of the granite and metamorphic hills in the distance.

Fort D. A. Russell, Cheyenne

SATURDAY, MAY 27

Last night was my first experience in camp life. Fortunately it was a still, bright night. With a good bed of hay on the ground and two pairs of blankets below and two pairs ditto above, I could rest [and] sleep very comfortably. Find it rather hard to break into this mode of life – not on account of its hardship and difficulties, but on account of the great publicity which must necessarily prevail when so many are congregated. Another obstacle, even greater perhaps, is the discrepancy in age and habits between myself and most of the company. Still I am bound to persevere. All the young gentlemen treat me with all desirable politeness and attention.

It seems to be decided that I shall take the oversight of collecting and pressing the plants. The other departments of collection are provided for, while this goes abegging. Mr. Adams offers to assist. I regret on every account that I must labor in a department which is so new to me; for although it requires but little scientific knowledge to enable one to collect and press flowers, still the pleasure of such a work is indefinitely enhanced by a thorough knowledge of it. There is one view of the care which may serve, however, to reconcile me the more readily to it, and that is that if I lack most in that department, I shall learn most in it by being thus compelled to attend to it.

After breakfast took a long stroll over the country around, collecting flowers and insects in company with Prof. Thomas and Mr. [*Alfred*] Smith.

The sun is very hot today, as it was yesterday in camp, though there is a fine breeze blowing.

The boys of the party have been playing baseball with the officers of the Post here – to the credit it is said, of the party!

Towards the close of day, as the sun declined, made a little excursion for flowers with Mr. Adams and put them in press.

SUNDAY, MAY 28

Had a good night's rest last night. The weather is superb. Rose early and after breakfast took a walk over the ground with Mr. Schoenborn [*Schönborn*]. I learn that it is contemplated when next we move to rearrange the occupants of the tents. Prof. Thomas will have charge of a tent with some of the younger boys. Precisely what my position will be I do not know, but I shall have good associates I know and plenty of room.

With a few young men I propose to go over to the town (Cheyenne) and attend church this morning. We did so, riding in an ambulance and attended at the Episcopal Church.

A Mr. [Piper?], Quarter Master's Clerk, formerly from Cleveland, rode over with us. He has been here several years – i.e. in the Western Territories – a very frank ingenuous man. . . . The sun is scorching hot today and yet there is a tolerable breeze.

A party with tents, belonging to Mr. Clarence King, surveyors of the 40th parallel, pitched near our camp yesterday.[5] Several of them are mexicans. They have very inferior tents etc. We shall have an addition of one to our party – a son of Gen. Duncan of this post.[6] He has prevailed our Mr. Hayden to admit him to the company. The Doctor is obliged to maintain the good will of their military men as he is to a large extent dependent on them for Stores, etc.

It is decided to start for Ogden on Tuesday, and in order to accomplish it, it was [*thought*] necessary by the manager, Mr. Stephenson [*Stevenson*], to load the cars today – Sabbath!? I am told that the Sabbath is but little observed while in the field – travelling and work goes on as usual. A man's conscience will be respected no doubt as to the amount of labor performed thus on the Sabbath, but considering the character of [*our*] party and our exposed circumstances it is quite probable that duty requires the doctor to move on rather than lie still. It is doubtless better for the party in every respect, all things considered.

On returning from Church today one could but dimly perceive the mountains in the West. The atmosphere is hazy and not as clear as usual.

I must write home today probably my last from Cheyenne. Towards night took a long walk over the hills and, if never before, they were wet a little with my tears.

MONDAY, MAY 29

We had a powerful thunder shower last night. It gathered darkness on the horizon during the evening and later it commenced to lighten in the South West. About 11 o'clock the shower passed, raining for a while very hard, but our tents are perfectly dry. This morning it is foggy and damp, and it remains to be seen whether the sun will disperse the clouds or not.

With Adams, I took a long walk of 4 or 5 miles and got a few new flowers. By 11 o'clock [*it*] cleared. I noticed that nearly all the Prairie dog burrows had fresh earth thrown out. Probably the rain washed earth into the holes last night – the cause.

As evidence of the dryness of the air in this region, we notice the fact that hundreds of dead horses and other animals drawn out upon the [hills] back of this post are almost perfectly preserved – dried up by the sun and wind. The flesh has been mostly removed (by Coyotes probably in part or Scavenger birds and insects) but the ghostly skeletons, partly exposed and bleached, but covered mostly with skin and hair, lying in profusion around, present a horrid and sickening aspect.

Pasturing on the same hills are many cattle, who, lying down in these crowded cemeteries to ruminate, can scarcely be distinguished from their dead and desiccated companions. Lying directly upon the white tertiary limestone which [crops out of] the sides of the hills around, is a stratum of Drift conglomerate of variable thickness (2 to 5 feet) made up of the debris from the granite mountains west. It differs in no respect from the loose drift above, only in being more or less firmly cemented. What the cement was which bound together in a heterogeneous mass these water-worn pebbles of quartz, red feldspar, hornblend etc., I failed to discover.

The drift of this region contains a much larger proportion of hornblend than mica, indicating that the mountains west are syenitic rather than of granite. I have met with more or less of mica bearing metamorphic rock, however showing that there is variety in the composition of the rocks in the mountain ridges.

At 12 o'clock P.M. this blowing [is] almost a hurricane. The air is full of dust, and now and then there is a little spurt of rain. We are rapidly breaking up camp. The wagons are taking off boxes and trunks and loading them on the [freight] cars. Only the sleeping tents, valisses and table fixtures remain for a start tomorrow after breakfast.

These winds are a common thing along at the base of the mountains. After dark the wind subsided somewhat but about 11 o'clock it commenced raining and rained hard nearly all the night.

Report No. 1: Ferdinand Hayden to Spencer Baird

CHEYENNE, W[*YOMING*] T[*ERRITORY*]
MAY 29, 1871

Dear Professor Baird:

. . . If those little Barometers come to hand, send them to Ogden, Utah, and they will be sent to us at Virginia City. We leave here tomorrow for Ogden. We have a splendid outfit – better than ever if anything. We put it on 5 freight cars. My party has reached the number of 28 persons. We shall have about 32 in all – enough in ourselves to fight off the Indians. Huse says he is too early for the birds' nests. My party is too large, but I think I shall manage to get through with it.

King's party is camped close to us.

Please take good care of all books or papers that may come to me.

Yours sincerely,

F. V. Hayden

TUESDAY, MAY 30: RAINING

Had breakfast in a hard storm of wind and rain. Could hardly be comfortable with three coats on. After breakfast, the tents were taken down in the rain, and we packed off with our valises to the Quartermaster's office while the boys assisted the men in getting the horses on board.

By eight o'clock the rain ceased and the sun came out for awhile. These hard showers, attended with high winds – little hurricanes – are said to be quite frequent at this season of the year, when the plains are becoming heated up and the cold air from the mountain passes rushes down the side hills with tremendous force. The wind last night passed suddenly from South West to West and then to North West showing that the storm was a sort of cyclone.

Reached Cheyenne with our extra train from the Post at about 11:15 A.M. Most of the boys will go on with the train sometime this P.M. and will be two days or more in getting on to Ogden. A few of us will go on in The Passenger Train at 1:50 – Mr. Adams, Mr. Schönborn, Messrs. Beaman, Hughes [*Huse*], and Smith.

Cheyenne is 6,072 ft above the ocean. Omaha only 966 ft. The rise from Omaha to Cheyenne, distance 517 miles by Union Pacific Rail Road, is nearly 12 feet to the mile, but it is so gradual as to be almost imperceptible. From Cheyenne to Sherman Station (summit of Laramie Mountains 8,242 feet above tide level) is only 33 miles, the grade is about 66 feet per mile.[7]

The ride of the east flank of the Laramie ridge from Cheyenne to Sherman and down onto the Laramie plains was one of extreme interest to me. We were slowly and with difficulty climbing up to the highest point on the Union Pacific Rail Road, and though the mountain scenery here is not so bold and striking as in many other parts of the West, yet as it was our first actual contact with the mountains, it could not fail to produce a deep impression on our mind.

The Laramie range which we here crossed is a clearly manifest anticlinal. The least skilled in Geology, in passing over hastily in the cars as we did, could not fail to understand it. From the newer tertiary beds we passed over the edges of older unaltered rocks, and then over metamorphic ridges all inclining to the eastward, their upturned edges pointing westward towards the central nucleus, and at last reached the granite (Red syenite) backbone of the range. This last is a splendid rock in texture and in color, and presents some beautiful studies for the geologist, especially in the manner of weathering.

Towering masses (remnants of the denudation which has wrought so

6. Sherman Station, May 30. U.S. Geological Survey, W. H. Jackson 4 [1869]

extensively and powerfully in all this part of the country) stand here and there like the hoary ruins of some mighty city, their sharper lines and angles being rounded and smoothed by the process of exfoliation, and their broad surfaces garnished with grey-green lichens.

It was a wonderful sight to behold. I could scarcely restrain myself from clapping my hands in extacy! On descending into the plain westward we passed successively over the same ridges from older to newer that we had passed in ascent; only that the dip of the strata had been reversed, their outcropping edges pointing now eastward towards the central axis.

From the summit we had an extensive prospect. To the eastward ran the great Buffalo plains extending to the Mississippi; to the South were the snow capped mountains which border the North Park including Long's Peak, 14,000 feet high; to the West were the Laramie plains or plateaus with its many streams gathered from the mountain sides; and to the North and North West stretched the Laramie Range (sometimes called here, but wrongly, the Black Hills) to whose summits we had just attained.

The air was very chilly. The rain storm which we had experienced in Cheyenne was here a snow storm and snow was yet standing in many places along the road side. It reminded me of my readings of Alpine scenery, for here were little rivulets running everywhere, clear and sparkling as the crystal; there were little flowers blooming in virgin purity and in close proximity to the snow drifts.

Among the rocks passed in this anticlinal were carboniferous limestone – Triassic or Jurassic, seed sandstone, Cretaceous and tertiary clays, marls, limestones, etc., covered every[*where*], more or less deeply, with Drift.

The Laramie plains, now beautifully grassed with variegated shades of green and richly watered, is fast becoming a favorite grazing district, and will undoubtedly erelong be everywhere dotted with ranches and herds of cattle.

But the country west of this plain, after passing the divide which separates it from the Green River and Bear River systems, becomes exceedingly desolate. The grasses disappear almost entirely, and nothing is seen for many weary miles but bunches of sage brush (*Artemisia tridentata*) partially covering the dry pulverulent earth. Very little rain falls in all this region. The Rail Road, for the most part, follows the meanderings of the few small streams that exist and thus the eye is relieved in part by narrow strips of green vegetation – where else all would be an arid desert.

It is said, however, that the soil in this great Desert, consisting mainly of clays of various shades, contains all the essential elements of plant life and that only water is needed to make the entire surface bloom and blossom like the rose. But great meteorological changes must take place before that can be. At present, it can be useful for grazing purposes only and this must be limited, I presume, to the few river valleys which here and there exist over this extensive plateau. It is said to be the feeding ground of deer and antelopes, and is not so destitute of life as would appear at first sight.

As we approached Green River from the Rock Creek Valley, we had presented over our right a wonderful exhibition of banded or variegated clays in an almost vertical bluff of great height. It was especially interesting to the geologist as suggestive of the changes involved in the first history of these strata both as it regards the water and source of the materials and the force and direction of the currents or the depth and condition of the water.

A portion of these surface beds over which we have passed were deposited when as yet the ocean prevailed, its saline waters penetrating all these valleys and washing the shores of the higher lands which, here and there, existed as islands in a shallow sea. This is proved by the character of the life of the age, as the fossils entombed are all such as belong to marine fauna.

Another portion of these deposits were made at a later period when the ocean had been excluded and the depressions had become vast inland lakes, surrounded by forest clad hills and grass covered plains as the lacustrine, fluviatile and [tonestrial?] character of the fossils imbedded abundantly testify. All this, though geologically speaking recent, was far in the past and

7. Burning Rock Cut, May 30. U.S. Geological Survey, W. H. Jackson 16 [1869]

great changes have since taken place, involving uplifts, foldings, volcanic eruptions, denudation and erosion on a vast scale, together with changes in climate and in life once and again.

The banded clays are in many places capped by a bright red sandstone which by atmospheric action has been wrought into a thousand fantastic forms. These are of special interest to the passing traveller, affording frequent relief to the monotony and weariness of the journey. Often they assume the appearance of ruined cities or of walled fortifications, of castles and towers, of human faces or figures, or other forms of animated nature. Many of these more striking forms have received local names and enter into the geographic description of the country, such as Castle rock, Sentinel rock, the Monument, the Pulpit, the Dial, the Witches etc. The word Butte (Bute) in the west is applied to any isolated outlying rock, which rises boldly from the general surface. Hence we have the Three Buttes, the Red Butte, the Black Butte, Church Butte, etc. The Black Butte receives its name from the dark and gloomy appearance which its dense covering of cedar trees gives it as seen from a distance; the Church Butte, from its fancied resemblance to a distant church pile.

Passenger on Union Pacific Railroad on way to Ogden

WEDNESDAY, MAY 31

Much that has been noted under yesterday's date is equally applicable to the Wonders which fell under our observation today.

During most of the day, the Uinta range of mountains, snow capped, were seen on our left having an East and West trend. Some of the higher points were visited last year by Dr. Hayden and party. The Utes – a tribe of Indians now friendly – have their houses and hunting grounds in that direction. At several places along our route Coal has been discovered and, to some extent, mined. The coal belongs to the great Lignite era (Eocene, or older Tertiary) and it is said to be nearly equal to the bituminous coals of Pittsburgh, Ohio and Illinois. It has been used on the Union Pacific Rail Road and, in many places in the West, as the beds are thick and easily accessible, they must prove exceedingly profitable to the owners of them. It would seem, therefore, that there is laid up in these comparatively barren hills an abundant store of fuel for any population which may hereafter find homes upon this great interior plateau.[8]

Near Aspen we found ourselves in the near vicinity of the Wasatch Mountains which form the Eastern border of the Salt Lake valley. The whole scenery presented a marked change. The vegetation was greatly improved, the hills were carpeted with grass. Trees of various kinds – the aspen, poplar, willow etc. – appeared in the valleys. The streams were more rapid and sparkling. Snow lay piled upon the mountains near, showing that these beautiful streams were perennial, their sources being in those ever snow crowned heights. At length we entered the far famed Echo Cañon – a cleft in the Wasatch range, where from the Observation Car we beheld the most wondrous views of this wonderful journey.[9] It was a rapid descent down a highly inclined grade in which little or no steam was used and in which the greatest skill and precaution was required. Long and high tresslework bridges were crossed; long and dark tunnels were penetrated; rapid curves along frightful embankments were passed. But these we scarcely noticed. On either side were precipitous mountain cliffs presenting an ever varying panorama of grand and beautiful visions.

At first the rocks were of the later formations, clay, shales and sandstone conglomerates of varying colors, and presented the most curious and won-

8. Trestle Work—Echo Canyon, May 31. U.S. Geological Survey, W. H. Jackson 23 [1869]

derful castillated forms. Every one admired, everyone exclaimed, all were in exstacy.

Castles, towers, antique ruins, giant cloud shadows, but left, I trust, upon my memory a most enduring impression!

At length we passed into the Weber River valley, where a new prospect was presented by a change in the character of the rocks. Older formations came up to view. Triassic, Carboniferous, possibly Silurian rocks, certainly metamorphic, whatever their age, appeared in extensive beds of slate of Mica, Schist, and Gneiss. All of which were standing almost vertically upon the upheaved edges.

The views presented by these highly inclined strata, if not as varied and beautiful as the castellated forms of the newer and weathered rocks, were at least more unique and impressive. Steepled towers, minarets, long and lofty walls stretching far up the mountain side, like the bony v[ia]ls of some vast thing, [as] if, life now passed in rapid succession.

At length all eyes are turned to the left, to see that very peculiar arrangement of two adjacent strata – which has received that somewhat significant, if not beautiful, designation, the Devil's Slide and which has been often told in story and photographed by the artist.

It is nothing more nor less than two parallel strata of metamorphic rock, several feet in thickness each, and separated from each other by a somewhat greater interval, which rise up from the general surface in two nearly vertical walls with even, clean-cut slides. The height of these walls varies in different positions from 20 to 40 feet. Commencing at the foot they stretch far up the mountainside all the way holding a perfect parallelism both in regard to comparative height and the interval that separates them. The upper or terminal edge of these walls is more or less irregular and jagged, while the sides are comparatively smooth. The space enclosed between these walls is dark and dismally suggestive. Such is the "Devil's Slide" of Utah.

No doubt his infernal majesty has long presided over these regions, but whether he has ever amused himself in sliding down these cold and jagged mountain sides is somewhat questionable. The warmer plains of [M. Kingdom?] might be more attractive.[10]

The Thousand Mile Tree (1,000 [*miles*] from Omaha) is passed, and still one more point of interest a few miles farther down the cañon [*is*] denominated the "Devil's Gate" where the Weber river rushes with headlong velocity through a narrow chasm between lofty converging walls and we emerge into the broad valley of Utah of which Salt Lake is the central depression. Turning to the north along the side of the Wasatch chain through which we have punctured, and we are soon at Ogden, our Western terminus. Thirty minutes later we are on board the train for Salt Lake City where we arrive at 7 o'clock in the evening.

Salt Lake City, staying at the Townsend House[11]

2

Salt Lake City and Ogden

Mr. Adams, who accompanied me to this city, and myself sallied from the Townsend House after breakfast to see this world renowned city. It has often been described, and a repetition would be useless. The features which first attract the attention of strangers, and which can never fail greatly to interest and please, are the great breadth of the streets and the ever flowing rivulets which sparkle along their sides. The streets are well graded and graveled and make excellent drives for carriages, while the mountain streams convey everywhere abundant supplies of water dispersing fertility and life and imparting to the atmosphere a delightsome sense of refreshing coolness.

Our first point was the Tabernacle.[1] We are admitted to the walled enclosure, and by applying at the office were politely attended by the person in charge who seemed happy to answer our main inquiries.

The Tabernacle is the great place of Convocation for the Mormons. It is a plain structure of peculiar form, huge proportions – an immense ellipse – the chief axes of which are 250 and 200 feet. Its roof is of shingle, an elliptical dome – looking for all the world like the cover to a soup dish.

Its form makes it a complete whispering gallery, and the speaker near one end, it is said, can be heard distinctly in any part of the house.

At the extreme next end is the organ – an immense affair now in process of building by Mormon artisans. The case is completed showing heavy ornamentation of carved work. Many additional sets of pipes are yet to be made.

Everything else about the building is vividly plain – paint even being discarded. On either side of the organ are the seats for the singers. In front

Panorama 2. Ogden Campground, June 3–10

9. Great Salt Lake City with newly built tabernacle, June 1. U.S. Geological Survey, W. H. Jackson 42 [1869]

directly of the organ is the poorly cushioned seat of President Young and his councillors.[2] In front and a little below this is the uncushioned seat of the twelve apostles. Next, below a similar seat for the civil officers or Officers of State, and still partly down in the same line, is the seat for the Bishops. On either side of these four slips or pews are the seats of the High Priests and Elders arranged nearly at right angles to others and of little less elevation.

Below all these are the slips for the people, arranged in four rows, of 32 feet length each, with broad aisles between. The women occupy the two central rows. Above, there is a gallery running all around the building except the end occupied by the organ. Here the women occupy one side of the house and the men the other. This arrangement is not a matter of *faith* with them, but is a custom, early introduced, to prevent their women from unpleasant contact with a rowdy set of California and other emigrants, which has from convenience been retained. They commune every Sabbath.

Within the same enclosure are the foundations of the Great Temple which is yet to be.[3] The foundation alone has been the work of many years. They are just ready to add somewhat to the superstructure by laying up a portion of the stone already cut and lying near. The size of the building is not so large as that of the Tabernacle, it being only 150 feet long by 100 broad. An Elevation plan, which was exhibited to us in the office, showed there immense towers in from the central one of which was 300 feet high while the main body of the building was to be 100 feet high. It is nearly rectangular in form and not oval.

The whole temple is to be cut of granite, highly ornamented, and it is this which makes it so slow of progress and so expensive. The granite (or rather sy[e]nite) is similar in size of grain to the well known Quincy granite of Boston, but the color lighter and far handsomer.

Leaving the Tabernacle grounds, we next made our way to the main entrance to President Young's establishment.[4] The grounds are very extensive occupying two or more entire squares and surrounded by a high cobble stone wall that completely shuts out the interior from the vulgar gaze. We were permitted to enter a small reception room in which were several ladies and gentlemen, strangers like ourselves. The room contained various paintings and engravings, among which were well executed painted likenesses of President Young and the chief Mormon dignitaries, most of whom are now living. We were informed that the President was not in, but would be in tomorrow from II to I o'clock. Fortunately, as we returned down the principal business street, we saw his carriage – we guessed it to be such – standing at the Print Store. We stopped and examined leisurely the Photographs and paintings displayed in the windows. Soon we saw Brigham Young himself – we knew him in an instant – come down the stairs and enter into conversation with persons in the store. We returned, made some errand, looked at the pictures hung upon the walls, but all the while we listened to and occasionally we glanced at, as the attention of himself and others being turned, we more intently scanned his person and physi[o]gnomy. We were entirely satisfied with the opportunity, and felt that we had seen the great lion of the city.

We then went to the museum to see the smaller lions.[5] Fifty cents gave us admission to see the smallest fraction of what Barnum grants for 25 cents. But this was mostly a show of Utah productions, ores, animals etc., and we came to study the west. Of [silver] and lead and other ores from the Utah mines, there was an abundant exhibit. Also a few splendid specimens of Chalced[dony], Rock crystal, selenite, common salt from a Salt bed in Southern Utah, and crystallizations from the Great Lake – Moss Agates, amethyst, etc.; [*also*] the Cloth manufactured here when excluded from the world; their early paper currency etc. There were some stuffed animals and birds. But that portion of the show which interested and instructed me the most was the exhibition of live animals. Of these the most strange were four Sea Lions recently taken on the Pacific coast near the Barbara Islands.[6] One, a female, was full grown or nearly so. The others there were younger, probably less than a year old. Their color was tawny and in the front vein of the head, especially of the male when the mane is developed, the resemblance to a lion must be very close. They were fed upon fish of any kind.

The man who had them in charge was an agent of Barnum and was exhibiting them here only for a few days. They played in a tank of fresh water, salt water not being essential so far as the man could determine. He hoped to get them through to New York as safely but was doubtful. The old one was 6 or 7 feet in length.

There was an old Dromedary which had been imported by the U.S. Government by the way of experiment;[7] five Bears, three of them Black (one of which was full grown), one a Cinnamon, and one Grizley. This last, though young, was said to be master of the pen. It was quite differently shaped – of a stouter build and more demonstrative. He had not yet acquired his Grizley hue. All these bears are frequently met with in the Wahsatch Range near by. There was one young Catamount (Puma), several Lynxes of two species, Foxes, Prairie wolves, Porcupines, Golden Eagles etc., all found in this vicinity. Here, also for the first time, I saw the Black tailed deer (mule) both stuffed and alive. A few monkeys and mackaws from South America and a cockatoo from Australia, completed all the exhibition of interest to me.

As to the general impression which Salt Lake City has made from this hasty visit, I would only note a kind of composite character – an oriental element and European alpine element, and an American element of the most modern type – these curiously blending into a harmonious whole the general or predominant effect of which is pleasing. Low buildings, many of them stone, large gardens many of which are enclosed in walls, with green trees and shrubbery, and the musical ripple of waters flowing every where, give it a dreamy oriental character; the snow capped mountains nearby and the herds of cattle pastured upon the plain give it an alpine and european character; all else is American. I have reason to believe that the Mormon population is largely foreign and from England, but the Miner and the Yankee agent is every where.

Salt Lake City is larger than I had supposed. It is said to contain twenty thousand inhabitants. The fixed population, I presume, would fall somewhat short of that. Owing to the width of the streets and the lack, as yet, of that compactness which usually characterizes cities, it covers at present a large area. The city is beautifully situated on a sloping plain with the Wahsatch Range of mountains on the East; the Oquirrh Range in the South west and the great Salt lake on the west and north. A more delightful situation for scenery could hardly be imagined. It is said to be perfectly healthy. The mormons under the rule of Brigham Young have displayed great industry and the change which they have wrought in this barren wilderness is wonderful to behold. Besides Salt Lake City there are numerous flourishing Mormon towns to the North and South and up in the cañons to the east. A larger and constantly increasing trade is carried on here. The mining interests of Utah have given a fresh impetus of late to all kinds of business, and large and fine blocks of stores are built or in process of building in the business portion of the city. The stores had a fresh and neat appearance and the stocks of merchandise were in many establishments quite extensive.

Of the domestic and religious character of the people I have made no personal inquiry: Sufficient has been written on those subjects by persons resident here. The city, so far as quiet, cleanliness and comfort is concerned, is certainly far in advance of many, if not most, of these western towns. As to their comparative morality, I cannot say, but my impression is that, bar[r]ing the peculiar institution of polygamy which prevails among the mormons, there is less of vice and immorality here than in most other places – I mean less of that open, obtrusive character which too often meets the unwilling eye or ear of a stranger.

This evening with a delightsome air and a bright full moon shining with unwonted clearness, I walked through various streets of the city – the business streets, as well as some of the more interior streets – in the vicinity of the Post Office and the theater, and I saw but little of that boisterous rowdyism which so loudly proclaims itself in many places and nothing at all was suggestive of vice or harlotry. A single walk of that kind may not be conclusive, I admit, but not withstanding I believe that an approximately accurate impression may be thus attained.

I should have mentioned while speaking of Brigham Young that he attained his seventieth year this very day, 1st of June. His Birthday was celebrated by a serenade from the Band. On the whole I shall leave Salt Lake City with very pleasant associations, and this independent of any knowledge of or sympathy with the peculiar religious institutions of the Mormons.

FRIDAY, JUNE 2

After breakfast I went out with Adams to gather plants on a hill back of President Young's grounds and in the valley below, as far as the Bath House at Warm Springs.[8]

This A.M. had an opportunity which I have long desired of seeing a mounted band of Indians, in all their native paint and glory. Some fifteen or twenty of them rode up Main Street in Salt Lake City, dismounted, made purchases (beads etc.), while several smaller parties were strolling about town on foot, entering stores, not so much to buy, so far as I could observe, as to satisfy their curiosity, for they occupied themselves mainly in pointing out to each other different articles of merchandise and commenting upon them in their own language. Some of the mounted party had skins along with them for a barter trade. These Indians were Utes, belonging to Kenas-ha's [*Kanosh's*] band – so I understood the name of chief – and occupy the country south and east, especially along the Uinta Mountains, as hunting grounds.[9] They often visit the City and other towns in Utah for trade, camping in the vicinity sometimes for days or weeks.

They generally know a little english and are considered as friendly to the whites. Most of the band which we saw consisted of young men and boys. When they first rode into town there were two women on ponies bringing up the rear, one of whom had a quantity of tent stuff apparently, bestowed upon a couple of long poles attached on either side to the pony like carriage thills and resting on the ground behind.[10] There may have been other women but I did not recognize them. They were all highly painted and ornamented with beads, feathers, etc. The prevailing color of their paint was a deep vermilion red, though some were painted with yellowish and greenish hues. This was painted upon their faces and occasionally upon their breasts and arms [giving] them a somewhat frightful appearance. Their dress, otherwise, consisted of a kind of suit of red flannel on sleeves, leggings, sometimes of [*torn page, missing word*] and Sometimes of deerskin; and always deerskin moccasins. Besides these, each Indian had a blanket, more usually of blue color, which was drawn carelessly around them, sometimes under and sometimes above their arms, and held together apparently only by their hands. They doubtless have some other way of fastening them in front when necessary to free the use of their hands. A few were armed with guns and one of them had a bow and arrows – but most were without either. One of their number [*torn page, missing word*] had so far departed from Indian custom as to wear a slouch white hat and a Blue Army Coat. He looked far less picturesque though he was more comfortably clad.

In P.M. we took cars from Ogden and found our Camp pitched near the Depot – all hands present.

Tomorrow the camp is to be moved farther away where there is pasturage.

Ogden – by the track

SATURDAY, JUNE 3
Slept alone in tent last night as my partners were all absent, Mr. Jackson at Hotel with his wife and the other boys on guard at the corral.[11] The wind

blew quite hard and it rained in the night, but I had an abundance of clothing and was warm.

A few Snake Indians are here in Ogden – painted and ornamented in a similar manner as the Utes seen at Salt Lake. (The Sea Lions are here too, on exhibition.)

The indians wear nothing upon their heads except ornaments. These consist of large feathers stuck in their hair on the sides or back of the head. All wear them of some kind. Those of the Eagle are most prized. The leader of the small band of Utes seen in Salt Lake had, in addition to Eagle feathers, two or three disks of polished brass of different sizes; the largest of which was at least 3 inches in diameter. These plates are round and the outer exposed surface slightly convex. The other side doubtless had projecting processes of some kind by which it was strongly tied to an irregular cue into which the back hair of the head was gathered. All the Indians thus far seen wore upon their wrists, arms or neck some kind of beads.

The Eye of the Indian is peculiar as it regards expression. There is a certain deep, dark, deceitful and determined expression, which added to the intense blackness of the pupil, is surely suggestive of treachery and blood. There is a sort of stoic fixedness which ordinarily presents itself in the Indian's eye. It is not a *stare*, it is not the index of *indifference* or *inattention*. It rather indicates the most watchful, cautious, plotting observation. An ophidian eye that cannot apparently be moved from its purpose, and yet, if closely watched there will now and then be detected a lurking twinkle bespeaking a consciousness of having satisfactorily formed some diabolical plot to be executed in the future.

That concealed twinkle that occasionally flashes up, like the dim and distant lightning flash upon the evening cloud seems but the precursor of the swift winged arrow, the bloody tomahawk or the scalping knife.

This dark and treacherous expression of the Indian's eye is greatly intensified by the blood-red paint so plentifully bestreaked upon their foreheads and high cheek bones which constitutes the frame of its setting.

Have pressed a large number of plants here at Ogden. This P.M. went up to the mountain side with Prof. Thomas collecting plants and insects. The distance was altogether greater than it appeared to our untaught eyes before the trip.

Ogden, on the terrace east of the city,
and 185 feet above the railroad track at the depot

10. Camp at Ogden, June 4. U.S. Geological Survey, W. H. Jackson 48

SUNDAY, JUNE 4

A beautiful day. Went over to the village in an ambulance with a few others to attend a Conference Meeting of the Mormons. This is the second and great day of the Conference and a large crowd was gathered. The occasion afforded us an opportunity to hear Brigham Young speak. The meeting was opened by singing and prayer under the direction of Bishop [*Willard*] Richards of Ogden. The prayer was offered by a Smith (Elias) a relative of Joseph Smith. The first address was made by D. H. Wells the Second Councillor – next to Young. His manner was rather tame and his tone monotonous. He stated that they accepted the whole Bible – the old and new Testaments. He referred to John's declaration in Revelation, "I saw an angel flying, having the everlasting gospel, etc." This gospel was revealed to the Mormons. He referred to their persecutions in the States and their settlement in the Utah Valley. They were a peculiar people, the latter day Saints, etc. I lost a part of the discourse by reason of the constant crying of the babies in the crowded congregation.

President Brigham is a somewhat natural orator. He has a pleasant voice, natural gesticulation, and a fine physique. He is decidedly a shrewd, talented man. He would make a successful politician anywhere. He has abundant self-assurance, and evidently loves power. He knows how to mount the popular wave – how to turn his sails to the popular breeze as well as any other man of this age. He is now just seventy years old, but has the freshness and vivacity of one ten years younger. He commenced his address by referring again to the persecutions of the mormons. Their principles were not understood. He welcomed investigation. The war now was for the truth. Many were ready for a Mob fight, but if they were not obedient to the truth, did not walk in the paths of righteousness, they would not reach heaven. He said that the Mormons had tried other religions and knew the truth. Other men followed the teaching of their priests and their mothers. He affirmed that any children of Mormons knew vastly more of religion than the Theologians of other religionists though they went to the academy, the College, and Theology Seminary. That all other sects were really infidel. They did not know the truth. They desired to know the truth but did not. The Religious world was in infidelity and it was the business of the Latter Day Saints to teach them the truth.

He said that everyday he was questioned, in his office, about the doctrine and practice of plurality of wives. He was rather facetious in referring to the curious manner in which the subject was introduced by visitors, especially by ladies. He said he felt no delicacy on the subject and could answer questions on that as freely as on any other. He regarded it as altogether a secondary matter. He was pained that so much curiosity was awakened in the minds of others. He thought it indicated something wrong in them. He would much prefer that they would ask him the way of life! Visitors would say, "Oh if it were not for your polygamy." He declared that they were persecuted and driven from the States not for this doctrine, for it had not then been promulgated. They were persecuted, not because of their belief in the Mormon Bible, but because of their belief and practice of the Old and New Testaments. He declared that the teachers of all other sects were made up of ignorance and impudence. They had failed altogether of bringing the world to practice morality. He said their government had been denominated a "One man's power." All other sects were divided among the various political parties, some one thing and some another, but he declared that a religion that did not control a people's politics and unite them in political action was of no value.

He denounced the mormon apostates, and attributed their desertion wholly to business motives. He referred to the running of the Rail Road from Ogden to Salt Lake on Sunday. He believed it best generally to observe the Sabbath. (It was God's revealed way.) But the Union Pacific Rail Road would run on Sabbath and therefore it was simply expedient and then good sense and duty to conform to that fact. He said the way was to be humble and teachable as a little child and God would show us all duty. The drift of his remarks on this head was that whatever was expedient and business-like was duty. He referred repeatedly to the matter of plurality, claiming that it was a question in respect to which he felt no particular interest. If a man did not want a wife, let him remain single. If he wanted one, let him marry one. If he wanted more than one let him take them. Whose business was it. But while he affected to be indifferent to the subject, it was manifest to me that it was the very particularly sore spot in Mormon doctrine and practice, which was constantly before his mind and in respect to which he felt bound to fortify himself and hearers.

In referring to the subject the fourth and fifth time he said that persons were so inquisitive often about his wives, ladies especially, that he presumed they would like to know with which of his wives he had slept the last night. He said he could tell them one thing: *He had slept with his own wife, and not another man's*. These sallies usually provoked a general smile of satisfaction and approval in the audience.[12]

The Mormons are made up very largely of persons from the old country – the lowest and most ignorant classes in England and Wales, with a few Danes, Swedes, and Germans. They are entirely ignorant of our Eastern civilization – of our churches, schools and political associations, and of course are the ready dupes of their better informed teachers.

And in estimating the character of their leaders it should not be forgotten that they have been the victims formerly of a senseless and unchristian persecution. There is doubtless a certain type of religious feeling which is very sincere in most.

Walked off toward the hills alone and had a precious season of communion.

Had a talk with Dr. Hayden about the wisdom of my proceeding farther. From what he informed me of the route and favoring circumstances I cannot doubt that it is my duty to persevere.

Report No. 2: Ferdinand Hayden to Spencer Baird

OGDEN, UTAH,

JUNE 4TH, 1871

Dear Professor Baird:

I write you a hasty note to tell you that all things have come, except the small barometers.[13] I am sorry they have not come for we need them very much. If they come they should be sent to Ogden as we hope to be at Virginia City and Fort Ellis from the 5th to the 20th of July. Wells Fargo Express goes to all these places. Of course the package must be made with great care. Should you find them, advise me at once by letter, Ogden, Utah. We expect to leave Ogden about Thursday (8th), and push right northward to Montana. Our team will consist of 5 wagons and 2 ambulances, 32 men all told, about 50 mules and horses, with 7 wall tents and several flies.[14] We make a formidable camp, and almost an army on the march.

We have been splendidly treated by the Army, especially Col. Reynolds at Fort Russell,[15] and the Union Pacific railroad Co. We transported 6 car loads of freight and animals (42) and 28 men for $693. If full freight and fare had been charged the cost would have been $3500 at least.

Schönborn is my chief topographer and takes hold admirably. We are going to take a Boat to the Yellow Stone Lake and a sounding apparatus, and make a most thorough survey of it.

It is quite pleasant in Salt Lake valley. The birds are just beginning their nesting arrangements. Huse has a few. All my party are laboring with great zeal and I presume my next annual report will contain a full survey of the Flora and Fauna of our route. I shall send direct to specialists such things as we collect by the time of our leaving Ogden. Nothing is to be sent to any one who will not pledge himself to have a report ready by January 1st 1872. Horn, Uhler, Porter, Cope and Leidy all are ready to take hold. . . . [16]

Yours sincerely,

F. V. H[*ayden*]

11. Ogden Canyon outing, June 5. National Gallery, VI, 168.tif

MONDAY, JUNE 5

Rose quite early and found it so chilly after sleeping that I took cold and begin already to suffer the penalty of a headache. I intend to take the charge of the recent shells that may be collected besides looking after the plants.[17]

Went about 10 o'clock in ambulance with Jackson and Dixon, Photographers, and a few others, up the Ogden Cañon – 5 miles. The River is

12. Picnic at Ogden Canyon, June 5. *Left to right:* Robert Adams (?), William Logan, George Dixon, George Allen, Mollie Jackson, and Charles Turnbull. Enclosed in letter from Hayden to Delano, June 8, 1871, National Archives, RG 48

considerable in size and very swift and the rocks on either side are lofty and very precipitous. A number of Photo-views were taken – one of the party at lunch.

Gathered various plants and a number of Helices, a species of H. Solitaria, if not a variety of the same. {These were formed among the scrub oaks on the sides of the cañon under the leaves.} Found a few dead small Paludinas in the sand of the river at one point {showing that they exist somewhere above in the cañon. Collected Tiger beetles and other insects.} The scenery up the Cañon is grand, though not so picturesque as that of the Echo Cañon.

As in the Weber Cañon the rocks are mostly metamorphic and the scenery wild and rugged. The trip was of a picnic character and very pleasant, though to me very tiresome. On returning through the village we saw several Snake Indians. I should have mentioned that Mrs. Jackson was with us today. She has come out to the Utah Valley for the first time to see the country and start her husband off on his long trip northward. She returns to Omaha tomorrow. She is a pleasant, lively and sensible lady, and quite a favorite with all.

TUESDAY, JUNE 6

After breakfast, took my first ride on horseback. My horse is the oldest one in the herd and was selected for me for its steadiness and reliability. On these accounts, too, it had received the cognomen of Sol – short for Solomon. I rode some 3 or 4 miles away and concluded that the horse would answer my purpose well.

{Rode to a small Lake 2 or 3 miles East of Camp. Collected plants, etc. Tadpoles and the larva of insects were numerous in the waters of the Pond but no mollusks were observed. The pond appears to have been recently made for irrigating or other purposes, and consequently there has been insufficient [*time*] for other forms of animals to establish themselves.

Obtained a few Post pliocene shells from a ditch bank – all of one species of Lymnea. Changed papers of plants.}

Had a grand bath in a brook that ran among the oaks clear and swift from the mountain side. It was a refreshing treat – one that I should like to enjoy every day. During the ride we called at a farm house where we were kindly treated to a bowl apiece of sour milk. The family consisted of a youngerly man 35 to 38 years of age, his wife, father-in-law and child. They have lived in the valley many years, and suffered many hardships. Now, however, they were getting into comfortable circumstances. I took the opportunity to inquire about the indigenous animals of this region. The old gentleman assured me that the Buffalo had not been seen in the Utah plain since the Mormon settlements commenced, but that their horns and skeletons were found, showing that they had once existed here. The Elk has occasionally been killed here, and formerly the antilope were somewhat common, though of late it was seldom seen. The Prairie dog (cynomys) is not found at all in this part of Utah, though it is rarely found in the more southern parts.[18] The grizly bear is somewhat common in the mountains and the black (with varieties brown and cinnamon) abundant. Bears will not attack men if not disturbed or wounded.

A species of Rattlesnake is quite common hereabouts and several have been killed by the party. They are small – 2.5 to 3 feet long.

These cañons afford glorious studies for the geologist. It would seem at first that the comparatively insignificant streams which now flow through them were altogether inadequate to their production; but the more one observes the action of water in eroding soil in every direction at lower elevations, and the more carefully he studies the details of form, in both cases, the more readily [*he*] will be constrained to admit that both are due to the same cause. The moderately deep cañon in the clay or sandy bench at the mountain base is a perfect facsimile of the profound cañon that cuts the main mountain range and exposes almost perpendicular cliffs one, two, or more thousand feet in altitude.

Everywhere the mountainside and summits are deeply furrowed and scooped by the erosive power of water, and the deeper cuts or cañons only show where the streams have been more abundant by union and therefore more efficient. It is true there may have been, in some places, a transverse fissure, more or less profound, made at the time of the uplift or folding of the mountain belts, and that these fissures have both determined the position and so far aided in the production of the cañon; but the more I observe these wondrous displays of Nature's forces amid the mountains, the more perfectly satisfied is my mind that atmospheric and aqueous causes are alone sufficient in the lapse of ages to scoop out their deep channels in rocks.

Undoubtedly the work was commenced at a period when the water (oceanic or lacustrine) reached a much higher level than exists at present. This fact indeed, has been demonstrated by Professor Hayden and other[s] from paleontological evidence, and they have even indicated the shore lines of those old cretaceous seas and tertiary lakes which confined the more elevated waters of those earlier times. But the erosive work which must then have been active in cutting down those old barriers slowly proceeded until, in time, the mountain barriers were channelled and in most cases the Lakes were drained. The Great Salt Lake of Utah Valley is indeed a partial exception. The Mountain barriers here have not been so deeply cleft as to allow of its perfect drainage.

Here the evaporation equals the precipitation. Owing to its considerable elevation and to its position between various mountain systems, the amount of that precipitation is relatively small, and thus we can easily see how in this very dry atmosphere the evaporation may keep pace with the fall of vapor. It is the impression here among the settlers that the climate is undergoing decided change – a change in every way favorable to the people. The warm season is prolonged and frosts less severe.

WEDNESDAY, JUNE 7: OGDEN CAMP

After breakfast rode down to Weber River with Professor Thomas. Collected all the varieties of plants I could discover in the valley immediately adjacent, and pressed them apart from those collected elsewhere. The weather is excessively hot, and during the ride I suffered from the heat very much.

Found a few shells, mostly dead. Professor Thomas found a few live snails – small size – two species, near to H. arborea and H. Striatella; also a small species of Lymnea.

{Inside of the tent the heat is absolutely insupportable. Changed papers of all plants in press. Mr. Adams, my Colleague in this department, is very kind and considerate in taking the larger share of the manual labor involved.}

. . . Wrote letter home.

Was disturbed by printing of Photos in tent and visitors till very late.

THURSDAY JUNE 8:
CAMP OGDEN, CALLED BY SOME CAMP STEVENSON

Not very well and the Doctor (Turnbull) recommended my aperient powders before breakfast and a breakfast of toast and milk.[19] Put up all the plants collected at Cheyenne, Salt Lake City and Ogden this far (sufficiently dry) to send East from this point (Rail Road). Collections in all departments thus far are forwarded east to Smithsonian from this point.

{A mishap has prevented the removal of our Camp to a station near the head of the Lake some 9 to 10 miles distant. Two horses and one mule strayed from the herd yesterday, and the search for their recovery has been going on all day. They have been heard from this afternoon.}

I am constantly trying to carry my mind back to the time when the broad Pacific, broader far than now, flowed over the site of these valleys and plateaus and perhaps of the mountains themselves; to a somewhat later period when these mountains were but a coast chain of Islands. When the Gulf and Pacific peacefully blended their waters in a broad shallow sea extending far north to the arctic. And when here, upon many a shallow bank and shelving shore, there lived and died a varied and beautiful oceanic fauna of which their entombed remains now abundantly testify. And this long after the Eastern, Northern, and Middle States, with their great central nucleus, the Appalachian range of mountains, had become permanently uplifted and established as the older portion of our continent. And, to a time more recent still, though long back in the ages of the past, when this newer portion of our Continent had been elevated, also from beneath the ocean waves and permanently delivered from the dominion of old Neptune. And, when the extensive foldings and plications of rocky strata, consequent upon this uplift, had become mighty mountain barriers sufficient to prevent the natural flow of the waters to their parent ocean, thereby causing the collection of all atmospheric precipitations, whether of rain or snow, into vast lakes, or continental fresh water seas, as much superior in magnitude to the so-called Great Lakes, of the East, as this great system of mountains, plateaus and plains in the West is superior to the Alleghenies, the Catskill and the Hudson River Valley. Here everything is, and always has been, on a grand scale as it regards scope and magnitude; and such even the great Lake basins of the tertiary epoch. At first only animals peculiar to brackish or estuary waters existed in these basins indicating thereby a transition state from the ruder reign of the Sea Gods to the softer and more [sound?] rule of the Nymphs and Naiads; but soon only freshwater faunas prevailed in the waters, while the hills and Valleys surrounding were clothed with the verdure of forest and meadow, and terrestrial life, more abundant and varied than at present exist, disported itself on every side. Such, indisputably, was the history of this portion of our country in some of the great geological ages of the past – a history written upon the rocks themselves in part, and in part upon tables entombed within the strata and thus wonderfully preserved – tables engraved by the finger of the Creator, himself, whether upon the tree trunk or leaf, upon scale, shell or bone, a fidelity in form and a perfection of finish is everywhere manifested, far surpassing the utmost skill of man in the work of imitation.

It is the province of the geologist and paleontologist to decipher these long buried records – hieroglyphical and unintelligible to the masses, but full of unerring truth and meaning to the initiated.

Report No. 3: Ferdinand Hayden to Spencer Baird

OGDEN, UTAH T[*ERRITORY*]
JUNE 8TH, 1871

Dear Professor Baird:

Your letter came today, I made some slips from papers which may aid you some, in forming an idea of our party, and I also send a photograph or two. You can make out some notes I think from what I send.[20] We leave Ogden Friday morning the 9th for Virginia City and Fort Ellis, Montana – about 430 miles.[21] The sources of the Columbia, Colorado, Missouri and Yellowstone rivers are quite close together. We propose to spend the remainder of the season in the valley of the Yellow Stone. Schönborn is a capital Topographer. He is perfectly at home with his instruments. I question very much whether King has any one connected with him that will equal Schönborn. I do not think he has had a fair chance before. He has fixed the Longitude and Latitude of this point, taken all the elevations needed, and he proposes to map a belt – 50 miles in width – to Fort Ellis, before commencing our systematic work. If I am successful in getting appropriations, I intend to spend the next 5 years in these northern regions. We are now prepared to take the materials for a Boat from Fort Ellis. We have a complete sounding apparatus and therefore intend to strip that region of all romance. We are prepared to take instantaneous views of the Hot Springs, etc.[22] All the geographical points will be well fixed. . . . Huse is doing a good work in Birds and eggs.

Yours, sincerely,

F. V. H.

Friday, June 9

Made up all the plants, thus far collected into a compact bundle, sewed them into a canvas sack, and forwarded them to Professor Porter of Easton, Pennsylvania, through the Smithsonian.[23]

After making up bundle, as above, went with Mr. Adams up into cañon nearby {collecting whatever came in my way, but looked in vain for shells}. Gradually riding higher and higher, we almost reached the top of the mountain. On return had a fine bath in a mountain stream.

The weather continues very warm – 88° in shade.

We expect to break up our camp tomorrow and move 8 to 10 miles westward.

3

To Fort Hall and the Divide

Idaho and Montana Territories

SATURDAY, JUNE 10

Broke camp and got off about 11 o'clock. Wagons seem overloaded – Everything full to overflowing. Many of us cut down our baggage. I made a cache of such things as I could best leave and left them with a merchant in Ogden (Woodmansee) taking receipt for the same.[1] We passed on West with train and cavalcade along the great thoroughfare and old overland stage road to California about 9 to 10 miles and made an early camp at the foot of hills near a pond called "cold springs."

Two men (Steve [*Hovey*], wagon master, and Dr. Turnbull) were absent in search of the three lost horses. I lent my horse and rode in the ambulance. It was terribly hot and dusty. We passed a camp of Shoshonies or Snake Indians with a herd of ponies. Several of the men followed us and came up with us while we were pitching our tents. They begged for sacks of flour, "Hog meat" they call it. The doctor declined but invited them to remain and have supper with us. They rode off without getting anything. They speak just a little English – are wild, filthy looking creatures.[2]

After our supper went out to gather flowers and still later took a fine shower bath under the drip of the Rail Road tank nearby. It was most refreshing and I took the time to change all my underclothes.

Water-tank, Central Pacific Railroad, near Warm Saline Springs

Panorama 3. Bear River Bay, Brigham City, and terraces at mouth of Copenhagen Canyon with wagon road, June 11

Sunday, June 11

Still in Camp made yesterday, within a few rods of Union Pacific Rail Road and near a pond called "Cold Spring." We are near the Western extremity of the Wahsatch range from the foot hills of which there issue both *hot* and *cold springs*. The R.R. station nearby is called "*Hot Spring St[ation]*." Steve returned last night with no news of the missing horses. Dr. Turnbull still back on search.

After breakfast, under the shadow and quiet of our tent lying supine just outside with the clear blue Canopy above, my communings with Heaven and with far absent friends through the medium of the dear Savior were sweet indeed. Took a walk with Adams upon the saline flats approaching the Lake and gathered a few plants peculiar to such a locality. The heat continues to be intense. After dinner went to the Rail Road bridge and washed and dried a few pieces of clothing, as we expect to be travelling steadily now for 10 to 12 days and shall have but little opportunity for such work.

On looking back towards Ogden, we can see the old Wahsatch Mountains, looming up near Ogden Canyon, their tops marked with snow drifts but bald and devoid of verdure. They look to be 2 to 3 miles away while in fact they are 14 to 15.

To the South West we can trace the Oquirrh Mountains for a great distance. To the North West the Goose [*Creek*] Mountains. To the North the Wahsatch mountains continue but are less elevated.

A break in the Wahsatch opens to us the Cache Valley which we shall probably enter tomorrow (or the day on which we leave this camp). It leads northward to Montana and we hope to find it cooler.

This valley is a perfect baking Oven – nothing less. It rapidly ripens such fruits as apples, pears, peaches, strawberries etc., and in a few weeks Mormondom will abound in these luscious and healthful fruits. Last evening and this evening the *spew spew* of the night hawk (chordeiles) reminded me of New England, but the barking cry of the coyotes on the hill sides and the smell of the saline flats on the Lakeside soon recalled me to my true position.

The mountains opposite reveal a series of terraces rising to a high bench 2 to 3 hundred feet covered with local drift, mostly quartzite boulders of all sizes. Beyond is the rugged mountain side with dark [colored] metamorphic schists and limestones below,[3] then a broad irregular newly horizontal belt of smooth faced quartzites of lighter color then conformable bands of a darker colored rock, the lithological character of which I cannot divine from their distance. The atmosphere has been hazy all day, but last evening I noticed the stars shone with unusual distinctness.

MONDAY, JUNE 12

The mosquitos troubled us very much last night. They abound in all the region of these salt flats or marshes. Some of the boys went to Salt Lake (2 miles) to bathe yesterday, and represent that they became so encrusted with salt . . . as to render it necessary to cleanse themselves in a stream of fresh water on their return. Soap floated on the water and was useless as a cleanser.

Broke Camp at 8 o'clock and rode on the old California stage road to Brigham City, 12 miles distant, when we turned north into Box Elder Canyon at a Danish Mormon Village called Copenhagen.[4] "Box Elder Park" is about 1,000 feet higher than Salt Lake. I rode horseback all the way (15 Miles) and was very tired and sore. Camped about 2 o'clock, rested an hour, had dinner and supper combined in one meal, after which we botanized, bathed, and wrote till dark.

The village and plantation of Copenhagen is circular in form, nestled here among the hills with seemingly no outlet. The dale or Park is about 3 miles in diameter and is beautifully watered by the Box Elder Creek – the system of irrigation being introduced. Some of the party rode to the top of mountains around. Many things were collected in all departments. Grasshoppers are abundant as also mosquitos.

Young Logan rode to the top of the hills and killed a large Rattle snake with fourteen rattles [(shelbtrim?)]. The boys got also two large snakes called "Bull snakes" (colubus).

Dr. Hayden brought down from the mountains many flowers and some dead helices which he thinks to be H. [cooperi?] – the same I think as those collected (alive) in Ogden Canyon. This is a beautiful Park some 4 miles long and 3 broad, which Doctor Hayden proposes to call Box Elder Park – inasmuch as the Creek and cañon are called Box Elder.

A beautiful stream of cold clear water ran near our tent. I could not keep from dabbing my hands and face in it and drinking a palm full now and then.

Copenhagen [Mantua] terrace, east of the town,
Box Elder Hole [today's Brigham City]

TUESDAY, JUNE 13

Up early and off with teams about 7 o'clock – (I concluded to take the ambulance to start with for I was so tired yesterday from my ride that I was unfitted for labor at the encampment – that is the labor of collecting.)

We passed out of the Park, and were nearly all the forenoon travelling along narrow defiles (cañons) till we reached Cache Valley where we immediately encamped.[5]

This valley is here from 3 to 5 miles wide and there are several considerable towns in sight. We are camped near Wellsville; Hiram [*Hyrum*] and Providence are other towns nearby.[6]

Traveled about 14 miles today. About mid-distance we passed a small enclosed park called "Dry Lake Valley" where were pasturing about 1,000 sheep besides a few horses and cattle in the care of two men.

We found in a saline lake there a few shells (planorbis) and fossil coral, etc., in the limestone which was abundant, the fossils indicated plainly paleozoic rocks. After camping found many flowers and shells which were properly cared for.

Shoshone Indians about all day, begging "grub." Encamped nearby.

{All the way of our march today the road on either side was a continuous and most gaudy flower garden, the predominating colors being purple and yellow, with various shades of green. It was for the most part, however, a repetition of a few species so that our collections were not so very enumerous as might otherwise be supposed.}

Cache Valley, south of Wellsville

WEDNESDAY, JUNE 14

Left our camp at Wellsville about 7 o'clock A.M. – passed down the Cache Valley about 18 or 19 miles and encamped near Smithville [*Smithfield*] – (1,000 inhabitants) on the bank of the Summit Creek, a beautiful stream tributary to the Bear River which is distant, they say about 25 miles. On the way we passed diagonally across the valley, leaving Mendon, on the South side below Wellsville and Hiram on the north. On reaching the North side of the valley we soon entered a considerable town of 3,000 inhabitants [*Logan*], the county seat of Cache County and the largest town in Cache valley.

We passed through a small town called Hyde Park a few miles farther down and finally through the town of Smith[*field*] – (1,000 inhabitants).[7]

Our campground is most splendid. A swift flowing stream of the purest water gives coolness and vitality to man and beast. We write now sitting by the water's edge under the shadows of a large Cotton wood tree.

These towns in Cache valley are all Mormon towns. Many thousands of acres of wheat are grown in this valley, dependent on irrigation. Each town has its Water Master and sub water masters who direct in the formation of ditches and when and how often each man's field shall be watered.[8]

Most of the land is overflowed twice during the season. The lower damper portions but once, while the drier gravelly portions are watered three times a season.

Wheat is much lower than it was before the Union Pacific Rail Road was built, but goods obtained in exchange are proportionately cheaper. All kinds of fruit are grown here and splendid vegetables. Grasshoppers are the great pest, and are killed by driving them into ditches or onto straw and burning them.[9]

The mountains on either side (East and West Mountains so called here) are made up largely of carboniferous limestone according to Dr. Hayden.

This method of farming by artificial irrigation grows upon me. It is attended with considerable labor but it makes crops sure.

Wrote home this P.M.

Smithfield near bridge over Smithfield Creek, Cache Valley

THURSDAY, JUNE 15

Got off about 7:30 o'clock and passed down the valley through Richmond and Franklin.[10] It was the intention and hope of all that we might reach Bear River tonight, but the weather being excessively hot and the wagons heavily loaded, the mules gave out when we had advanced only 18 miles, rendering it necessary to encamp by a muddy ditch in the middle of the plain, as we were crossing from the North to the South side. This was a great disappointment, of course, but there was no remedy. After the tents were pitched, I laid down to rest before dinner and fell asleep for a few moments. On awakening my head commenced aching severely – I think from the intense heat of the sun. Thermometer: (3:30 o'clock): 97°.

There is very little game hereabout. One of the men shot some prairie chickens. We passed two fine streams this morning – the water abundant, clear and cool. Would that we had that luxury at our camp! We obtained a few shells (Lymneas, Physa and Planorbis) at the streams on our way. We obtained but few plants – nothing new.

Grass Creek, Cache Valley

13. Bear River Crossing near Bridgeport, June 16. U.S. Geological Survey, W. H. Jackson 51

FRIDAY, JUNE 16

A splendid morning but no regrets at leaving this camping ground.

Rode 15 miles on horseback and then took the ambulance for a few miles until the camping ground was reached, some 18 miles travel for the day.

{Crossed the Bear River at Bridgeport about 10 o'clock, when a few varieties of shells were collected – snail, lymnea, etc.[11] The usual quantity of plants was collected and pressed, among others several brought down from the top of the mountain by Dr. Hayden.}

We are a little north of Oxford, the northernmost, but one of the Mormon towns in this valley, in a beautiful valley abundantly supplied with grass and water. {No shells found at this locality.} Temperatures have been gradually rising during the day and the night is cooler.

At our camp this evening got plenty of game – prairie hens, etc. Had opportunity for another good bath. Returned early with thoughts upwards and eastward.

Grasshopper Creek

SATURDAY, JUNE 17

Another magnificent morning. Passed up to the head of Cache Valley through the "Red Rock Gate" – two buttes of red rock near each other – over the divide into Marsh Creek vale, the waters of which flow northward to the Pacific through the Snake, Lewis and Columbia Rivers.

A long tiresome ride with a few springs of water. We reached the Corrinne [*Corinne*] Stage Road near Carpenter's about 3 o'clock (21.5 miles) and camped.[12] Here we found a variety of shells – Anodons, Lymneas, Physas,

14. Camp near head of Cache Valley (75 miles north of Ogden), June 16. U.S. Geological Survey, W. H. Jackson 49

Planorbis, etc., besides some interesting forms found in the Alluvial banks, some left above the water.

Meet with Indians in small numbers very frequently.

During my ride yesterday I was alone for several miles and had a good opportunity for communion. I could not help pouring out many tears upon those thirsty hills.

Marsh Creek

SUNDAY, JUNE 18

We move on today much against my inclination, but it cannot be helped. A Mormon brought into camp the mule and one of the horses lost at Ogden, having followed us all the way for that purpose. One of the horses, it was ascertained, had been killed by falling over a precipice.

We have come from Ogden about 120 miles.

Our route today gave us an interesting variety in geological scenery. We have lofty mountains on either side, with high foot hills, rounded and grassed partially, and the narrow valley of the Port Neuf River near the center, along which our road (Stage road) runs. The road is put and kept in pretty good condition by the stage company and toll gates with heavy tolls are a part of their compensation. The stations for relays of stage horses are about the only signs of civilized life. At Murphy's Station (some 10 to 12 miles back, where we struck the Port Neuf River) we came upon a heavy show of igneous rock – brownish black basalt. We crossed several belts of

15. Red Rock Gate with ambulance carrying Jackson photo equipment, June 17. National Gallery, VI, 173.tif

this old lava in a few miles and, after that, it continued on the west side of the river as a black ragged bluff some 20 to 30 feet high all the way to this our camping ground.[13] It is nearly level and occupies the lowest portion of the valley. It must be somewhat recent therefore (probably Tertiary epoch) as the valley must have been previously worn to its present depth. In many places it was distinctly columnar in form as a photographic view, taken on the road, will show. Dr. Hayden says the mountains on either side dip westward, making, what is called, a Monoclinal with regard to each other. He knows nothing of the ranges east or west of those immediately bounding this valley.

At a point in our road where the Photographs were taken many shells (living) were collected both from the modern marl beds forming the banks of the stream and from the stream itself. Some shells (dead snails, Helices etc.) were gathered at our camping ground, but comparatively few flowers were obtained.

Took a long walk alone and had my thoughts transferred to a far distant spot in the east – Home, great home!

First Camp on Port Neuf River

MONDAY, JUNE 19

Left camp at 7:30 o'clock and passed northward a mile or so where we obtained two photographic views of the trap ridge – one including a fine cascade, gathered a flower and some dead helices to commemorate the spot. Made my way to a mound just at the edge of the Fall and getting down to the water bathed my weary head.

I have mused long upon the origin of this basaltic eruption. May it not have been that in the folding of the Sedimentary strata, now appearing in the mountains on either side as metamorphic rocks, an extensive rift was made which was filled immediately with lava from below and that the broken strata above have been washed away. This view would suppose the igneous rocks to extend downwards to an indefinite distance.

Against this view, however, is the conclusive fact, I believe, that the columns at the top of the ridge stand nearly vertical indicating the upper or surface portion of a lava stream – igneous overflow. This latter seems to me must have been the original mode of formation, but an impassable river separates me from the ridge, and I cannot well study it. I do not know, as yet, what Dr. Hayden thinks of it.[14]

Helices and other shells are found abundantly in the marly strata at the bottom of the valley, but not a live helix has been found here. Not so – within an half hour of writing the above, I was so fortunate as to find several live specimens of the same helix just at the water's edge at the first fall (upper). A Photograph of the Fall shows me reclining on a rock near the spot.

{Got but few flowers today – a few new species taken care of by Mr. Adams.}

Made only 16.5 miles today, but it was exceedingly hot and dusty. Our camping ground was on the same stream as last night – Port Neuf. The mosquitos are terribly troublesome. How we are to sleep I do not see. We have each a small piece of mosquito netting to throw over the face.

Evening had a long talk with the Dr. respecting the geology of the western world and of geology in general.

Second Camp on Port Neuf River

TUESDAY, JUNE 20

{Soon after leaving camp we entered upon the broad valley of the Snake or Lewis River. Camped near Landers Station on Indian Reservation 14 miles from Fort Hall.[15] In a small stream (Ross Fork) near camp found a few Paludinas of the same species evidently of those found on the Port Neuf River.

Flowers were formed today on the dusty plain, but on account of the high wind prevailing in camp they were not pressed.}

There are many terms used in this western world quite new to eastern ears though universally employed here. A man who drives an ox team is denominated a "Bull whacker," one who drives a mule team is a "mule skinner." Hence they talk of *whacking* bulls and *skinning* mules with all seriousness. One who carries goods across the country is a "freighter." We meet numbers of these freight trains, both ox and mule every day. Usually two or more large teams travel together. Their dust may be seen rising from the plain for a long distance. Today we passed a large drove of cattle on their way to Montana.

Have travelled but 12 miles today – encamping early in order to communicate with *Fort Hall*, where our letters were directed to be sent from Ogden. Hope therefore even to hear from home.

Have been afflicted with severe headache for several days probably from overheating.

Can hardly get rested on my hard couch at night and feel stiff and tired. I seem to myself to be of but little use to the expedition. Besides I am ill at ease with the company – feel melancholy and discouraged, and either from widely different education or from dissimilar personal sympathies, cannot but regard myself as quite out of place in such association.

I do not need company myself – my communing[s] are above and always sweet and precious but I fear that my motives are misunderstood and my presence with company less welcome.

Had this afternoon, a slight exhibition of what is so frequently witnessed in Egypt and Arabia – an immense cloud of dust driven by the wind. Our tent, which was almost blown away by the force of the wind, was completely filled with sand and fine volcanic dust.[16]

Wrote a letter home this P.M. and mailed it at this station.

Ross Fork, near the bridge [*today's town of Fort Hall*][17]

WEDNESDAY, JUNE 21

"Jim" Stevenson returned in the night from Fort Hall and brought letters. I of course rose early to devour them – one from Home. . . .

We change our previously intended course somewhat and go by the way of Fort Hall which brings us nearer to the mountains on the East, and saves us in part from the fine dust of the stage road on the plain and affords us better water though it is less direct.

{Moved over the divide separating Ross Fork valley from Lincoln Valley in which Fort Hall is located. At the very summit of the hill saw considerable masses of igneous rock apparently in place – some of the rock nearly looked like porphyry from the road, but I had no time to examine it. Gathered and picked flowers but obtained no shells.

The igneous overflow here must have been very extensive, and it is quite probable that it occupies a large part of the snake river valley west of this.} (5 o'clock P.M.) Camped at Fort Hall, to stay, it is said, until day after tomorrow.

Received this afternoon another letter from home dated the 11th. . . .

Have just seen two Indians – called Bann[o]cks – one was highly painted. They speak a different language from the Shoshone or Snakes.[18]

The old Fort Hall, I learn was situated some 20 miles from this Post, and was not a military station so much as a Fur company's trading post. This post has been recently established, the buildings are now nearly completed. There is but one company of troops located here at present. The officers in Command are Captain Putnam and Lieutenant Wilson. By invitation I took supper at Post and spent the night. (Invitation repeated and urged next night – declined.)[19]

Fort Hall

THURSDAY, JUNE 22

After breakfast went out two miles in company with the officers, Prof. Hayden and a few others to see the warm springs which supply the irrigating aqueduct with water.

There are three or four springs of variable temperature (averaging about 75° Fahrenheit) which issue from the hills near each other. The waters are highly charged with lime and travertine is abundantly deposited in the vicinity. Some mosses and plants were collected and a few shells found at the springs. They were very minute and in form like paludina. Whether young or full grown I could not determine, but presume the former.

On returning saw some fine specimens from Montana belonging to Mr. Stanley, the Post-trader here. The best were Chalcedony – He kindly gave me a nice specimen of Obsidian which I broke and divided with a few friends.[20]

Lieut. Wilson stated to me that the black igneous rock – Lava – extends 200–300 miles south westwardly according to his own personal observation – that the American Falls, fifty miles hence (950 feet high), and the Shoshone Fall, still further down (212 feet high), flow over this rock and their deep cañons below are cut out of it. From all that I can learn, this portion of the United States is composed of igneous rocks to a much larger extent than our geographers and geologists have imagined. The "Three But[t]es" as laid down in Colonel R[a]ynolds map are all in sight from our tent. They stand

16. Fort Hall with shadow of Jackson's camera, June 21. National Gallery, VI, 175.tif

out as isolated mountains rising from the shoshone plain and can be seen at a great distance. Their position with regard to each other was not correctly laid down in the map referred to as they were only seen at a distance and from one stand point by Col. Raynolds' party.[21] A corrected map will be made and published as the result of our Schönborn's observation.

{About 4 o'clock P.M. every day this week there has been a gathering of clouds in the S. West, West, or N. West attended with some lightning and thunder and with much wind. The wind, of course, has been very troublesome in camp.}

Report No. 4: Ferdinand Hayden to Spencer Baird

FORT HALL,
JUNE 22D

Dear Professor Baird:

We arrived at this point in safety, and stop to rest a day. We reached this point, 175 miles north of Ogden, June 21. All the party are well. We have made fine collections in all departments, worked up a [belt] of country, so far, full of interest. It has been very hot and dry every day. The difference between the wet and dry bulb is 25 to 34°.[22] Heat is 95° to 105° in the shade by day. We are now in the Snake river valley. Tomorrow we resume our march for Virginia City which we hope to reach about the 8th or 10th of July and we hope to leave Fort Ellis as soon as the 15th for the Basin.

I have received letters which inform me that Col. J. W. Barlow, Chief Engineer of General Sheridan's staff, has been directed by the General to join my party at Fort Ellis. Also Thomas Moran, a celebrated artist of Philadelphia, and Mr. Bierstadt, will join me also, to make studies for pictures.[23] Henry Elliott has sketched the whole route in his peculiar style. I have worked out the Geology and Mr. Schönborn, with two assistants, has worked up the Topography in good style. Photographs of all important scenery have been taken, about 30 negatives, and I do not know what else to write you, except that we are all in good health and spirits and moving on at the rate of 15 miles per day. You can call our expedition the "Yellow Stone Expedition." I will keep you posted from time to time. . . .

Yours sincerely,
F. V. Hayden

FRIDAY, JUNE 23

. . . Took a long ramble over the hills in search of flowers and shells. Got farther away than I was aware, and was overtaken by a considerable shower of rain which wet me nearly through, but it was so refreshing that I did not quicken my pace.

On coming in sight of the Camp I observed an unusual stir and found them making a hasty preparation to start off – contrary to previous expectation. Having lost my dinner, I was invited by Capt. Putnam, on whom I called to take my leave, to sit down for a repast with him, Dr. Hayden and a few others. We had oyster soup and other good things. On our way we were overtaken by another shower and it grew colder so that as a result I find that I have taken considerable cold. At our Camp on Blackfoot Fork (7 miles from Fort Hall) we found excellent food and water.

The sandhills around gave us a fine botanical range and we collected largely of plants – some of which were quite new to us.

A few shells (living) only were found, but aplenty of the bleached paludinas and cyclases were picked up from the surface of the ground everywhere.

Had a questionable night's rest, as the character of my dreams, now recalled, indicate – trouble, pain, anxiety.

The Blackfoot is a deep rapid stream which we cross on a bridge. It comes down from a canyon on the East, some 50 or 60 miles long.

Blackfoot Fork, at the Bridge [present town of Blackfoot][24]

SATURDAY, JUNE 24

Broke camp earlier than usual – 6 o'clock, and were off for the crossing of the Snake River itself. The Blackfoot is said to have deserved its name from the tribe of Indians of that name. The Blackfoot Indians of the present day, however, are far to the North of this valley – about the head waters of the Missouri. The three beautiful beauties (But[t]es) are distinctly seen in our ride today standing out from the plain to the west of us.

Reached Camp on Snake River at 1 o'clock. The River is crossed at this point on a bridge known as Taylor's Bridge. The Stage station nearby is called Eagle [Rock] Station [Idaho Falls].[25] The river banks are of basaltic rock and a small island of the same rock gave facility for the Construction of a bridge. I understand it is private property. The river is about 4 or 5 hundred yards wide and runs with great velocity. No man or beast could cross it in its present high stage. A high rate of toll is charged for passing. It is almost the only place where the Snake River can be crossed.

17. Taylor's Bridge (today's Idaho Falls), June 24. U.S. Geological Survey, W. H. Jackson 1511

We find this basalt in all our journey here in Snake River valley. Indeed it extends for 2 or 3 hundred miles, if reports are true.

This volcanic rock presents every variety of form from compact to Scoriaceous [*crustlike*] and is in many places semi-columnar.

From our camp this evening Prof. Hayden pointed out to me with his glass the *Three Tetons* some 80 or 100 miles away near the head waters of the Snake River. They are volcanic peaks and perhaps indicate the direction from which this vast amount of lava has flowed.[26] This lava eruption was comparatively recent as is proved by the fact that in numerous places it is seen to overlie the white sand rock of the Pliocene age which every where in this region forms the lower benches of the mountains.

Collected and pressed a large number of plants today and obtained a few shells from the river. They are a species of Unio – approaching *U. arcuata* and a small Paludina.

Had a shower as usual in the P.M. This time it was quite heavy.

The Bridge here and the rocks adjoining were photographed at various points.

Taylor's Bridge, Snake River [Idaho Falls]

SUNDAY, JUNE 25

The party got off this morning a little after 6 o'clock. I remained behind with the ambulance and the photographic corps to enable them to complete their series of views at the bridge, and under shadow of an old gnarled cedar I thought me of the dear ones at home and of the privileges they enjoy this Sabbath. I do not believe that there is now any necessity for travelling on the Sabbath. There is no danger to be apprehended from Indians and the only pleas must be to gain time for work. To be sure our animals had a day of rest on Thursday last while we lay over at Fort Hall, but we – the men of the party – have no Sabbath. But to me every day is in a sense a Sabbath and nothing can interrupt my communion with Heaven or separate me from love of Christ! Even such treatment as I have received from certain parties in Oberlin (professed Christians not only but ministers of the Gospel) cannot in the least shake my confidence in God though I confess it almost destroys my confidence in man.[27]

Got into camp about 2 o'clock – 22 miles from the bridge. The camping ground is a very neat plain, but drinkable water is wanting. A teetotaler is often obliged in this country to see others drink while he goes dry. But I would not be the slave of such habits as are commonly indulged in here for all the country itself. The habit of some of the young men of our party pains me not a little, but the circumstances of all are peculiar and the temptation strong.

Far to the South East [*Allen means northeast*] we can see very distinctly looming up from the horizon, like a conical cumulus cloud, Mt. Madison, one of the loftiest peaks of the Rocky Mountain System. It stands near the corner boundaries of Idaho and Wyoming – [ ] feet high.[28]

Basaltic lava here and there all the way today. This outflow of lava at the close of the tertiary must have covered, at the least calculation, 30 thousand square miles of this valley.[29]

I have seen enough lava, for here it is everywhere in this broad valley, but I *do* want to look down into some real crater and see the furnaces of old vulcan actually in blast! Shall I ever see it? I expect not.

The largest outflow of lava recorded in modern times, if my memory serves me, was that of Skapt[a] Is[land] of Iceland, and that covered only about 500 square miles.[30] Five Hundred to thirty thousand! The old tertiary eruption was, indeed, to any of recent date, as this vast Rocky range is to little Iceland itself! The palm to the past.

Market Lake[31]

MONDAY, JUNE 26

Such an experience as we had last night I shall never forget. I have heard of Mosquitoes before, *many* of whom would weigh a pound! But I have never seen them before to be counted by the million, crowding the air like the fine dust of an African Simoom. We are encamped upon a level plain – an old marsh with pools of water standing on every side and thus torments are generated beyond all computation. Our camp presented an unusual sight last evening after sundown. Every man was obliged to give himself up to self defense. Some had their mosquito netting around their heads – others their blankets or overcoats. All were in Motion, raving about the camp like so many madmen, and looking like so many masquerades. The horses and mules were wild with excitement, running about stamping and kicking. Everybody laughed, but every body was tormented beyond endurance. We shall probably be troubled with them hereafter, especially in the valleys and plains near the water courses. So many men and animals attract them forcibly. We spent a miserable night, though protected in part by netting.

Traveled about 18 miles today and camped by a clear stream running from the West. Collected a few flowers and pressed them. Found a few Planorb[ie] in a pond by the way, but no shells in the stream where we camped. Have had the three Tetons and Mt. Madison in sight most of the day.

The road has been very heavy today – deep sand – and our progress, the latter part of the way, very slow.

I forgot to mention in my yesterday's memoranda that I wrote a letter home and had it mailed from the stage station near our Camp last night. All my surroundings make me intensively homesick.

Camas Creek

TUESDAY, JUNE 27

Better night's rest, as the mosquitoes were not as thick. At 5:30 o'clock the camp is breaking up. It is a beautiful morning, but it bids fair to be warm. It is my custom now to ride horseback for an hour or two in the morning and then take the ambulance for the remainder of the day's march. My hands are very sore and trouble me not a little in my work.

Our Camp here is on a small river called Camas from the Indian Quamash, the name of the plant, allied to the Onion, whose bulbs are edible. The Shoshone are engaged now in collecting the "Camas root."

We are still about 30 miles from the mountains and must make one more camp on the plain, but we are all longing for the end of this monotonous march over sandhills, desiccated marshes, and basaltic ridges. Made only about 19 miles today and camped by the side of a deep ravine worn in the basaltic rocks. This is a water channel through which the water flows to the river when sufficiently high, but at present and during all the summer long the water, if any is left, stands in motionless pools. It looks clear but it is warm and insipid. This, like all the streams in these plains, is really a canyon, that is, the sides are as nearly perpendicular as the nature of the rock will admit, and the surface abrasion is so small that a person standing at the distance of ten rods from the sides would scarcely suspect the presence of any channel at all, although it is ten yards across and more than that deep. The explanation is that most of the water flowing in those streams comes from the melting snows of the mountains, and as very little rain falls upon the plain itself, they merely cut their way deep in the rocks without eroding their banks and shaping them into hills and valleys with sloping sides. . . .

We are approaching the mountains in the North of this great plain. Tomorrow should bring us to their base. The ravine or channel here is called Dry Creek, because for the most part it is without water. After dinner I botanized a while, bathed and strolled away for thought.

A cave was discovered by one of the herdsmen about a mile from Camp and some of the party entered it with candles. It is worn out in Chambers and water Channels form the [ ] underneath the lava sheet. It was explored for a distance of a quarter of a mile or so. One of those who visited it thought that chambers were in the lava and supposed that they were natural cavities formed in the cooling of the lava, and not the result of erosion. Dr. Hayden intends visiting it tomorrow morning.

Dry Creek, near Hole in a Rock[32]

WEDNESDAY, JUNE 28

A splendid morning. I am sitting on the top of a basaltic column and looking eastward where too are my thoughts and my heart! The camp is breaking up – horses feeding [*on*] grain, wagons being packed with tents, etc., etc., a few, like myself, writing.

18. Pleasant Valley with George Allen on the left, June 29. National Gallery, VI, 178.tif

[*Later*] The more I see and learn of this lava the more fully I am satisfied that 30,000 square miles is a small estimate for the extent of surface which it covers. We travelled but 16.5 miles today, but the change in every respect has been great. Two hours closed our weary travel upon the plains and brought us to the foot of the mountains. For the next four hours we were slowly winding our way among the hills up Beaver [*Head*] Cañon, and camped in Pleasant Valley. This is a most romantic spot – a small depression or enclosed vale among the mountains through which runs a clear pebbly brook. The mountain declivities are peculiarly rounded and grassed over while the ravines are studded with pines.

{Found here a large variety of flowers, quantities of which were collected and pressed. The flora of these mountains is almost entirely distinct from that of the plains. The vegetation here appears very similar to that observed around Ogden and Box Elder Canyon, though many new species are found here. A single Helix was found here upon the hill top.}

I have suffered extremely here with Head and earache at this camp, and was able to render Mr. Adams but comparatively little assistance in the care of the plants.

Had quite a hard shower this P.M. which made the ground wet about camp but got to bed early and slept my headache away. So that on awakening I found myself feeling quite well and like work again this morning.

Pleasant Valley [*Monida*]

19. Red Rock Mountains near Junction Stage Stop and the junction of the Overland Stage Roads, June 30. U.S Geological Survey, W. H. Jackson 56

THURSDAY, JUNE 29

After the Camp broke up went with the Photographic corps on a hill overlooking the vale and changed the papers of pressed plants, while Jackson took pictures. I believe I was included in one of them.

The hills in this passway to Montana are all of igneous character; but there are other varieties of rock boulders (principally quartzites) indicating a different character to the higher mountain masses around.

The air is cool and delightfully pleasant, and we shall not soon forget this "Pleasant Valley" and this *Thursday morning*!

The igneous rocks of this cañon are quite different in color (bluish not blackish) and texture than those observed in Port Neuf and Snake river valley. It contains two abundantly stellar crystallizations of some white mineral which I cannot now determine; and a brownish variety of very high luster. Perhaps they are different shades of the same mineral. (Perhaps a glassy Feldspar?)

After 12 miles travel today in which we were rapidly ascending we came to the summit of the Chain – the Divide [*Monida Pass*][33] – and for 8 or 10 miles farther we remained nearly on the same level as the very sluggish movement of the waters along the side of the pass plainly indicated. The side hills and the valley bottom were still lighter colored igneous rocks – in some localities it was a white vesicular trachyte.

At our Camp this P.M., five miles from the divide, we have excellent grass and water, and it is understood that we remain over here one day to recruit.[34] Collected and pressed a large amount of plants.

Also found in the streams a number of shells – lymneas and physas.

Junction stage station is near our camp.[35]

Wilson's ranch near the Junction

FRIDAY, JUNE 30

Train laid over today. After breakfast went up on the mountain side in company with the Photographers. Had a glorious time, though I did not reach the highest point (which many did); but from my elevation I could see a great distance. Got back tired, but had a large quantity of flowers to press and shells to collect.

Found the highest mountains near to be mainly of carboniferous limestone but capped with red sandstone, probably triassic. Mr. Moran, an artist from Philadelphia, joined us by stage.[36]

PART TWO

GEORGE ALLEN'S

AND

ALBERT PEALE'S JOURNALS

4
To Virginia City and Fort Ellis

Montana Territory

Allen

Got an early start, and although I was not feeling very well, as a consequence perhaps of drinking too much cold water after my exertion yesterday and loss of sleep, yet I commenced my horseback ride in good spirits and enjoyed the kaleidoscopic changes of scenery on our route exceedingly. The latter part of the way I rode in the ambulance and came into camp after 23 miles of travel with a blinding headache. These nervous headaches will be the disappointment of my hopes, I fear, and compel me to turn back. They seem to me to result in part from constipation – my daily trouble – and in part from unavoidable exposure to extra heat by day, or cold by night, or currents of air at all times. The fact is I am too old and infirm for such a mode of life, and it was folly in me to undertake it. I trust, for the sake of the anxious and waiting ones at home, that I may live through it.

For myself, if it were the Lord's will, permanent release would be sweet to me. "Thy will be done."

We have left the stage road for a shorter route to Virginia City – 40 to 50 miles.[1] {Camped near a divide, or summit, between two valleys. The rocks nearby are massive gneiss standing out boldly from the hills. On our route today we passed immense hills of basalt on our right. There was also much white [oölitic] limestone in the hills flanking the valleys and in most cases capped with conglomerates. Gathered and pressed flowers and found a species of Lymnea shell in the brook near our camp.}[2]

Panorama 4. Nevada City, Alder Gulch, Virginia City, and descent into the Madison Valley, July 4–6

Peale

Rising about 4 o'clock this morning I found it very cold and dressed therefore in a hurry. We got on the way about the usual time. The ride all morning was cool and pleasant. I wore my coat most of the time. Our way lay through the mountains, along little streams – now up hill and now down. After travelling 23 miles we encamped on Wild Cat Creek at an elevation of 8200 ft. We passed a higher point just before coming to camp. I got 2 specimens of a phonolitic rock, also a number of limestones and sandstones of pliocene age.

I spent the afternoon trimming my specimens and packing a box of minerals and rocks in which Charlie [*Turnbull*] helped me. It was rather cold tonight after the sun went down.

Wildcat Creek

SUNDAY, JULY 2
Allen

I am feeling much better today – no headache.

The train has made but about 6 miles today, and that may be the reason why I have stood it so well. On our way we passed into and through a very narrow wild and rocky canyon, which made it hard for our teams and wagons.[3] I rode in the ambulance with the Photographic corps, and while they were taking Photographic views in the canyon, I gathered some flowers, enjoyed the scenery and mused in my thoughts of home and heaven. How many times of late have I thought of the Psalmist's fervent admiration of mountain scenery!

{Encamped in a beautiful valley through which passes the clean and rapid waters of the Blacktail Deer Creek.}

This afternoon I have had the leisure to write a letter home but cannot mail it until we reach Virginia City. Hope to receive letters from home in a few days. My hands are exceedingly sore, badly fretted and chapped, bruised and begrieved with dirt, and I feel all over like a Rocky Mountain savage as I am.

My letter savored too much of dissatisfaction and I guess I must not send it, lest it worry the dear ones at home.

Gathered a few shells and pressed the flowers collected in the morning.

Peale

This morning we did not start quite as early as usual and only came 7.4 miles. We are encamped on Black-tail Deer Creek. Our way was through

Wildcat Cañon downwards. It is a beautiful cañon, the rocks standing out boldly on either side. They are mostly gneissic and hornblendic. At one point we came to quite a number of porphyritic rocks, of which there was a great variety.

This afternoon I spent writing a letter to the *Press* and to Dr. Mills which Jim will take to Virginia City tomorrow ahead of us as he goes for the mail.[4] The Doctor [*Hayden*] and Mr. Schönborn went out this afternoon and not coming back by the time it got dark, Charlie and Jim [taking] a lantern and wood, went to the top of the hill near us and made a fire. They [*Hayden and Schönborn*] however, soon came in, wondering what the light was.

Black-tailed Deer Creek[5]

Monday, July 3
Allen

Made a journey of 22 miles today, and reached the Stinking Water Creek for camp. This is a singular misnomer, for the creek, at least where we camped, is swift, clear and sweet. There is a nearby stagnant stream rising from a spring in the same valley and possibly the name may have risen from this circumstance, or it may be due to the character of the water in other parts of the valley.[6]

The road in the early part of the day lay over a succession of broadly rounded hills, the sweep of which presented curves of magnificent proportions. The hills were capped with basalt.

We at length entered a narrow ravine (cañon) where were many fine exposures of rocks, some of which were photographed.[7]

At our camp on the "Stinking Water," I gathered a large number of fluviatile shells – Planorbis, Physa and Lymnea, and pressed such plants as had been gathered.

Excellent sections of Drift hills are presented in this valley, and the erosive action of water is clearly seen.

Cotyle riparia [*bank swallows*] abundant.

Peale

Jim and Dawes left this morning about three o'clock for Virginia City and we proceeded on our way about 7, up over hills of recent formation . . . {formed when this basin was covered with water by the deposit at the bottom of the lake. Reaching the summit} suddenly a great sight burst into view. We stood on what seemed to be the rim at the top of a vast amphi-theatre at the bottom of which was a line of green showing the course of a stream.

20. Camp on Stinking Water (today's Ruby River), July 3. U.S. Geological Survey, W. H. Jackson 60

At the sides {converging towards the centre} were hills of modern formation rounded and covered with grass, the white {sandstone} rocks being exposed here and there through it, while on the top as a flat capping lies the basalt {looking as though placed there with rule and compass, so mathematically exact did it seem}. In the distance we could see a blue snowy range.

We proceeded down the cañon getting lower and lower past towering masses of rock {mostly granites, interspersed with red, blue, and gray porphyries, giving variety to the scenery that is seldom seen in any land}. We emerged into another lake basin with the same modern hills of white rock mixed with limestones. The name of the cañon we were told was the Devil's pathway. {We pitched our tents near a ranche, the first we had seen for some time, on the Stinking Water river.} I got 30 specimens which kept me all afternoon trimming. I got into camp late for dinner but through Charlie's thoughtfulness, found my dinner reserved with a cup full of milk.

Stinking Water River [Ruby River]

THURSDAY, JULY 4TH!!
Allen

Made Virginia City (18 miles) today. When about half way we met Stevenson returning with the mail. For me there were two letters from home – Mary's and Rosa's[8]. . . and a *Harper's Weekly*.

We passed through the City and camped a mile beyond. The people were

21. Virginia City, July 4 or 5. National Gallery, VI, 187.tif

busy in celebrating the Fourth – a procession with ladies representing the States and territories, speeches, firing of cannon etc.

The valley for miles has been dug over and washed for gold. How valuable the works are at present I do not know. While Americans were busy in the celebration, a few chinamen were at work.[9]

We first struck the valley at a small mining town called Nevada, three miles from Virginia (below). The town of Virginia is the center of business for this region. It is a long straggling business street, with a few other side streets for residences, stables etc. There are a few handsome stone edifices – stores I judge – but most of the buildings are low, cheap and temporary.[10]

We lay over tomorrow, and I shall go back to town to do business and to learn more of the place.

There are a few Indian lodges near our camping ground. They are hideous, dirty, painted creatures.

This morning I had an opportunity while riding by the side of Dr. Hayden to obtain his mind about continuing with the party beyond Virginia. He seems to desire that I should remain, and Perhaps I may be more useful when the party divide and a Section goes up to the head waters of the Yellow Stone. He suggested that when the party got through with the season's work I should return by stage to Corinne rather than continue with the train. Of this I had before thought, and purposed it possible to accomplish.

May the kind Father direct all my thoughts and acts!

Peale

I was on guard this morning from 12 P.M. to 2 A.M., when I turned in. We were wakened by a salute fired by the teamsters with needle guns about 3.30

o'clock. We were through breakfast by 5. Steve traded one of the horses for a poney at the ranche. We had a good deal of amusement seeing him try to mount for the first time.

We were soon on the way, the rocks being of the same modern character for some distance until within about 10 miles of Virginia City when they began to assume more a quartzitic and granitic character – in fact becoming auriferous. At one place I found a man by name, David Loyd, formerly of Pittsburgh, mining by the hydra[u]lic method {working industriously alone in a gulch, picking out the pebbles and washing the gold bearing earth through the flume. He told me he was making three dollars a day}.

We came to Virginia City about 11 o'clock having passed first through Nevada [*City and*] numerous places where mining has been carried on. {The piles of bare pebbles and ditches of water with upturned barrows showed us we were in the midst of placer diggings.} All was quiet however, everyone, with the exception of a few Chinamen, having gone to Virginia [*City*] to celebrate the Fourth.

Virginia is a regular mining place. We saw quite a number of Chinese in the streets. As we got into the city we found a parade forming. The American Flag was flying. A brass band headed the procession consist[*ing*] of three or four lodges of Good Templars, and a wagon containing a number of young ladies representing the different States and Territories. Each [*band*] member . . . seem[ed] to be trying to play a different tune. We followed [*the procession*] up the main street to where it was photographed, after which we formed in double rank and joined as a cavalcade. By the time the parade was over our wagons had arrived and we followed them to camp about a mile above the city.[11]

About 8 or 9 miles below Virginia we met Jim with the mail.

I got five letters; 2 from home, one from E. W., 1 from Clara, and 1 from the Dr. [*Mills*].[12] Also received 3 papers, a *Press* containing my 1st letter, an *Inquirer*, containing Adams's letter, and a *Dispatch*. I spent the afternoon writing home, to the Dr. and to E. Quite a number of our boys went down to the City to a ball given tonight in honor of the 4th. We travelled about 18 miles today.

Springs, near Virginia City

WEDNESDAY, JULY 5
Allen

Remain in camp today. A circumstance has happened today which makes me feel very anxious to change my plans somewhat. Prof. Thomas intends in a week or two to take the stage for Corinne and the cars thence to California and then return home. I do want terribly to accompany him, and shall try to bring it about.

Rode up to city in morning. Found letters from Mary and Frederic in the Post Office. . . .[13]

Went to the gold placer mines in the gulch and spent one of the pleasantest days of my life. A gentleman by the name of Marshall, originally from Massachusetts, for awhile studied at O[*berlin*], a teacher, extensive miner etc., took special pains to show us the entire process of gulch or placer gold mining.[14] He is very intelligent and clearly comprehends what he attempts to explain. Several photographic views of a mine belonging to a Mr. Hart, cousin of Mr. Marshall's, were taken by the Photo Corps. One of them included some chinamen at work for Mr. Hart.

Ate a good hearty meal at the mining cabin cooked by a young brother of Mr. Hart's, recently from Massachusetts (a "Pilgrim"),[15] and took tea with Mr. Marshall. Mrs. Marshall was from near Worcester, Mass. They have one little girl, five years of age, Nellie, and it really does seem so good to see and hear a little child again! The kindness of these Western friends I cannot soon forget.

The placer mines extend along this valley for 16 miles. It has been estimated that 15 millions of gold have been taken out from these gravel beds. This gold was discovered in 1863 and in 1864–5 some 5000 miners were at work. Now there is not as many hundreds. The privileges are owned by few persons and the work is done more systematically and economically than formerly. Hundreds of fortunes have been made here by miners, but in nearly every case the money has been recklessly squandered. The moral character of all these mining towns is deplorably bad. Theaters, Dance houses and Saloons are the leading Institutions of every such place. Whereon gold "is struck" and miners congregate these spring up as readily as weeds in a neglected garden.

Mr. Marshall gave us a full account of the conditions of this and other mining territories in the west so far as it related to the doings of the *Vigilant Committees*. The "Vigilantes," composed of order loving (really *law loving*) persons, were obliged to associate and take the law into their own hands, in order to [*provide*] the protection of life and property against a banded set of robbers and cutthroats, who at one time here were so powerful as to elect as sheriff and Deputy sheriff men in league with themselves.

"Road agents" (highway robbers) were everywhere. Any man who was known or suspected to have been successful or to have any "dust," was marked and secret plans concocted for his robbery. He was shot at night in his cabin or on the highway if he attempted to leave the country by stage or horseback. The Vigilants banded in opposition, marked their men, and by their union and energy, soon had the leaders hanging by their necks. They were in communication with similar Committees to other parts and a murderer or robber was pursued to death most relentlessly.

Order again prevailed. Life was safe. The regular custodians of law ostensibly assumed the reins of government and the usual forms of trial returned to use.

Mr. Marshall, however, asserts that the fact of the organization of the V.C. in full force, as known to the rowdies, is the power behind the courts that enables them to maintain the outward forms of government and in any case punish the guilty. He characterizes severely the public officers appointed by the President of the U.S. for Montana – Governors, Judges etc., excepting from blame only Edgerton (first Governor) and Potts (present Governor).[16]

Mr. Hart presented me with a "prospect" of gold – result of washing a single panful of dirt. Also gold alloyed with mercury. Got also a small "prospect" from Marshall's mine.

{Mr. Adams packed a box of dried plants for shipment east from this place.}

Peale

This morning I went down to town with the Squire [*Cyrus Thomas*] and spent all the morning in the Governor's office writing. Governor Potts had placed pens, paper, envelopes, and stamps at our disposal. I wrote out some mineralogical notes of our trip from Fort Hall to Virginia City. I also wrote Clara, to Coleman Sellers,[17] and to Mother again, having received another letter from her this morning. I took dinner at the International Hotel, the Squire having given me 75 cents.

This afternoon, Dr. Hayden took me to Judge Lovell's office where I looked over some specimens of gold and silver ore.[18] He took us to his house to show us some specimens from the Yellowstone and I was introduced to his daughter, Miss Fannie Lovell. I spent some time in conversation with her, having a very pleasant time. I found that she used to go to school in Burlington, N.J.; while [t]here, a Miss Winn came in and I was introduced.

{Judge Lovell presented Dr. Hayden with the enormous fossil tusk of a mastodon, and some other fossils which were found in a gulch near the city.}

A Mr. Castner gave me some specimens of copper ore from near here. The remainder of the afternoon I spent helping Jim pack [*the*] mastodon tusk, carrying baskets of sawdust and going to camp for old saddle blankets and gunny sacks. {From all I could learn in the short time afforded me, it seems that the placer mining is the only kind that pays well here as yet. Let, however, facilities for transportation, such as a railroad would give, be afforded, and there are ores here in the mountains, now worthless, that would become valuable as if by magic.}

I took supper with Jim and Adams at a restaurant. We had oyster stew and beefsteak – cooked nicely. Adams and I rode up to camp and found all in bed.

THURSDAY, JULY 6
Allen

Rose early and wrote a letter to Son Fred and my Diaries for yesterday. After breakfast had a long talk with Dr. Hayden and found him well inclined to the idea of my accompanying Mr. Thomas on his return and expressed a desire that I should go on to San Francisco with him as I was now so near and could so easily accomplish it.

Accordingly it was decided that I should go on to Fort Benton with the Train and remain a week or two and then join Mr. Thomas.[19] I cannot express the relief I feel at this conclusion as I am fully satisfied that further connection with the expedition could, from the nature of the circumstances, be of little use as it seems plain that I cannot go to the Yellow Stone Lake and work there with them. I am under very great obligation to Dr. Hayden in this whole matter. He has consulted my ease and my comfort – has shielded me from many annoyances of camp life and this not on account of any satisfactory returns that I could make to him. Indeed, I have been suffered to go along with the expedition for my own improvement and pleasure rather than from any efficient labor that I could render. I trust I fully realize my position and am truly grateful.

Spent the day mostly at the Mines near Virginia and washed my first pan of dirt and got a good show of color . . . valued at 75 cents and small fine garnets. The process – "prospect" – is carefully preserved as a memento of my success.

Towards evening rode in the ambulance to camp some 12 miles East on the Madison River. On the route from Virginia to camp we passed over a series of broad and lofty hills capped with basalt. This valley of the Madison is exceedingly beautiful. On reaching camp found our ambulance had suffered a mishap and been considerably damaged. I felt ashamed at my failure to discover the difficulty. "Dummy" was driver.[20]

Found a quantity of shells at River near Camp – Lymneas and Physas. Mosquitoes troublesome.

Peale

This morning I went down to town and packed a box of specimens to send on, making two that I have prepared. Got a letter from Clara, also a paper. Judge Lovell gave me quite a number of specimens. I met Miss Lovell in the street. She spoke. The Squire took a room at the Hotel. He leaves us and will go to Helena and then to California. I took dinner at Hotel with Charlie and Jim.

I met an old High School graduate of Class of 1852, who is Col. Demling [*Deimling*].[21] I took dinner at the International Hotel again. Charlie stays behind to get the mail tomorrow. Elliott and I started for camp together, stopping twice on the way. I got two specimens of sandstone and one igneous. The view as we reached the top of the last hill between us and camp was grand. We were looking down into the Madison Valley in which we could see our camp. Away beyond was a beautiful range of Mountains [*Madison Range*] with two or three isolated peaks, one being especially distant. We stopped under a tree on some rocks while Elliott sketched it. The wind was blowing at the time, making it very pleasant.

After a ride of 10.08 miles we got to the camp on the Madison River with the Mosquitoes. The Madison is a rather wide and very rapid river. I learned that Goodfellow's ambulance had upset on the way, throwing him out, also Duncan, who was in it. When the other ambulance came in later, it was found to be damaged also, the spring being bent and key bolt out. To crown the misfortunes, the ridgepole of the fly was broken.

The mountains this evening at sunset were beautiful, being of purple and golden hue. The terraces in front of the range are wide, distinct, and very long {one above the other, resembling fortifications}. The valley is as pretty as any we have seen. The grass is excellent.

First Terrace above Madison River

FRIDAY, JULY 7

Allen

Today made about [15.7] miles through a high, hilly, rough country with but little of interest – at least I was but little interested in that matter after we left this valley of Meadow Creek – a small creek, emptying into the Madison. Up to that point I rode Mr. Jackson's horse which shook me pretty well, and that or something else unknown to me, brought on a suddenly relaxed condition of my bowels, attended with cramps or severe grip-[p]ing pains in the stomach which compelled me soon to take to the ambulance where I rode some 12 miles.

On arriving at Camp I remained in ambulance until the boys had prepared a tent and for the rest of the day I kept perfectly quiet. {Was so unwell to be unable to attend to any business, but my assistant made some additions to the collection of plants.

The weather is cool and delightful, and tonight, though camped by a low meadow, we are not troubled at all with mosquitoes.}

Peale

We were a little later than usual in breaking camp on account of having to shoe some of the horses. We followed the river for some distance when we ascended a terrace and left the River to the right. It cuts a cañon for itself through the mountains. I rode with Prof. Allen. We got a glass of milk through the kindness of Smith who happened to come up while near a ranch. I rode to a ranch about [*half*] a mile up from the road but found no one about.

We soon arrived at Meadow Creek Valley, a beautiful little place with numerous small streams and one main one, Meadow Creek, running through it. It is a very fertile Valley, there being plenty of good grass and quite a number of trees. There are 14 families settled in it, the oldest settler having been here 7 years.[22] We passed his house and found his wife busy making cheese. There is a quartz mill here which he formerly owned but has just sold. I visited it but had no one to explain it to me.

From there we began to ascend the mountains and we had a long climb. We passed several mines but no one seemed to be working in them. The rocks are all quartzites, granites, and gneiss. I got specimens.

Soon after passing the summit we encamped in Hot Spring district, having travelled 15.77 miles. I spent the afternoon trimming specimens. Charlie got in towards evening with the mail. There was nothing for me, however.

Hot Spring Creek [*today's city of Norris*]

Saturday, July 8

Allen

I feel much better though I have some headache and am quite weak. Rode all day in ambulance. It has been quite cool (50°) so that most of the party put on extra coats.

When at length we reached the camping ground it was raining quite hard. Tents were put up in haste and all were soon under cover except the herdsmen, who doubtless found some shelter of either bush or tree.

The route has been more interesting today than yesterday though my position in the ambulance has forbid my obtaining the full benefit of it. We were camped last night in what is called Hot Spring Valley,[23] and today we passed the spring itself. The spring has the temperature of about 124°, Fah. with a circumference of ferruginous scum. Several Gold mines are in the vicinity. The water of the little creek is utilized in a novel manner. Wheels placed horizontally are made to revolve by the current for the purpose of affording machine facilities to the miners, and are called Rasters.[24] They serve to carry a stone wheel running in a narrow trackway to crush the quartz.

After passing a high divide (with a high and perfect cone-shaped mountain in the rear background) we came again to the Madison River which we passed over on a bridge some 200 feet long.[25] The river current was swift and must have been considerably deep. If the Jefferson and Gallatin Forks are any wise as large, the Missouri, at their junction 40 miles below, must already have a broad and deep channel.

Several ranches were passed today both in Hot Spring Valley and in that of the Madison. Having attained the East bank of the River and crossed Cherry Creek we soon (in a mile or two) struck off to the right and passed over another divide into the small valley where we encamped (Elk Creek).

Adams gathered plants today and I obtained a few shells (Physas) near the Hot Spring. Got Beaver Wood on Elk Creek.[26]

Peale got specimens from a quartz mine and gave me one or two. They had two shafts 100 and 120 feet deep, connected. It pays fifty dollars to the ton. It is called "Red Bluff Lode." Hot Springs District. Montana Lode is 4.5 ft. wide, dipping at a high angle to the North East.

Peale

I was on guard this morning from 1 A.M. until 3 o'clock. After breakfast, I went to some warm springs near camp. There were 3 or 4, the highest temperature being 76° and the lowest 64°. The temperature of the atmosphere at the time of observation was 48°.

The main spring was 2 ft. in diameter and 4 inches in depth. The rock above was syenite.

We soon reached a ranche near which there was a large hot spring which was about 4 ft. by 10. The highest temperature was 124°, the lowest 110°. Temperature of the air was 50°. . . . We passed several arasters or mills. A little further on we came to Bradley's ranche. Here I branched off and went to the right about a mile with a man who happened to be going that way in order to visit a quartz mine. When I reached it, Mr. J. J. Lown, {the

22. Madison River Bridge, July 8. U.S. Geological Survey, W. H. Jackson 911

proprietor}, took me down into it.[27] I slid down on two saplings laid parallel to each other, holding a rope with one hand and a candle in the other. Reaching the bottom we went through a passageway to the other shaft at a distance of 100 ft. Beyond this there is a shaft 45 ft. down to water level. One of the shafts is 105 ft. deep and the other 110 ft. The lode dips to the North and strikes East and West. The width is 2 ft. to 7 ft.; average 4.5, and [*it*] pays $30 to $65 per ton. [*one blank line*] The hanging wall is granite and the bed rock is gneissoid. They have been mining for 6 months. About 8 men employed and pays $3 per day. I took dinner with them. Mr. Lown gave me a can of California peas, and I started for Bradley's where I procured a bottle of water from the Hot Spring and proceeded over the hill to camp.

It was a wet, disagreeable ride – the rain and wind beating in my face almost all the way. I soon came to the Madison River again, which I crossed on a bridge near where there lived a man who had just got back from the

Yellowstone River with fish. The ride along the Madison, which I followed for some distance, altho cold, was beautiful. The river is wide and winds through between a number of round hills from the sides of which the rugged syenites project in sharp ridges.

After riding some distance, the road left the River to the left and went across a number of hills till I reached Elk Creek, where I found Camp, after going 18.8 miles. I found Charlie busy cooking wild currants. I spent the time until supper was ready in packing my specimens.

I got quite cold tonight.

Elk Creek, near fork of roads

SUNDAY, JULY 9
Allen

Rose early and found the storm which shut us in last night, quite passed. The morning was indeed a glorious one in contrast with the evening and worthy to be commemorated as the Lord's Day. . . .

To the South West a lofty chain of mountains lay glancing in the sunlight – its peaks glittering with the snow just fallen – for our rain of the valley was snow upon the mountain tops.

We have made 21 to 22 miles today, the first half of the way being a passage over the divide which separates us from the Gallatin River. The summit of this series of hills gave us a widespread and most significant prospect. We could see the lofty hills which separated the Jefferson and Gallatin rivers, and over which we have been passing for many days, gradually diminishing in h[e]ight to the North West. A grand amphitheater of mountain chains on the East and West and far distant North showed us at a glance the position of the three "river junction" and the commencement of the Great Missouri.[28] This dioramic view, so vast in scale – extending 50 or 60 miles to the Northward, and as clearly defined in the morning sunlight, deeply impressed itself upon my mind and will not easily be effaced.

The hills along our route presented a few green water-channels to the eye, and those were very small. The rocks exposed in the higher hills were granitic so far as I could judge from the roadway, and the lower hills were undoubtedly of tertiary age as their color seemed to indicate. On reaching the foot of the hills we soon came to the West branch of the Gallatin which we crossed on a long, rough, log bridge.

The river was skirted with a belt of cottonwood some 75 to 100 rods wide, and really seemed quite home-like. The road from the bridge to the City of Bozeman (8 miles) runs diagonally across a nearly level prairie, some of which is, and all of which will soon be under cultivation by the irrigating process.

The East branch of the Gallatin is much smaller than the West.

Our camp is nearly 4 miles from Bozeman and about one mile from Fort Ellis by road. Bozeman is a small, irregular town – quite immature in appearance like all these new western towns.[29]

This valley is well grassed and on the whole is the most inviting place that I have seen in these parts. There are now many settlers (some nice wood houses) on the prairie out of Bozeman.

{Learned in conversation with several gentleman the following facts: Gallatin County has about 25,000 inhabitants. About one fourth of the land in this valley is now preempted, and in July 1872 Government withdraws the privilege.[30] All the valley proper may be readily cultivated by irrigation. The lower flanking hills could, at greater expense, be also brought under cultivation and would afford a warmer and more eligible soil. Wheat, squaw corn, potatoes, turnips, etc., grow readily and yield large crops. Grazing facilities are unsurpassed. Excellent mill privileges exist about 10 miles north of Bozeman – the water issuing in a strong and unfailing current from a large spring on the hillside. Four mills (gristmill, sawmill) are already in use on the stream separated from each other by an interval of only 100 feet each, and the power might be indefinitely increased. [The] valley is from 5 to 12 miles wide.}[31]

It is now thought that [our] Train will go about 30 miles further before the party for the Yellowstone will pack and [that they] will leave here in about four days. I do not yet know when I shall return to Virginia [City].

Peale

We were on the way early this morning. On looking back we could see that it had snowed on the Mountains last night. We commenced ascending the hills and the higher we got the grander was the view. We soon caught sight of the Gallatin Valley lying below us and after riding some time reached it and crossed the West Gallatin River, which is quite a wide stream whose banks are covered with quite a forest of beautiful trees, the site of which was very satisfying to us. Passing through the trees we emerged upon a well cultivated plain with numerous streams passing over it and saw a two-story house with back building, the first we had seen for a long time.

After a long ride over a wide plain we came to Bozeman, through which we passed just as the people were coming from Church. About three miles further on, we came to Fort Ellis and encamped about a mile above it in a

23. Fort Ellis with mountains in background, July 9. U.S. Geological Survey, W. H. Jackson
64

bed of flowers. I wrote to Clara and to Grandmother this afternoon and commenced a letter to Mother and to Uncle John.

First Camp near old saw mill, on East Gallatin River, Fort Ellis

MONDAY, JULY 10
Allen

Finished a letter home which I commenced yesterday and sent it to Bozeman to be mailed. Also one to Prof. Thomas at Helena. I now expect to go back to Virginia [*City*] on Wednesday. After doing up my tent work for the day I took a field glass and went up slowly to the top of the highest accessible mountain just north of the Fort and camp, and there took a survey of the country.

To the South West was a chain of lofty snow-clad mountains [*Tobacco Root Mountains*]; to the North West, the beautiful valley of the Gallatin; to the North East, high hills and distant peaks beyond [*Bridger Range*], and to the South East and South were rugged mountain tops [*Gallatin and Absaroka Ranges*] stretching far away towards which my eyes were directed with the utmost interest, for here lay the head waters of the Yellowstone, the lake itself, and all the wonderful phenomena of waterfalls, cañon, geysers, mud volcanoes, etc., the terminal point of the expedition and the main object of the whole survey. I looked as Moses looked from Pisgah towards fair Canaan, but like him I am by my circumstances forbidden to enter.[32] I am even now writing upon the top of this mountain. I am reclining upon the root of a large fir tree (2 feet diameter) just on the southern slope to exclude the cool penetrating north wind and yet be in the shade.

Woolen undershirts and drawers and woolen outer shirt and stockings with heavy woolen coat, vest and pants – and yet here in the middle of July I am scarcely comfortable. I have been cold of nights with three thick Canadian blankets over me and my woolen shirt and drawers on. Such is Montana in the mountains. It is said that the winters are not very cold, but I do not believe them! No doubt however, it is a healthy country.

Here and now, doubtless, is my last experience in climbing the Rocky Mountains. My face will soon be turned southward and homeward. Stage and Rail car will soon remove me from these glorious scenes.

I have come far to gaze upon these mountain peaks – their broad swelling foot hills – their beautiful terraces – their pure sparkling mountain streams. It has cost me something in home comforts and [t]ears, but I do not regret it. I am a thousand times repaid. These visions of God's glorious work in the rock structure of the globe, which I have been permitted to enjoy, are indelibly impressed upon my memory, and I trust have awakened in my heart emotions of gratitude and sentiments of adoration which could not otherwise have been experienced. Thanks to my Heavenly Father and thanks to the kind friends who have thus favored me!

Here upon this mountain top, far away from all human sight and hearing I have poured out my soul in exstacy to God – "Nearer my God to thee" because [*I am*] lifted up from earth and brought closer to the skies. O my Savior, deal gently with me ~~a little longer~~ while I return to the dull plain of human life to tarry a little longer! Home, dear sweet home!

[Peale]

Our camp was moved this morning down nearer to the Fort. The Doctor, Capt. Norton, Lt. Jerome, Dr. Campbell and I went up to Spring cañon to see a coal mine which we found abandoned.[33] The coal is lignite. We found quite a number of fossils – shell and leaves of plant. We went down the cañon, which is beautiful, to the Fort. I spent the afternoon watching the boys play baseball with the soldiers.

Second camp near Fort Ellis on East Gallatin River

TUESDAY, JULY 11
Allen

Went to the Fort last evening with Dr. Hayden and was introduced to Capt. Ball and his lady.[34]

This morning had pleasant talk with various members of the party as most of them were about starting for a small lake some 12 miles away, and I should not see them again.

Packed my things and made ready to leave in afternoon.

I feel in some sense quite sad at leaving the party. Though not by any means congenial to my feelings, yet, after all, there is with their wildness and profanity a frank and manly independence and a kind quality of heart in many of them which serves as a bond of attachment. The great center of interest – the Yellowstone – is just before them, and I feel it hard not to participate in the pleasure of exploring it; but duty calls me another way. I am persuaded that it is best that I should go, and hence – farewell to camp, to camp friends and camp life. . . .[35]

[*The remainder of the expedition narrative is supplied by Albert Peale's journal and by Ferdinand Hayden's letters to Spencer Baird. Today's official place-names appear italicized in brackets beside journal descriptions of well-known features. If the place-name was bestowed in 1871, an H follows the name if Hayden's party assigned it and a B if given by the Barlow party.*]

TUESDAY, JULY 11

This morning I wrote to Mother again and to Uncle John, while waiting to go to a lake 12 miles from here.

About 11 o'clock Jackson and Dixon, with a pack mule, and the Doctor [*Hayden*], Mr. Moran, Capt. Norton, Lieut. Jerome, Dr. Campbell, and myself started for the Lake [*Mystic Lake* H].[36] After following a road for a while we soon struck a trail which we followed for 6 miles to the Lake. We had to dodge fallen timber and trees the whole way which was now down hill and now up hill. The Doctor and I got some fossils. The view as we reached the last hill was beautiful. The Lake lay at the bottom of the valley while back of it were slopey hills covered with pines. Higher yet and forming the background was a high mountain with bare spots and snow. Jackson, Dixon, Moran, and myself, determined to stay all night. So the rest of the Party left us about 5 o'clock. We had blacktail deer for supper. We all tried fishing and although there were plenty of fish we could not get a bite. Towards evening Mr. Moran and I started down the lake to explore it and found there was a canyon at the lower end and a series of falls – the water falling 500 feet in the space of a quarter of a mile. The view was grand as there was a deep gully in the foreground with sharp projecting rock, while there were pine covered hills rising high in the background. We returned to camp where Jackson had a large blazing campfire around which we sat

24. Mystic Lake Camp, July 11. National Park Service, Yellowstone National Park

for some time and then wrapped ourselves in our blankets and went to sleep.[37]

Mystic Lake

WEDNESDAY, JULY 12

We rose at 4 o'clock and made our breakfast on trout which Capt. Norton and Elliott caught yesterday. After breakfast Jackson took some views in which I was then packing my saddle bags. I paid another visit to the Canyon and about 9 A.M., started for Camp reaching there at half past 12. After dinner I packed the fossils I had procured and then went over to the Fort and waited in Lieut. Jerome's quarters for an officer in order to get a coat and boots, Lieut. Grug[a]n coming along after some time.[38] I got an order from him and got my coat and pair of boots, (No. 6) for which I paid $8.21. I took [*the*] coat . . . to a tailor at the Fort and left it for him to put . . . inside *my black overcoat*. I got my clothes from the wash woman today paying

$1.00 for washing and mending and left two towels and wash rag with her. I turned in early this evening.

Fort Ellis

THURSDAY, JULY 13

I woke about 5 A.M. and got up and wrote, finishing Mother's letter and commencing one to the *Press*.[39] Charlie left two letters for me in the tent last night about 12 o'clock. When the horses were brought in this morning my horse was taken to town to be shod. I saddled old Solomon and went with Elliott, who rode a mule up Spring Cañon and got some fossils of leaves. We got back to camp about half past 1 o'clock. On the way I stopped and got my towels paying 25 cents.

It was very hot this afternoon so I took a bath in the creek and then went over to Lieut. Jerome's quarters and wrote some of my letter. I met some of General Barlow's party. They are to go along with us. On my way back to camp I stopped and got my overcoat. The tailor charged me $2.00 for putting my black coat inside. I went to bed early.

Report No. 5: Ferdinand Hayden to Spencer Baird

FORT ELLIS, MONTANA
JULY 13, 1871

Dear Professor Baird:

We arrived here last Sunday morning and are now getting ready to enter the Yellow Stone Valley. We are having our Boat made at [this] place and [will] pack it on a mule. We [will] make a permanent camp on the Yellow Stone about 50 miles from Fort Ellis and nearly 100 from the Lake and send backwards and forwards for supplies as we need them. We shall send to the Fort for our mail about once a week. Colonel Barlow, Chief Engineer of General Sheridan's Staff and Captain Heap, Chief Engineer of General Hancock's Staff are here with assistants to make an exploration with my party.[40] We have one company of the 2nd Cavalry between us as escort. We are well furnished with everything we need for success. The three aneroids came safely. . . .

Nothing remarkable has occurred while everything may be said to be remarkable. The whole country is wonderful. We are continually at work at something. I know but little what Huse is doing. I think not much – something perhaps.

As soon as we discover anything of importance I will write you and be glad if you will notice us in *Harper's* as much as possible.

Prof. Allen and Mr. Thomas are both gone. Prof. A. gave out. He is too old for this kind of work. . . .

Yours etc.,

F. V. Hayden

PART THREE

ALBERT
PEALE'S
JOURNAL

5

From Fort Ellis to Bottler's Ranch and Mammoth Hot Springs

This morning I never woke until Dan [*Gibson*] called us. I finished my letter to Clara and sent it and also the one to Dr. [*Mills*] with the letter to the *Press* enclosed. We did not get away from camp until about 10 o'clock. We have a hunter and a guide now, the latter being a Mexican.[1]

{We commenced to ascend at once, and soon found that we were going to have some very rough travelling. Instead of good stage roads we had a mountain trail, winding over the hills, passing now by rough projecting rocks, and anon descending into beautiful little valleys. The mountains rose around us on all sides, covered with dense forests of pines.}[2]

The rocks we passed today were sandstone. I got some fossils of plants on the way. After a ride of about 9 miles over a very rough road through the hills past the head of Spring Canyon and the coal mine we visited a few days [*ago*], we camped about 2 o'clock on a little creek. The weather is very hot. Negley, Huse, Moran, and Dawes took the wrong road, but Dawes and Negley suspecting they were wrong turned back and followed our tracks. Huse and Moran came into camp some time after we had eaten dinner. Charlie staid behind at the Post and will overtake us tomorrow with the Escort and Barlow's party.[3] Jackson, Dixon, and Adams, who staid back in Bozeman, came into camp a couple of hours after the tents were pitched. . . .

This evening I went to the top of the hill (or rather mountain) back of Camp to see, at the request of the Doctor, whether or not the top most

Panorama 5. Butter Keg Canyon (today's Yankee Jim Canyon) with Yellowstone River in the foreground, July 20 rocks were igneous. I found that they were and also got a number of fossil leaves which I spent the evening labeling and packing.

{At sunset it commenced to rain, and the last rays of the sun struggling through the clouds lighted the hills with a crimson tint, which, with the dark green of the foliage and the sombre lowering clouds in the valley beneath, formed one of the finest scenes it has been our fortune to behold.}

Spring Creek, branch of East Gallatin River, on Indian trail

SUNDAY, JULY 16

Last night I was on guard from 11 o'clock P.M. til 1 A.M. Instead of having the horses in correll [*sic*] they were herded so Logan and I were both mounted, I on a mule. We neither of us had a watch so we guessed at the time and I hit the time to the minute – waking Steve [*Hovey*] who took Turnbull's place.

Early this morning I went to the top of the Mountain again for fossils. Crossing over to one that was higher, I had a view of the Yellowstone River in the distance, winding through its valley [Paradise Valley].

Our train got away from camp about 6 o'clock. I went back to our old camp and took the road after the train, coming up with them after going about 3 miles. They were at a miry place: several of which they had passed over and which was what kept them so long. While they were getting the wagons over, I amused myself in getting some wild strawberries which were quite abundant all through the grass. We soon came to a creek over which we had to make a crossing. One of the wagons almost upset and we had to hold it up with ropes while it was pulled over. At 1 o'clock we had come 6.5 miles. After going 2 miles further we camped on Trail Creek.[4]

This afternoon I wrote some labels and wrapped up some specimens for the Doctor. I commenced a letter to Mother. Charlie has not overtaken us yet. José, one of our hunters and guide, is in our tent. He sleeps at the feet of Negley and Duncan. Some of the boys went out hunting but did not bring in anything. We saw two antelope this afternoon. Bob Bushnel shot at them from too great a distance however. José came in and says he killed one but did not bring it in. Smith had the asthma when we got in camp and I gave him some Ammon[*ium*] Carb[*onate*] which relieved him somewhat. It was showery all afternoon and this evening rained quite hard. Rocks today sandstone and igneous. {On one of the mountains, near our . . . camp, was a curious projection of rock to which Dr. Hayden gave the name of the "Pope's Nose."}

Trail Creek, 80 feet above the surface of the water

MONDAY, JULY 17

We were up at 3:30 A.M. and on the way by half past five. It rained a little when we started and looked as though it had rained quite severely during the night. The first part of the road was pretty hard – we having to do some digging and road making. We had also one steep hill to go up when we had to double the teams. With a great deal of horse whipping and hard pulling the wagons all reached the summit. Charlie caught up to us and told us he left the cavalry 8 miles behind us this morning about 4 o'clock and General Barlow and wagons 9 miles behind [them], the latter having upset one wagon near the coal mine and the cavalry had to send back a pack train for grub. Barlow carries an umbrella and stopped two hours yesterday for lunch.

We soon got out of the canyon into the valley of the Yellowstone which we followed for some distance over igneous rocks and past them until we got to Boheters's [*Bottler's*] ranche where we encamped having come 16.03 miles today.[5] We stopped at the ranche and got a drink of milk all around and then went into Camp.

Our hunters came in with plenty of Antelope today. José found the antelope he killed yesterday flyblown.[6] We met a fisherman and bought some trout from him so we had antelope and fish for dinner. We are encamped in a place with high grass that will make good bedding. The mosquitoes are thick and I have to write under mosquito netting. After dinner I went up to the ranche and saw some men who have been mining and looked at some specimens. As they had just been churning, which they do by water power, I got a drink of buttermilk. They have quite a dairy, milking twenty-five cows. The mosquitoes got thicker again this evening and we had to smudge them, that is, build a fire of buffalo chips. I wrote some more in my letter to Mother this afternoon. Charlie says that Col. Barlow carries an umbrella and stopped two hours at noon for lunch. I [fixed] mosquito netting over my pillow tonight.

At the ranche they have a great many skins – Bear, Antelope, etc.

Bottler's Ranch, 80 feet above the Yellowstone River

TUESDAY, JULY 18

This morning I helped Jim [*Stevenson*] fix a box for his pack mule and also fixed leathers to my pantaloons to keep my belt from slipping up. Lieut. Grugan and Capt. Tyler came up this morning with the cavalry – forty men. They took dinner with us. Some time after, Col. Barlow and his party

25. Bottler's Ranch with hanging animal skins, July 17. *Left to right:* unidentified man, the two Bottler brothers, Albert Peale, and Clifford Negley. National Gallery, v2, 203.tif

arrived. Col. Barlow had his umbrella strapped on his saddle and Capt. Heap was the most comical looking man. He has a buckskin suit with fringes and has a lot of traps stuck about his person. He is a small man. They are all encamped with their three wagons upon the hill back of us.

I got a small box this afternoon and fixed it with leather straps and then picked out what chemicals I will need going to [*Yellowstone*] Lake. Cam, Duncan, and Negley went out fishing and brought us a great many. I wrote to Mother finishing my letter and took it over to the ranche so as to have it go in the morning.

While sewing with the awl this morning I accidentally ran my foot on it and it penetrated about an inch. I bathed it in cold water and put court plaster on it.

There is a peak [*Emigrant Peak*] opposite our camp across the river that is a mile in height. The mountains are beautiful at sunset. Jim and Jackson, with Moran, got here from the [*Crow*] Mission about 1 o'clock this morning.[7] I woke up when they came in.

WEDNESDAY, JULY 19
I woke this morning with a slight headache and spent the day reading, packing my chemicals, and getting things ready to start tomorrow. Jackson, Mr. Moran, Dixon, Christman [*Crissman*], José and Alec Sibley started with

26. Emigrant Peak with the survey map in foreground, July 18. National Gallery, V2, 204.tif

two pack mules {in order to obtain pictures of the various objects we expect to meet with along the road}.[8]

The rest of the mules were tried [*out*] today. The Doctor brought in some specimens of igneous rocks this afternoon. My head not being better I spent the afternoon laying in my tent.

Report No. 6: Ferdinand Hayden to Spencer Baird

BOTTLER'S RANCHE
VALLEY OF THE YELLOW STONE
JULY 20TH, 1871

Dear Professor Baird:

I send you a note on the moment of starting for the Lake. We are now 65 miles below [*downstream from*] the Lake and have made a permanent camp, as we cannot get our wagons any farther. It is now about 6 o'clock in the morning and in half an hour we shall be on our way, and on the 23d we hope to put our Boat on the Lake. We have examined the Yellow Stone range of Mountains, one of the finest ranges I have ever seen on the Continent. Henry [*Elliott*] has sketched them finely. We have fixed up a pair of wheels for the odometer, and our instruments for Topography are superb.[9] All is well with man and beast. We have been greatly successful so far. The weather is fine, grass of the best kind. We are reveling in game and trout. Our Boat and sounding apparatus we carry with us. We shall pass on into the head branches of the Missouri and Columbia and connect at several points with Col. Raynolds' work, so that we claim that our map will be as good as any ever made by the Engineer Bureau.

The geology is largely basaltic, some of it recent volcanic. Still it is very interesting in its character.

The Yellow Stone Valley is very beautiful and fertile and free from dangers from Indians, so far as we can hear. Our company of 2d Cavalry is camped quite near us. There is the greatest interest everywhere in the success of our expedition. The photographers started yesterday, three in number.

Will write again the first opportunity. Will send Draft for the three Barometers when you send bill. We have made arrangements to have our mail sent over to us from Fort Ellis.

Yours truly,

F. V. Hayden

27. Lower Canyon of the Yellowstone (Yankee Jim Canyon), July 20. National Gallery, v2, 206.tif

THURSDAY, JULY 20, 1871

I was on guard this morning from 1 A.M. until 4:30. At 3 o'clock I went over to the Ranche and wakened Mr. Bottler. After breakfast, which we had early, we packed our mules and horses. Charlie helped me. I put one of my blankets under my saddle and made a roll of the other two which I put behind my saddle. I strapped my picket pin and rope on the front, one on each side. My clothes, soap, and towel, I put in my saddle bags, with my [gun] across my shoulder and hammer in my belt I was equipped. We got on the way very soon, the Cavalry and Col. Barlow preceding us a little. But few of our packs required any fixing after we started, although General Barlow's party had to stop very often to fix theirs.

Charlie is left in command of the permanent camp with Duncan, Negley, Huse, Loucks, Bob Sherman, Bob Bushnel, and Ed Flint.[10]

It commenced to rain soon after we started and I had to bring out my coat. Our course lay up along the Yellowstone River on its [west] bank. The rocks at first were all igneous of a variety of shades quite a number being red. Also an igneous conglomerate. As we came near the mouth of the Cañon [*Yankee Jim Cañon*][11] the rocks became gneissoid, passing into granite at times. We are encamped in the midst of the Cañon having marched 14.5 miles. The cañon is beautiful high masses of gneissic rocks standing out in bold, rugged relief while here and there are slides of rocks, the River is of a deep green color and runs close to the Mountains on its right banks which are very high. {One of the features of the river . . . [*is*] the abundance in it of delicious trout.}

We have just come over a very steep rocky hill which gave considerable trouble to Goodfellow with his odometer wagon, especially as it was also loaded with a cask of butter. {One of the pack mules fell over the edge, but fortunately went down but about one hundred feet before he was rescued.} The Cavalry and General Barlow are on the opposite side of a little creek from us.

We took our dinner in picnic style, each finding a shady place for himself. The Doctor and Jim have a tent. We have three flies with us, under one of which Schönborn, Beaman, and Smith recline. The other is used by Logan, Adams, Carrington, Elliott and myself. After dinner I took a walk up the mountain and found the rock to be gneissoid, garnetific in many places – the garnets very generally imperfect, however. This evening I arranged a list for guard duty. We had trout and prunes for supper which, with a good appetite, were not bad to take. I retired to sleep under the fly with my saddle for a pillow.

First canyon south of Bottler's Ranch [*Yankee Jim Canyon*]

FRIDAY, JULY 21

We left camp early this morning and at once began climbing until we were out of the canyon. The river below is of a greeni[sh hue] and dashes over the rocks scattering the foam as it goes. We soon began to climb hills again and were surrounded by igneous rocks among the broken fragments of which I found quite a number of chalcedon[y]. We soon emerged into another broad expanse of the valley after passing a small lake [*known as both Lake Seven and Cutler Lake*]. There is but little vegetation along the river, a few trees (pine and quaking asp[*en*]) being thinly scattered on its banks. The valleys themselves are covered with a fine dust probably originating in the finely powdered volcanic rock as in the Snake River valley. They have scattered over them sage bushes but even they are few and far between.

Proceeding a little farther, passing huge towering masses of stratified limestones, we came to Cinnabar Mountain, so called from the color of some of the rocks. Here we came to Devil's Slide. This grand piece of nature is composed of two ridges of rock, one of igneous rock, the other of quartzite, each about 30–50 feet in width and both 200 feet in height. They are separated about 150 feet, {the rock between having been washed away in the lapse of time through the action of the weather. Standing in the gorge

28. The Devil's Slide, July 21. U.S. Geological Survey, W. H. Jackson 72

and glancing upward along the solid perpendicular wall, a feeling of awe comes over one, and our minds naturally revert to the time when these masses must have been forced into their present place.} On each side, at intervals, there are the remains of similar projections. In the centre of the first space to the left, running from the top to the bottom and distinctly outlined, was a broad red streak about 20 feet in width. These dykes must have been thrust up when the strata above were in position. That there was a terrible convulsion here at some time in the past is proved a little further along, where the strata has been so twisted as to lie in three different directions {in a space of 200 feet}.

Our way wound around over hills past another small lake till we reached the mouth of the [*third*] canyon . . . {impassable for the horses}, so here we left the River and, turning to the right followed Warm Spring Creek [*Gardner River*][12] at the mouth of which there is quite a deep, short, narrow canyon. Proceeding along the creek some distance we came to a spring of hot water near which there are one or two huts with sick men who have come here to be benefited by them. Here we turned to the right and began to ascend the hill. As we progressed the ground beneath gave a sound as though it were hollow. We soon passed another warm spring covered with a hard crust that has been deposited by the water.

A little further on and we were greeted with one of the grandest sights imaginable. Before us rose about 600 feet a mass of white sediment arranged in separate terraces looking like a vast frozen cascade [*Mammoth Hot Springs Terraces*]. Each one of the terraces has a number of hot springs, while in beautiful basins (formed of the deposit) – some of them white, others red, others of a delicate pink tint – rising one above the other were innumerable pools of water, some hot others warm and others still cold. About 300 feet above our camp there is one large circular basin about a quarter of a mile in diameter filled with pools of water which boils up in various places over the surface. It is beautifully clear, seeming to be of a greenish-blue color. About 75 feet higher is a ridge, all along which there is a narrow rift in which we can hear the water boiling. On one side of it there are two fountain like jets of water. The deposit extends up the cañon getting higher and higher and overgrown with pines. At one time the springs must have existed here, then afterwards they ceased here and burst out further down. So they must have continued for years and perhaps centuries. The hills below are composed of hollow crusts of the deposit. In many places there are holes from which there issues out hot air and steam. In some places there is a very slight deposit of sulphur. Looking into the chasms in places crystals of sulphur can be seen encrusting the sides. In other places, again where the water has bubbled up, there are tubes of the crust with delicate fringes on the outside.[13]

At the front of the springs the sediment has spread out into a flat area from the centre of which there rises, about 75 to 100 feet in height and 10 feet in diameter, a column which we have named the Cap of Liberty from its resemblance to one.[14] Back of us on the side of the hill is another resembling a beehive and so we have called it [today's *Devil's Thumb*].

There is a ranche here. {Mr. J. C. McCartney and Mr. H. R. Hore [*Horr*], with commendable foresight, have taken out a claim for 320 acres, which covers a considerable portion of the springs. They expect to commence the erection of a two story hotel next week. It requires no stretch of the imagination to see this place in the near future thronged with invalids drinking this water and bathing in it for their health. When the Northern Pacific Railroad runs through this country, this will be one of the places that no tourist will think of neglecting, for it will rank with any natural curiosity that the world can produce.}[15]

It has been rainy all afternoon. At sunset the view from the top of the

29. Hot Springs on Gardner's River (Mammoth Hot Springs), with Thomas Moran, July 21. National Gallery, v4, 217.tif

springs was very pretty, the white sediment in the foreground, the hills near us of a golden green color, while the Mountains, in the far distance, of a dark blue color with red exposed spots in places, while the clouds stood in masses on their sides.

In front of camp on the other side of the creek below us there is a curious mountain [*Mt. Everts*]¹⁶ with a level top sloping off abruptly at the end like a huge [fence?] while on the sides the strata stand out seeming to be supported in places by columns of rock. In one place the strata end abruptly cut off by a layer of [regular] basaltic rock. The sides are cut up into ravines with a few pines here and there over them.

The temperature of the hottest water in the springs is 160°F., from this it [ranges] down to cold water. The temperature of air at observation was 70°F.

A little to the east of south of us there is a high peak of vertical rock of a red color [*Bunsen Peak*] while running back from it there is a mountain covered with pines the dark green foliage of which forms a beautiful contrast.¹⁷

This evening one of the soldiers was sick and they sent down for me to come and see him. I went up and gave him some medicine.

Hot Springs, White Mountain [*Mammoth Hot Springs*]

30. Liberty Cap and bathhouses of J. C. McCartney, July 21. Scanned image from Aubrey Haines. *The Yellowstone Story* 1:197. Courtesy of the Yellowstone Association

SATURDAY, JULY 22

This morning, Smith, Dummy, and I, under the guidance of one of the Ranche men, went up the gulch to a hot spring. It is 20 feet high by 50 feet long and 30 feet wide. On top the water bubbles from a couple of small cones and has rounded off the sides. From a number of curious formations formed by the water we called it Oyster Shell mound [*today's Orange Spring Mound*].[18] On the way back I collected specimens and Smith and I took a bath in one of the numerous bath tubs that abound among the springs. The temperature of the springs down at the road is 130°[19]. . . . [*It is*] 170 feet to the top of the first [terrace] from Camp – Elevation of Camp 7,000 feet, [*and*] 370 feet to the top of the mound highest up the Canyon.

After dinner I went over towards the ranche and got some of the water and specimens. Getting back to camp I was caught in a rainstorm. I made a qualitative analysis of the water and found a small quantity of Hydrogen Sulphide, sulphate of magnesium, and small amounts of carbonate of soda. Lime is pretty abundant, alumina is also present in quantity. There is probably carbonate of potass[*ium*] present also.

This evening I mixed some medicine for a man over at the ranche. Jo brought in part of an antelope that he killed today. One of the men of General Barlow's party brought in a bear and two cubs which he killed.[20] Jim and Jo started after the remainder of the antelope that Jo killed. They expect to stay all night. The Doctor started out on a trip also. I wrote to Mother this afternoon and sent the letter over to the ranche. Adams commenced a letter to the paper [*Philadelphia Inquirer*]. I got some pills and gave one to Dan. I saw to my patient over at the ranche.

SUNDAY, JULY 23

I spent all morning writing on a letter to the newspaper over at the Ranche. I wrote on a slate composed of the sediment from the Springs which, placed on three pine sticks, formed my table. Adams finished his letter. After going to Camp for dinner I returned to the ranche and finished my letter to the *Press*, enclosing it to Dr. Mills. On the way over I came across Jackson who was photographing and was taken in a picture with Mr. Moran. After finishing my letter I started for Camp and overtook Jim and was taken in another picture with him and Sibley. I collected some more specimens which I took to Camp and packed with what I got yesterday. After supper I took them all over to the ranche. While there the men gave me some meat of a young cub. It was the first Bear meat I have eaten. It was roasted and tasted deliciously. Nebraska Bill went over to Camp with me and I wrote a letter to Charlie by the light of a huge fire asking him to send up some medicine for Bill. He was sheriffe along the Pacific road during its building and saw some pretty rough times.[21] He told us some of his adventures. Jim and Jo brought in some more antelope this afternoon. The Doctor, Mr. Schönborn, Elliott, and Col. Barlow were out almost all day coming in about supper time.[22]

{We are the first organized party that has ever visited these springs, and we have made a stay of two days in order to explore them more fully.[23] Tomorrow we expect to push on for the lake.}

6

To Tower Falls, Lower Falls, Yellowstone Cañon, and Yellowstone Lake

MONDAY, JULY 24

I was on guard this morning herding the horses from half past 1 to 4 A.M. when I came in and woke Steve and Dan, turned in and got about an hour's sleep. After breakfast I helped the Doctor pack some specimens which Henry Greve and I carried over to the ranche on horseback. When we got back to camp they were just about moving out.

The first part of our course lay down hill and across two rapid creeks at one of which one of the packs became loose and I helped fix it again. We soon began to ascend and followed a small creek [*Lava Creek*] up the gorge on the side of a mountain the rocks of which were sandstones capped with a huge layer of basalt, fragments of which were strewn over the side of the mountain and along our trail.[1] After a ride of about 4 miles we came to a place where the capping extends across the gorge forming an abrupt perpendicular wall broken only at one side opposite that on which we were. Here the water rushes down forming a beautiful fall [*Undine Falls*] half hidden by the forest of pines. Ascending upon this platform of basalt and looking back the scene was grand.

Great Mountains in all directions, most of them rounded in form, others, rising in sharp peaks, formed the background, while in the foreground, far beneath us, lay the valley through which we had just passed. The central feature of the scene was the Hot Spring we had just left. Turning around, the scene in front was entirely different. Instead of the grandeur we had just been looking at, we gazed upon low rolling hills covered with beautiful verdure with here and there scattered trees, principally pines [*Blacktail Deer Plateau*].[2] It reminded us of Pennsylvania fields. All that was wanting to complete the picture was houses, barns and fences.

Panorama 6. Mouth of Tower Creek, Baronett's Bridge, foot of Grand Canyon, and East Fork of the Yellowstone, July 24–28

Proceeding a short distance I saw a fall [*Wraith Falls*] some little distance to the right. I found it to be a beautiful cascade. The water flows down an incline formed of basalt which is arranged in ledges in the most regular manner. These ledges cause the whole mass of water from top to bottom to be a mass of foam and causing it to look like snow from a distance. On the banks reaching high up are huge masses, rising like vast chimneys. The resemblance is more striking from the horizontal fissures in the rock as one almost imagines they are built of brick.

Turning back, I soon reached the trail. My pony put his nose to it like a dog and raising his head with a neigh started on a lope after the train. After a ride of a mile or two I came in sight of them. After a ride of 8 or 10 miles we camped at the mouth of a small gully down which runs a stream of good cold water. We pitched our fly under the trees. Schönborn, Smith, Beaman, and Carrington, with Barlow's party, did not come in. They must have gone another direction. Jim went out to hunt for them but was unsuccessful in finding them. Capt. Tyler sent out some of his men after them also.[3]

Elliott and I, after dinner, took a ride of about 12 miles. We saw two antelope and flushed three flocks of grouse. [*We got*] on the top of one of the highest hills about here, one which commanded a view of the entire country all around, and the scene beggars description. It was slightly hazy which softened all the lines and made it beautiful. The rocks we passed over were igneous in character. Getting back we found Jim had brought in some fossils.

Small Creek near Yellowstone River bridge [*Baronett's Bridge*][4]

TUESDAY, JULY 25

In the night our stock stampeded twice, getting frightened at something. I did not even wake, although some of the party did. They made a great deal of noise. They succeeded in getting them back. {They must have been scared by a bear, for on riding over the hills . . . we noticed signs of Bruin in various places.}[5]

After breakfast I wrapped and labeled some specimens for the Doctor. We got a note from our other party, through Capt. Tyler's sergeant, saying, they were all right and encamped on the Yellowstone.

We got away from camp about 8 o'clock and after travelling some miles we came to Jackson who had just gone into camp. A little further on we came across Barlow and with them found Schönborn, Carrington, Beaman, and Smith, who went along with us. We passed through a good bit of fallen timber and came to a very deep narrow canyon [*The Narrows*] the walls of which reach down perpendicularly about 500 feet. Its narrowness makes it seem deeper yet at the bottom, bounded by the hard wall on either side. The river flows of a deep green tint, covered here and there with white froth.

Dismounting we led our horses down the side of a deep mountain over a rough trail and crossed Tower Creek, encamping on the right bank. After dinner I went to look at Tower Falls. They are very fine. The water makes a semicircular turn then forms a series of small falls and then rushes over the precipice falling 156 feet [*measured today at 132 feet*]. Above these there are a number of towers which rise to the height of 100 feet above the water. My first view was from the top of one of these towers and the depth to where the water fell seemed immense. Afterwards I went down the side of the canyon to where the water fell and stood in the spray. Looking up, the sight was grand. The width of the water is about 20 feet. The precipice it falls over is perpendicular. After visiting there I went down to the edge of the River where a small creek empties into it. Here, there are a number of warm springs [*Calcite Springs*] only one of which is defined. It is about 2 feet in diameter and about 18 inches in depth. Its temperature is 127°F. From several places Carbonated hydrogen escapes, in others H[*ydrogen*] S[*ulfide*]. In many places there is a deposit of sulphur, in others a black deposit at the bottom of the stream, probably carbonaceous.[6] In others there is a white deposit tasting strongly of iron, as indeed, is shown by its changing to the oxide in places.

It was dark when I got back and we picketed horses. After a cup of tea I turned in.

Tower Creek on Yellowstone Lake Trail

WEDNESDAY, JULY 26

When I woke I found it was quite cold, indeed, enough so for frost. I went down to the Springs again and got some specimens. Elliott was with me and he and I seeing the Doctor on a hill not far from us went and joined him.

We rode along the edge of the river for some distance when we struck across to the trail to the right which led across a ridge just below Mt. Washburn. On the way we passed two herd of antelope, one containing eight. The other was too far away to count them. Joe Clark was after them. After a long ride we reached the top of the mountain. We were up 10,590 ft. (a.b.) [*aneroid barometer*] and we were well repaid for our steep climb.[7] The scene in its vastness beggars description. We commanded a view of the entire country for miles. Far to the north we could see the mountains back of the hot springs [*Gallatin Range*], also Cinnabar Mountain, and even the

31. Tower Falls, July 25. U.S. Geological Survey, W. H. Jackson 78

lower canyon of the Yellowstone through which we came. In the northeast the mountains [*Absaroka Range*] presented a very rugged appearance, their ragged edges running along the horizon until we could trace them no farther, while in every direction rose high peaks which, from their jagged appearance, were evidently volcanic in origin. Glancing still farther along, [more] to the south, we could see the Lake spreading out in the sunlight, studded here and there with Islands. Beyond the Lake far to the south is a small range of snow covered mountains to which the Doctor gave the name of the Yellowstone Range.[8] The wind blew terrifically, so much so, indeed, that [*Elliott*] and I were both obliged to lie prone and both hold his paper while he sketched the Mountains.

Leaving the summit we began the descent, Elliott leading the two horses and I walking behind with a switch to keep them going. When we reached the trail we were overtaken by Wood, Prout, and one of the men with the odometer of Col. Barlow's party. Our way lay through timber, a great deal having fallen, making our progress slow and tedious. In some places we had pretty steep climbing. Most of the party went over to the [*Lower*] Falls. I spent the afternoon testing the water from the springs. Our camp was on Cascade Creek.

Cascade Creek, 1.5 miles north of lower falls, Yellowstone River

THURSDAY, JULY 27

This morning Elliott and I started for the [*Lower*] Falls with the intention of descending to the bottom of the cañon, a thing which all the hunters and trappers say cannot be done. { . . . [*We*] wished to get the depth of the cañon in order to estimate the height of the falls; . . . so with a barometer in pocket and ropes across our shoulders, we proceeded to the edge, and tying our horses commenced the descent.} We tried in one place getting within about 200 feet of the river when the walls descended abruptly so that we could not go further. Going back to our horses we rode a little further down the River and tried again. This time, after 1 1/4 hours climb down a place inclined about 80° we reached the bottom. I had one slight slide on the way but fortunately caught my foot against a rock which kept me from going further. {All was silent except the roaring of the water as its waves dashed upon the solid rock at our feet. Far above us the trees along the edge seemed like a line of grass while far below it, and yet above our heads, floated a number of hawks disturbed by our descent.}

We took measurements with the aneroid barometer and found that the canyon was 1,000 feet deep where we descended. The falls, therefore, must be about 400 feet high.[9] They are very pretty, indeed, and the sun shining on the spray formed a beautiful rainbow. On the sides of the rock where the spray dashes there is quite a good deal of vegetation of a beautiful green color. The Cañon is grand. It is cut through igneous rocks of various kinds and in places is stained of a red color from the iron of numerous springs. In

32. Lower Falls, July 27. U.S. Geological Survey, W. H. Jackson 82

others, it is bright yellow from infiltration of sulphur.[10] In others, it is green from vegetation and in still others pure white. The rocks are weathered so as to form columns, towers etc. Along the banks, from top to bottom, the river rushes through the narrow space at the bottom as if chafing against its imprisonment. It dashes against the rocks in great waves covered with foam, and were one to fall in, he could be dashed to pieces among the rocks at the bottom.

Getting some water from the only spring we could get near {and a specimen of rock from the water's edge}, we commenced the ascent, collecting as many specimens as I could carry. Some I had to drop afterwards as, along some of the ledges, both hands and feet were needed to hold on. {After two hours of hard work we reached the top almost exhausted.}

We took a small lunch and rode on stopping above the little falls [*Upper Falls*] which are very pretty. . . . {What they lack in sublimity they gain in picturesqueness.} I caught two very large fish but we found, afterwards, that they were infected with worms and not fit to eat. We rode on through a little timber, soon coming out into a beautiful little savannah, after which we rode along the bank of the river which spreads out very widely here amongst the pines, the bank sloping off from us to the waters edge. We soon emerged onto a broad plateau [*Hayden Valley*][11] covered {with grass, and intersected by numerous streams, which become quite wide as they approach the river}. In many places the ground was very miry, indeed, and we had to proceed carefully to prevent our miring.

We crossed a small stream, Alum Creek, strongly impregnated with alum, and after riding about 3 miles came to two white conical hills, each 250 feet in height [*Crater Hills*].[12] At the southwestern base of which there is a huge boiling sulphur spring [*Sulphur Spring*] encircled by a beautiful rim containing a great deal of sulphur, and is fashioned into beautiful shapes. The temperature of the water in this spring is about 197°F., and, along the course of the stream running from it, there is an abundant deposit of sulphur. The spring is about 12 feet in diameter. A little to the west of it there is an opening from which jets of steam come out, making a noise like a high pressure engine. This Spring the Doctor named the Locomotive [*Locomotive Jet*].

A little to the South, after passing through some timber, we came to a mud spring [*Blue Mud Pot*] the contents of which resembled a mass of rather stiff batter through which the steam came bubbling, keeping it in a state of constant agitation. The mud is of blue color, and where each jet comes forth, forms a series of concentric rings, giving it a beautiful appearance, if one can imagine a mud spring to be beautiful. All about the vicinity of this latter spring there are numbers of others, the deposit in some being yellow, in others a dirty green, in some white, and some red. Leaving these springs we saw a smoke over the hill which we supposed to come from Camp so we hurried toward it but found it to be simply some burning sage brush. Finding the trail, we followed it along the River, crossing the wide mouths of three creeks, and found camp situated in some pines on the bank of the River, near a number of mud springs. After dinner I started out with a bottle and my hammer to explore them.

Immediately back of camp I found two crater-like mud springs at the bottom of which, through a bluish mud, the steam was bubbling like boiling mush. There were also two large pools of water fed by a number of springs on the side of the hill. The water tastes strongly of alum and is of dirty greenish color. These springs come through clay instead of through limestone as in the hot springs back on the Gardiner River. After reaching the top of the hill, I could see steam rising from the ravine below, and descending, came first to a sort of cave or grotto which extends 10 or 15 feet into the side of the hill in sandstone. From this gushes forth every few seconds a puff of steam and water which is very clear and flows down a small channel [*Dragon's Mouth Spring*]. It would be a delightful place for a vapor bath.

Proceeding a little further, passing a pool of alum water, I came to a huge mud crater at the bottom of which, about 20 feet down, I could [*see*] every now and then (when the wind blew the steam aside) a seething mass of mud [*Mud Volcano*]. The trees all about this place are coated with mud showing that it throws out mud sometimes to a considerable height. Here I met Elliott, the Doctor, some of General Barlow's party, and one of their guides, an old trapper who has been in this country before. He took us over to another spring [*Mud Geyser*] which he assured us would commence spouting about sundown. We sat down on the bank to wait, somewhat incredulous, for the water was quite placid with the exception of the centre which bubbled a little. Soon however the water began to rise gradually, until suddenly, it was thrown into the greatest agitation, becoming very muddy. The water was thrown up about 10 feet every few seconds and a cloud of steam rose from it continually. We gazed on it with wonder. After continuing about twenty minutes it stopped as suddenly as it began and the water became as smooth as the most placid lake, the water, however, still very muddy. The trapper says this happens four times a day.

We returned to camp wondering what wonder this country will produce next. This is the nearest approach to a geyser that we have yet seen and must be caused by the accumulation of steam and gas far beneath the surface. When a sufficient amount of force has accumulated, it begins to make its way upward, thus causing the water to rise until at last it overcomes the resistance of the mass of water above and forces its way out, throwing the water through which it passes into violent agitation. When the accumulated steam has escaped, the force being absent, the water subsides again. The constancy of the heat at the point where it is formed, and the constancy of the amount of water, will account for its periodicity.

33. Mud Geyser Crater, July 28. U.S. Geological Survey, W. H. Jackson 96

After picketing the horses I went on guard at 8 o'clock. About 10 o'clock it commenced to rain, and at half past 10, when I wakened Steve, it was raining quite hard. As I had borrowed Adams overcoat I did not get wet.

Mud volcanoes, Twenty feet above Yellowstone River

FRIDAY, JULY 28

This morning I packed up all the specimens which I had collected as well as those the Doctor got, Henry Greve helping me. I then saddled my horse and took the trail back to the Hot Springs at Crater Hill whither the Doctor and Mr. Schönborn had preceded me. I found them at the [huge] boiling Sulphur Spring. We visited all the springs, collecting specimens from each. After exploring them fully, we took the trail and went back to our camping ground to find camp moved. Goodfellow, Smith and the odometer cart were waiting, however, for Mr. Schönborn. We found that Col. Barlow was still in camp and not going on until tomorrow. From them we learned that the mud geyser had spouted twice today rising 20 feet this morning.

We kept on along the trail which led along the bank of the river, sometimes through the pines, and now and then out into open places, giving us a splendid view of the river. The Doctor went ahead of me and I soon lost sight of him. After riding about 6 miles I got to the Lake and saw camp ahead of me.

The Lake is beautiful and the wind which blows pretty strongly every afternoon keeps the water dashing on shore in a succession of waves. The day is beautiful and our fly is pitched on the bank, commanding a good view of the water with the Mountains beyond. We call our place Lake View.[13] The lake is about [ ] miles wide here, and there is an island about the centre. Jim and the rest are busy fixing up the boat. Some of the rest are going to make a raft. I helped a little on the boat and we launched it. It rides very well. It is made of an oaken frame covered with tarred canvas. The oars we made from the pines here.[14]

I wrapped up some of the specimens we got this morning. In one of the springs we saw this morning there is a sort of a thick scum floating around on top. The specimens from it, on drying, have a sandy appearance and feel, which must be the reason it floats instead of mixing. It will not pulverize finely enough. I noticed also that the edges contained a good bit of water which would be another proof.

I commenced a letter to Mother this afternoon. At sunset the view looking out on the Lake was beautiful. The mountains beyond were of a purple tint, changing gradually to deep blue as the sun went down. As I write now, the moon is shining brightly and is reflected from the surface of the water, which is now considerably quieter, the wind having gone down. The lake is 9,000 feet above the sea.[15]

First Camp on Yellowstone Lake, 14 feet above the surface of the water

SATURDAY, JULY 29

Jim [*Stevenson*] and Elliott started off in the boat this morning for the island. They used a blanket for a sail. I spent the entire morning and part of the afternoon testing water from the different springs. I mixed up some medicines for Smith.

Sometime after dinner the boat came back. They went all around the island and say that it is a thick Jungle and that the tracks of game are abundant. The boat worked splendidly. Elliott named the Island "Stevenson's Island."[16] They brought back some rock from one of the bluffs which they say are 10 feet high. I wrapped up the remainder of the Specimens from Crater Hill, after which I took a bath in the Lake. Lieut. Grugan and some of his men started for the Island this evening on a raft. They expect to stay all night. The sunset this evening was very pretty and by moonlight the Lake was lovely indeed. Mosquitoes were thick.

34. The *Annie*, with Stevenson (*left*) and Chester Dawes, July 28. U.S. Geological Survey, W. H. Jackson 1268

SUNDAY, JULY 30

This morning Jim and Beaman went out on the Lake to take soundings. I spent all morning in writing a letter to the paper [Philadelphia Press] with the exception of a morning walk along the beach.

After dinner I finished my letter to the Paper and wrote a note to Charlie, finished my letter to Mother, and wrote to Dr. Mills. . . . One of the men from Bottler's Ranche came in today and says that the Indians attacked and killed three men down near Bozeman.[17] He brought a letter from Charlie to the Doctor, but I did not see it. He, I believe, started for Fort Ellis for provision[s] and hearing the news turned back.

Towards evening Adams and I took a long walk along the Lake on the beach getting a few flowers. It was very much like walking along the sea shore. There was quite a surf which dashed up at our feet. Having been quiet all day it seemed very much more like Sunday does at home.

7

The Geyser Basins

MONDAY, JULY 31

I got all my things together this morning, and with the Doctor, Mr. Schön-born, Elliott, Dic, John Raymond, Goodfellow with the odometer, and José as guide, started for the head waters of the Madison. We went over to Col. Barlow's camp but he was not ready, and as the men from the ranche were just starting out, we concluded to go with them as far as they went our way.[1] We had no trail and our way was through thick timber a great deal of it being fallen. It was hard work for the odometer and Goodfellow. About noon we left the trappers and struck off on our own hook to the North West. Almost all our way was through the heaviest sort of timber.

In the afternoon we came into the valley [*Hayden Valley*] in which Crater Hills lie and in sight of Mt. Washburn again. Here we struck the trail of Barlow's party which we followed about 10 miles when we overtook them and went into camp together. We found an escort of four soldiers and a sergeant with them for us; as they were not ready when we started they came with Barlow. The rocks along our way today were all igneous. In many places there were masse[s] of almost pure obsidian. We passed a number of places . . . where hot springs once existed. Nothing is left but the white, glaring deposit [*sulfur*] from which steam and gases were escaping. On the road today we saw an Elk but he was too far off to shoot and he soon saw us and trotted off.

We are on one of the branches of the Madison [*Nez Percé Creek*] the water

Panorama 7. Lower Firehole Basin from the northeast, Three Hills, and Twin Buttes, August 4 of which is quite warm, probably from warm springs. It does not taste much however. {After a ride of thirty miles it was almost sundown when we got in and a hungry set we were.}² We all went to work and had supper in short order. Even the Doctor helped build a fire. We [*had*] not stop[*ped*] for dinner, and our elk meat with bread and coffee tasted splendid. The Doctor, Mr. Schönborn, and I retired under the shelter of the fly which the soldiers put up for us. Elliott slept outside.

Nez Percé Creek, six to eight miles east of
*its junction with the Firehole River*³

TUESDAY, AUGUST 1

I woke just before sunrise and just as he made his appearance above the hills I jumped up to find it somewhat cool. Mr. Schönborn put a tin cup of water under a tree last night so as to have a cool drink this morning. Sure enough when we got up this morning it was cool, being coated over with ice. {Looking at the thermometer we discovered that the mercury recorded 28°F. Indeed, in this country, spring and summer are crowded into the month of August. The flowers in bloom are the same we saw in May at Cheyenne.} I wrapped up a few plants and rocks for the Doctor this morning. The Doctor, Mr. Schönborn, and Col. Barlow started off on a trip and we stayed in camp, letting the animals feed until we started. The Doctor came in about 10 o'clock, bringing some specimens from a spring, the highest temperature of which was 199°F. I took down the temperatures. José and some of the members of Col. Barlow's party went out hunting this morning. We waited until they came in . . . about four o'clock. José saw a buffalo and wounded him but did not get him.⁴

It was nearly five o'clock before we got started. Our way led along the bank of the river [*Nez Percé Creek*], through open timber, crossing the stream at times which was somewhat miry in places. We passed a place where there were two hot springs with beautiful clear water. In one, however, the water flowed into a sort of basin in which there was an abundant deposit of sesquioxide of iron. Passing on further between two walls of igneous rock about 300 to 500 feet we emerged upon a plain on which we found four hot springs, the first being about [4] feet in diameter the next 2 feet the next 1 foot and the next somewhat irregular being about 15 feet long and averaging 5 feet wide. A little further on we came to a small mud spring about a foot in diameter with thick mud in the bottom. About a foot from the surface it was boiling somewhat. I got some of it. We went into camp on the river near a hill covered with pines [*Porcupine Hills*] which rises conically from the plain.

Lower Geyser Basin – just south of Nez Percé Creek,
about a mile east of its junction with the Firehole River[5]

WEDNESDAY, AUGUST 2

When I got up, there was ice on the under side of my blanket. After breakfast, Elliott started off and the Doctor, Schönborn, and myself started off around the springs. We came across Elliott near the geysers [*Fountain Group*]. The geysers are intermittent in their action. One of them spouted up about 60 feet and after a time stopped entirely [*Fountain Geyser* H]. Above this we came to mud springs, some of which were red, some pink, and others white [*Fountain Paint Pot*]. {The mud is of all . . . consistencies. The steam escaping through the mud has reduced it to an extreme degree of fineness, and in pushing its way through some places throws it back in forms resembling the leaves of a lily.} We followed a string of hot springs away up a ravine taking temperatures and collecting specimens. All the springs and geysers seem to contain a great deal of silica and iron which is deposited in different places.[6] Some soldiers were collecting near a quiet pool when suddenly it began to spout and they left suddenly. We did not get in until near 5 o'clock, when we moved about 2 miles to where Col. Barlow was encamped in front of geysers. As we came into camp we could see a huge volume of smoke in the direction of the geyser to which we gave the name of the Giant [*Great Fountain*], showing that it must be spouting. . . .[7]

José came in today after hunting all day without any game.

Geyser hill near the Fountain Group

THURSDAY, AUGUST 3

It was very cool again this morning when I got up. I slept under a pine tree as the place the fly was put up was so rough that I concluded I could find a better place. We had slapjacks for breakfast. I cooked one for myself and therefore enjoyed it very much. The Doctor, Mr. Schönborn, and Col. Barlow and some of his party started out early.[8] I stayed behind to pack specimens and watch for the spouting of the Giant [*Great Fountain*] Geyser. Seeing smoke in that direction, I started with one of the soldiers as escort. We went to the sulphur springs that I visited yesterday and got a specimen of sulphur near them. There are three or four of them.[9]

When we got to the Giant [*Great Fountain*], everything was quiet. Supposing the spouting was all over, after collecting specimens and pebbles from pockets around the basin, we turned to leave but had gone only a short distance when it commenced action. It spouted about 60 feet although it looked a hundred. The volume of smoke was immense and as the water broke into spray, high up in the air, the sight was grand. The eruption lasted about 20 minutes when all became quiet again and we left. The basin of this geyser is very large, although the place from which it spouts is only about 20 feet in diameter.

Reaching camp again, I resumed work on my specimens until dinner time, when Elliott, the Doctor, and Schönborn came in. José was in, having been on the hunt for game all morning without success. After dinner I finished packing specimens, after which, the Doctor and I started off down the river passing a number of hot springs on the way. One stood on the bank like a chimney rising about 2 feet above it. On looking into it, it seemed to have no depth. Proceeding some distance down, we turned across through the woods and came across a number of mud springs, near which there were some small cones from which steam escaped [*probably present Microcosm Basin near Rush Lake*]. Breaking these open there were veins of sulphur and of iron running through the pieces making handsome specimens. On the way back we were almost mired. We attempted to go through a place but the horses sank in so that we were obliged to make a wide detour in order to get over to camp.

When we got in we found that Elliott had killed a duck with his small pistol. The Doctor, Col. Barlow, and I rode up to the geysers. In the meantime it had commenced to rain.

When we got back we had roast duck and what they call hell fire stew for supper.[10] José came in without any game. Col. Barlow sent over a fly to put up at the end of ours and both Elliott and I turned inside as it looked very threatening. The thermometer this morning early stood at 28°F.

FRIDAY, AUGUST 4

When I rose I found it very foggy and cold. {One would not have to exercise his imagination very much to think himself in some great manufacturing centre, for vast columns of steam rise about him in all directions.} As soon after breakfast as it began to get somewhat clearer, the Doctor, Schönborn, and myself started down the river taking the temperature of the springs, geysers, and mud springs.[11] We went over the whole ground. We saw a cascade in the mountains [*Fairy Falls B*]. It falls 250 feet and underneath it is a deep cavelike projection running under the rock over which the water falls. It looks as though the water were falling over a natural bridge.[12] There are two hills [*Twin Buttes* H] which slope toward the edge of the water on either side, while the mountain ran along back of it covered with pines. The stream was not very wide although it fell 250 feet, the water being lost to sight among the pines. On getting back to camp we took dinner and then, packing, started after the other party.

We soon came to some huge springs [*Grand Prismatic Spring*] – the largest we have seen yet.[13] There was one about 200 feet in diameter. Just below this there is a huge depressed spring down in a crater 20 feet deep. There was an immense volume of steam which obscured the water, which was beautifully clear and blue showing huge boulders in the bottom [*Excelsior Geyser Crater*]. The water from these springs was considerable in amount and flowed over into the river in a beautiful cascade lined with sesquioxide of iron.[14]

We got off the trail and, after hunting around for it about an hour, we came across it and followed it up the river, passing a number of hot springs, till we came to camp in the midst of the geysers that Lt. Doane described [*Upper Geyser Basin*]. Elliott showed us a sketch of one which he says must have gone up 200 feet at least.[15]

We had a soldier with us as escort today to hold the horses. We had squirrel and partridge for dinner as José got no game.

Upper Geyser Basin, on the west side of the
Firehole River opposite the Grand Geyser

SATURDAY, AUGUST 5

After we turned in last night, one of the geysers commenced to spout. Although we could not see it, we could hear it, for as the water fell it shook the ground. We could feel the vibrations as we lay upon our blankets. Towards morning I woke shivering with the cold. I crawled under an extra fold of blanket and went to sleep again.

After breakfast the Doctor, Mr. Schönborn, and I, with two soldiers to hold our horses, started off to take the geysers below camp. I carried the thermometer and took temperatures. The first one we visited was the one that spouted so high last night. We saw the Grotto also. One of the small geysers we came to spouted every 10 minutes. The Doctor was gathering some specimens near it when it commenced to spout suddenly. He left as fast as possible. This we called the Soda Geyser [*Jewel Geyser*]. Some of the huge springs go to an immense depth and on looking into are { . . . filled with water clear as crystal. . . . The tint seen is a most beautiful blue. I can compare it to nothing but the blue of a clear sky, and even then you must imagine the color intensified. It seems as though the cavity were lined with a portion of the heavens above us, convoluted and rolled over the projecting ridges on the sides of the spring, each of which throws} back the sunlight dispersed into its constituent colors. Wherever the water has a chance to stand and cool it deposits the iron – the red color of which contrasts prettily with the white of the siliceous deposit.[16] In some places, where pine trees have fallen, the branches with the cones on have become coated forming beautiful specimens.

Following the other fork of the river, we found a number of springs (one of which was immense). There is one of the geysers we can see from Camp that spouts every hour. It must be Old Faithful. We saw the Giant also this morning.[17] About noon one of the geysers near camp spouted, throwing up an immense volume of water to the height of 25 feet, the steam going much higher. It was like some huge fountain. The [mass?] was very wide.

This afternoon, Mr. Schönborn and I started out with a soldier as escort to finish the survey of the Geysers, I taking the temperatures which varied from 130 to boiling, past 196. Elevation here is 8,200 feet.[18] We visited the Castle which is the prettiest one of all. {It is situated in the centre of a large and gently sloping mound of the siliceous deposit. Its crater rises above this about twenty-five feet, fashioned in turrets, whence its name. Some of them are broken down, as though the "Castle" had been subjected to a bombardment. It is about fifty feet in length, and is encrusted with a bead-like formation. The water gushes from it every few hours, making a great deal of noise.}

We also visited Old Faithful . . . {and well it deserves its name, for it spouts with great regularity every hour, throwing the water to the height of one hundred and fifty feet. It does so seemingly without effort, making no noise}.

We came across one beautiful spring. It consisted of an outside basin of about 15 feet diameter, lined with red, while inside was a small corrugated border rising about 6 inches of a bright yellow color. Inside of this, looking into the regularly sloping [cavern], the tint was a beautiful blue.

One little jet of steam near Camp rose about 20 feet with scarcely any intermission [*Saw Mill Geyser* H]. The spring expanded when the Steam reached its utmost height and the sun shining on it was reflected in its constituent colors. I procured a bottle of water from the Grand Geyser opposite Camp.

I had one of the soldiers as my patient today and gave him some medicine

35. A distant view of the crater of Castle Geyser. Hayden and Peale observed the Castle in eruption on August 5; this photo was taken by Jackson on August 8. U.S. Geological Survey, W. H. Jackson 109

from Col. Barlow's Camp.[19] It was cloudy all afternoon and rainy in the adjacent mountains.

{Our rapidly diminishing stores [*warn*] us . . . to turn towards the lake. . . . We brought provisions for six days . . . [*are*] unable to obtain any game, and . . . resort to squirrels and . . . other small game . . . reducing ourselves to one biscuit a day.}

SUNDAY, AUGUST 6

Last night about 10 o'clock the Grand Geyser spouted and I had an opportunity of seeing it in the moonlight. The Doctor came in while it was going on and said it went fully 200 feet.

In place of bacon we had a rabbit for breakfast, which tasted very good. After finishing our meal, I helped pack the specimens. All the mules being packed, we started for Yellowstone Lake, bidding farewell to the geysers. The Doctor was behind. On coming up he told us he had a farewell salute from "Old Faithful"; he spewed 150 feet.[20]

Our way led through fallen timber, some of it pretty bad. After 8 miles travelling, having passed a beautiful little lake, we arrived at the summit of the first ridge, 9,600 feet above sea level.[21] It was a pretty steep climb to the top of it, over a volcanic sand composed of broken down obsidian which composed the only rocks about us. I got some specimens. Ascending a point about 100 feet higher, we began then to descend and soon caught sight of a lake which at first we supposed to be Yellowstone Lake. We soon saw that it was considerably smaller and heart shaped. It was Heart Lake, the one that Doane called Lake Besse, but the trappers and hunters in this region have always known it by the name of Heart Lake. It is about 5 miles wide. [*Peale and his party were at today's Shoshone Lake, not Heart Lake.*][22]

. . . After passing along its shores, against which there was quite a surf beating, we struck into the woods, Schönborn leading. José said we were going too far to the right, but still we kept on. After a while Elliott left us in disgust. One of the horses of the escort gave out and had to be led. Towards sunset Schönborn and the Doctor came to the conclusion we were lost so we decided to camp at the first water. The soldier and horse with José stayed behind to rest. About a mile and a half further we came to a small lake about 1 mile wide and 2 long which was not down on the map and must be the headwater of one fork of the Snake River.[23] We are away to the south of the Yellowstone Lake. We travelled about 22 miles through the timber, some of it of the worst description. I tore my green blanket on some tree. We had bacon, slapjacks and tea for supper. José came up with the soldier and his horse. We had to supply the escort with grub.

In coming down to Heart [*Shoshone*] Lake[24] the Doctor led the party through a miry place. One of the mules became mired and had to be unloaded and taken back around through the woods the way Elliott and I went in the first place. After we left the lake and ascended the ridge, we heard a shot fired which we supposed was fired by some hunter. Hearing another and looking around, we found that Coxe, one of the soldiers, was missing. We fired and shouted at intervals, he answering, and in about a half an hour he came up. Another of the escort was driving one of our mules when he got kicked in the ankle. When we got to camp I bandaged it for him and told him to bathe it in cold water.

Small lake [Lost Lake?] about 2 miles northeast of
Madison Lake [Shoshone Lake] and 4–5 miles from Yellowstone Lake

MONDAY, AUGUST 7

This morning we started early, José in the lead. We had gone but a mile and a half when we reached the shore of the [*Yellowstone*] Lake and found we were about 3 miles south of camp which we could plainly see.[25] We followed the bank having to ford some little in places. We overtook Carrington and

Logan who were on the beach gunning. They told us that Lieut. Doane had come up and ordered most of our escort back to fight the Indians. Getting into Camp we found that Jackson, Smith, and Lieut. Doane had gone over to the geysers. The escort were ordered back to escort the surveying party sent out by the Northern Pacific Railroad. Lieut. Doane will command those left with us.[26]

I found a paper with my third letter in it. It had a large heading and the Doctor thought it very good. Smith took my letters over to the geysers with him. I wrote to Mother and finished my letter to Charlie and gave them, with my letter to Mills and the Paper, to Logan to take back to Bottler's to mail. I re-packed all the specimens that we brought over from the geysers.

Elliott spent most of the afternoon in fixing the boat for a trip all around the Lake {to explore and chart [*it*]}. He will take Carrington with him. After Elliott was through, we took a bath in the Lake from which, however, we did not derive much satisfaction as the water on top was hot from a deep hot spring near the Lake, while underneath it was cold [*Winter Spring*]. It was cleansing, however.[27]

We found the party here living on two biscuits for dinner with what meat they could get, and one biscuit and one cup of tea for supper. After I picketed my horse I went over to the hot springs close to camp and got specimens which I put up by the light of the campfire.

Fourth camp on Yellowstone Lake, [*at West Thumb*]
south of the Hot Springs, 10 feet above the surface of the lake

Report No. 7: Ferdinand Hayden to Spencer Baird

YELLOW STONE LAKE, WY

AUGUST 8TH 1871

Dear Professor Baird:

Your two letters of June 16th and July 3d were brought us from Fort Ellis by Lt. Doane who has just arrived to take command of our escort and accompany my party the remainder of the season. In my last I told you we had made a permanent camp at "Bottler's Ranch" on the Yellow Stone River about 140 miles below the Lake. That was as high a point as we could go with wagons. We then took a pack train and proceeded up the Valley.

The first great group of springs we came to was on Warm Spring Creek, Calcareous, the most beautiful we have yet seen or expect to see. There were no real geysers but deposits of lime 150 to 200 feet in height, looking in their forms like water flowing over a moderate descent and gradually congealing into ice. Indeed, Photographs will appear like the [ebullitions?] of ice about Springs on a mountain side on a grand scale. Lt. Doane did not see them at all, consequently we have explored them for the first time.

We [went] around the Tower Falls, upper and lower Falls of the Yellow Stone, Crater Hills, and Mud Springs, and found that all the descriptions given by Lt. Doane and others fell far short of the Truth.

We arrived at the banks of the Yellow Stone Lake July 26th and pitched our camp near the point where the river leaves the Lake. Hence we brought the first pair of wheels that ever came to the Lake with our Odometer. We launched the first Boat on the Lake, 4.5 feet wide and 11 feet long, with sails and oars.[28] We have now explored the north and west sides of the Lake, made soundings of about half the area – over 40 – and find the greatest depth 300 feet. We do not expect to find it over 500 feet deep on the East and South sides where the water is deepest.

We find a channel running [nearly] N.E. and S.W. for about 45 miles [long], a portion of which has been sounded. A chart of these soundings will be made. Points have been located with a prismatic compass all around the Lake. A man stands on the shore with a compass and takes a bearing to the man in the Boat as he drops the lead, giving a signal at the time. Then a man in the Boat takes a bearing to the fixed point on the shore where the first man is located and thus the soundings will be located on the chart. Henry Elliott and Mr. Carrington have just left in our little Boat, the "Annie," while I am writing to you, to be absent several days. [Elliott will] make a systematic sketch of the shore with all its indentations, with the banks down, indeed, making a complete topographical as well as a pictorial sketch of the shores as seen from the water, for a circuit – of at least 130 miles. He will also make soundings, at various points.

One of the islands has been explored. We have called it Stevenson's Island, as he was undoubtedly the first human that ever set foot upon it. It contains an area of 1500 acres, densely wooded, in part with pines, with an under growth so dense that Messrs. Stevenson and Elliott could not penetrate many portions of it. This under growth consists largely of gooseberry and currant bushes loaded down with fruit: this 3 miles from any shore yet several Elk, with Beaver, Deer and Wolves; No Rabbits were seen. There were mice or moles as their traces were seen. The highest portion of the Island is not more than 50 feet above the water. There are some other small island[s] which we have not yet examined. We are passing around the Lake commencing on the west side. Our first camp was near the point where the River leaves the Lake. We then moved around to the south west side at the Hot Springs as it is located on Doane's chart.[29] We shall move again soon – to the South East side. From these points [will] be made side trips to the sources of the Missouri, Yellow Stone and Snake Rivers. We are discovering and locating several beautiful new Lakes, generally about 3 miles long and 2 wide.

We returned yesterday from an 8 days trip, explored the different branches of the Madison, examined all the Hot Springs and Geyser region, made charts, located and took the temperatures of over 500 Springs. The area called the Geyser region on the Firehole and other branches of the Madison river we estimated at 5 miles in width and 20 in length, or covering an area of 100 square miles. This does not include a large number of other localities where there are quite large areas covered with springs. We make separate charts of them.

We are making most abundant sketches and Photographs of everything. Henry Elliott has been most diligent. Every cone, Pyramid, the springs in operation etc., are all sketched. We found the Hottest Springs or Geysers to vary from 188° to 198°. The boiling point here is somewhere between 194° and 196°. A great majority of the springs ranged from 140° to 175°. The Springs are of two kinds: silica, sulphur and iron, or silica and iron. The Hot Springs of the Madison are mostly silica and iron, and the inner white deposits have no trace of lime. On Warm Spring Creek [*Mammoth Hot Springs*] the deposits were nearly all Lime.

The Elevation of the Lake is about 8,500. My little aneroid reads as I write to you, 8,600 feet, but when the observations of the Mercurial Barometer are worked out, we think it will be about 8,500 feet.[30]

We found everything in the Geyser region even more wonderful than it has been represented. One of the Geysers threw up a column of water [approximately] 8 feet in diameter at least 200 feet, once in 32 hours. Old Faithful, whose crater stands on a hill at the head of the Firehole Valley overlooking all the rest, plays about every hour, and the morning I left he gave me a [parting] for 10 minutes in which he held up a column of water, 6 or 8 feet in diameter, 150 feet with the utmost care and with very little noise. There are a hundred or more of the Geysers that throw up [*water*] 10 to 50 feet. Some are playing all the time, others are intermittent [and] I do not think have any regular periods.

The trout in the Lake and the streams of the Yellow Stone Basin are most abundant. Above the Falls and in the Lake about half of them are filled with intestinal worms. It is a sort of tape worm from 6 to 14 inches long. They are mostly found lying in the abdomen, but many of them have worked into the flesh and imbedded themselves, and sometimes lie just under the skin, having worked through from the inside. I have saved abundant specimens in all forms.[31]

We do not find many animals or Birds here. We have some. Game is so scarce that with the best of hunters we cannot be supplied with meat. I have two good hunters and I think they have not killed more than three or four animals for the past two weeks. It may be that the altitude is too great and winters too severe, for lower down on the River, [small] game is abundant. We find a few of the *Lepus bairdii* but have not succeeded in getting a good specimen.[32]

I send this back to you by James [Stevenson] who returns to our permanent camp for supplies. This is about 40 miles from Fort Ellis. I do not know when the letter will reach you but soon I hope.[33] We are all well. We'll finish our Lake Basin Survey and then go down the Yellow Stone on the East side between the sources of the Yellow Stone and Big Horn Rivers. We hope to reach Fort Ellis about the 1st or 5th of September. Schönborn does splendid Topographical work. Write at once.

Yours Truly,

F. V. Hayden

I will send you some Photographs soon.

8

On and around Yellowstone Lake

From Base Camp at West Thumb to Steamboat Point

This morning I got up about 4 o'clock. I packed the remainder of the specimens while those who went back to Bottlers' ate their breakfast. It was very cold this morning. I helped in the packing of the animals. Elliott and Cam Carrington started in the boat very early this morning. Jim, Beaman, Dawes, Logan, Adams, Dixon, Mr. Chrisman [*Crissman*], and John Raymond, Alec Sibley, and Jo Smith, started back with the pack train [*to Bottler's Ranch*]. After they had been gone about an hour or two the Doctor and Schönborn missed an aneroid barometer and made Steve saddle and go after the train to see if Beaman knew where it was. He had gone but a short time when they found it. We did not get breakfast until rather late. We had prunes, bacon, bread, and coffee.

After breakfast, the Doctor, Schönborn, and myself started out to go the rounds of the hot springs along the Lake near camp. I rode Dick (Negley's horse) and the Doctor rode his extra poney. While the Doctor and Schönborn went around taking the temperatures, I held the horses. The area of springs here is not very great and we soon finished them after which we struck up into the woods and came across a small lake [*Duck Lake*] about half a mile long and about a third of a mile in width. It is not far back from [*Yellowstone*] Lake and is very pretty indeed. Coming back to camp I went on the hunt of my hammer which I dropped from my belt while running after the Doctor's poney which ran away to the herd. Fortunately I found it after a short search.

Getting back to Camp I spent the remainder of the morning fixing my fly of which I was the sole occupant until night when Jackson came into it. I spent the afternoon reading and writing. Towards evening I helped Mr.

Panorama 8. Head of Yellowstone River and North Shore of Yellowstone Lake with Steamboat Point ("Earthquake" Camp) on far right, August 19–22

Schönborn make a base line along the shore of the Lake.[1] I also got a bottle of water to analyze tomorrow. This morning one of the soldiers saw three bears but was afraid to shoot. His excuse was that he had but one cartridge.

While we were at supper, Lieut. Doane and Col. Barlow's party came in camp and some little time after, Smith, Jackson, and Dunning arrived.[2] Smith gave me my letters: one from Clara dated July 5th, one from Mother dated July 11th, and another from Dr. Mills, dated July 14th. I read them by the light of the camp fire in front of the Doctor's tent. I read of the death of Uncle George and Will Patterson with regret. I was not surprised at Uncle George's death as I had expected it. Lieut. Doane sent us a supply of provisions. He sleeps in the Doctor's tent and eats with us. Mr. Moran went down the Madison, on his way back to Philadelphia, with the soldiers who went back to Fort Ellis.

WEDNESDAY, AUGUST 9

This morning I packed some specimens then wrote a note to Mother and Clara conjointly in answer to those I received last night. Then I put in a package with two of the Doctor's and took both packages over to one of the men who started down with Col. Barlow's pack train for provisions. The remainder of the morning I spent in examining the water from the hot springs near here. This afternoon, we started for the South end of the Lake, Lieut. Doane leading us. Our way was almost entirely through timber, the most of it very fair, occasionally coming out into open grassy places. We passed a number of small lakes. One of the packs getting loose two or three times, Steve, Dick, and Geiselman, were obliged to stay behind. Not coming up soon, we stopped and shouted and fired both needle gun and pistol.[3] After some time they came up and we proceeded on our way. After travelling [ ] miles we went into camp on one arm of the Lake at the foot of the snow-capped Mountain, in a ravine on a little creek.

It was very cool this afternoon and when we got in, Jackson, Kelley, and myself built a huge fire which will keep burning nearly all night. We saw an elk on the way. Lieut. Doane shot at it but missed him. We had scarcely got in camp before José and Clark came in with a blacktail deer, some of which we had for supper. It was very tender and delicious. Some time after making camp, Col. Barlow and party, with the soldiers, came in. Kelley will sleep in our tent fly in the center.

Before Red Mountain [This campsite was west of Flat Mountain at the main bay of Yellowstone Lake.][4]

THURSDAY, AUGUST 10

This morning I woke to find my toes cold. When I got up at sunrise I found the thermometer stood at 15.5° to 16.5°. We soon had our fire – which kept on all [*last*] night going right lively and were not long in getting warm. After breakfast I lay around in the fly while Jackson fixed some chemicals after which He, Kelley, and I, with the photographic pack, went to the top of a hill near camp and took a picture of the Lake. I was in the picture. We got back to Camp about 11 o'clock. The Doctor, Lieut. [*Doane*], and Schönborn started off on a trip to the Mountain [*Flat Mountain*] back of Camp. As we got in Camp, Col. Barlow's party started off towards the head of the Snake River.[5] This is, I believe, our forty-second camp.

José and Jo Clark started off again this morning for game. Geiselman found a kind of mole and I fixed it, skinning and putting it in arsenic. The Doctor came in about one o'clock and we hurried with dinner and then got ready to start. Our way was over the mountain back of camp. We had pretty bad timber to go through. By evening after several delays on account of the packs, we arrived at a valley where we encamped. We built a large fire in front of our fly. I fixed up the plants got during the day and also some rocks, got during the day by the Doctor, they being volcanic with the exception of one which was a limestone. I retired early as I had guard duty to do, borrowing Steve's overcoat.

Camp at head of Snake River [Actually, they were northeast of Heart Lake.][6]

FRIDAY, AUGUST 11

I was on guard last night from 11 o'clock to 1:30 A.M., when I woke Hamill of our escort and turned in. It was beginning to get pretty cool. We got on the road about 8 o'clock and started on our way around the Southern end of the Lake. We travelled all day until after sunset when we camped on the bank of Bridger Creek [*Yellowstone River*]. We had some pretty bad timber to go through. We were on the shore of the Lake twice when we built fires and left marks on the trees telling where we were so that if Elliott and Carrington happen to see it they may find us. We saw a wolverine in one of the open spaces we crossed but it got in the woods before any one could get it. The Lieut. shot a duck, which, with a rabbit that Steve caught, we had for supper. It commenced to rain in the afternoon and kept up so until night. In crossing Bridger Creek, Smith attempted to cross first where there were quicksands. He got in too deep and was obliged . . . {*molens volens*, to dismount in the middle of the stream. He reached the shore thoroughly wet, and minus his saddle-bags, which floated down stream, bearing with him the surplus clothing, much to the merriment of those safe on the bank}.[7] The Lieut. did not get in until we had been in camp some time. José and Clark started out again this morning, saying that they would not come in until they got some game. We passed a number of beaver dams and saw several of their houses which rise above the water about 3 or 4 feet in a conical shape made of sticks.

Camp on Bridger River [upper Yellowstone River][8]

SATURDAY, AUGUST 12

I woke this morning to find it hailing and raining. The Doctor and I fixed up the flowers before breakfast. We had bacon, coffee, and biscuit for our meal after which I skinned a young rabbit and prepared it with arsenic. By the time I was through the packs were ready and we started. Our way, at first, was through willows which were very thick and wet. It was raining almost all the time we were on the march. The latter part of our journey was through timber, emerging out an open place on the edge of the Lake. We camped so as to be in a conspicuous place for Elliott to see us if he happens to be on the bay. We built a fire of sage brush. While helping I singed my hair and part of my side fuz[z]. Jim shot a pheasant, taking off its head. When we got in camp we found that one of the horses (the Doctor's bay poney) was missing, so Steve and Dick went after him.

We all went fishing and soon caught enough for dinner. I caught one. The water was [al]most too rough and it was snowing so I did not fish very long. We had several snow storms during the morning. In the afternoon it cleared off, but there was a strong wind. Jackson and I went fishing again. I got one fish out of water, but it got back. Jackson caught three. The bait having given out we stopped. Jo Clark came in this evening with a goose and said that José had an elk and that they had killed three, but we [*had come*] too far for them to bring them in. Goodfellow shot six ducks.

Camp on terrace [Terrace Point], Yellowstone Lake,
80 feet above the surface of the water

SUNDAY, AUGUST 13

We had a stew made of ducks and goose for breakfast. Jackson, Kelley, and myself went to the top of the mountain back of camp. Jackson took six pictures of the Lake; I am in three of them. The view was splendid and the day clear. I got a number of specimens of volcanic breccia. We were up all morning. The Doctor, Schönborn, and Lieut. [*Doane*] with Dick, one of the soldiers, and two pack mules, started off on a side trip expecting to be gone four or five days.[9] I traded Saddle bags with the Doctor, his being torn. José came in this morning with about [100] pounds of Elk meat. I spent the afternoon wrapping up specimens and flowers, after which I took a good wash in the Lake. John mended the Doctor's saddlebags and I put my things in them. We are reduced now, again, to one biscuit a meal. The thermometer this morning stood below the freezing point again. This afternoon, John Geiselman thought he saw a bear and got Jo Clark to go up with his rifle. He shot five times, hitting each time, when they found it was a black stump. Steve [*Hovey*] and the corporal of our escort went ahead today to pick out a camp. They got in after dark, bringing with them a female eagle which they shot on a nest near the trail. Smith moved into the Doctor's tent as did, also, Jackson.

Monday, August 14

This morning, Jackson, Smith, Kelley, and myself started on to the camping place that Steve picked out yesterday. We had very fair travelling, being part of the time in the woods and part along the shore of the Lake. We had scarcely got on the way before we flushed up some pine hens, of which Kelley killed two. We crossed a creek, the water of which was very strongly impregnated with alum from beds some distance up the side of the mountain. We came across the eagle's nest which Steve saw yesterday. It is at the top of a large dead tree and made of sticks, about 6 or 7 feet in diameter. Smith succeeded in wounding a male bird, a genuine bald headed eagle. Its tail feathers are white also, while the body and wings are black. The female we got yesterday is larger, measuring from tip of one wing to the tip of the other, 7 feet. It is of a black grey color. The male measures 5 feet from tip to tip, and has powerful talons and a rather yellow beak. We succeeded in bringing him in alive. Smith shot him in the wing. He has a brilliant sharp eye.

We crossed a stream with two beaver dams on it. When we got to the point Steve visited yesterday, we found Elliott and Cam with the boat. They were cooking so we added our store of chicken and made slap jacks. As we had no yeast powder, we made them thin. They had plenty of tea, but only one cup besides the one they made tea in. We had one, however, so we managed to make out, six of us using three cups. We made a gravy from our chicken and had bacon also. The whole dinner was splendid.

36. Peale overlooking Yellowstone Lake and Promontory Point, August 13. U.S. Geological Survey, W. H. Jackson 104d

The Lake was very rough. The waves coming in were equal to waves on the sea coast. Elliott says they were able to take but three soundings, it being rough all the time. {The wind once was so strong that the mast was broken off and carried away.} The boat rode splendidly. They saw the fire we built on the hill. They beat Jim and the rest of the party getting to the mouth of the river, an hour before Jim did. {A second party, Mr. Alfred Smith and Private Starr of our escort, was organized for the purpose of taking soundings.}[10]

While we were eating dinner, Steve rode up and said they were going into Camp about 100 yards back from the Lake. When we were through we went over and found Camp in a beautiful place at the edge of the trees looking out on a beautiful little park with a stream of water running through it.

Steve sent Jo Clark back on the trail with a pack for the meat he left behind. I spent the afternoon reading. Jo Clark came in after dark without the meat, saying that it had been eaten by some animal.

Camp Hovey, on Yellowstone Lake [*Signal Point*][11]

TUESDAY, AUGUST 15

I was on guard this morning from half past one until four o'clock, when I turned in and slept until half past seven, and got up for breakfast. All our flour has been used and we have to live on meat, coffee, and tea. Jackson,

37. Goodfellow and the odometer, August 14. National Gallery v3, 301.tif

Kelley, and I started over to the Lake with the pack to take pictures but it was too smoky.[12] We found Smith on the beach, and as the Lake was perfectly calm Smith and Kelley went out in the boat.

Jackson and I came back to Camp and I assisted him in taking pictures. We photographed Goodfellow and his go cart. He also took two pictures of myself and horse, the second of which was a failure as Toby moved.

Smith came in having gone to the promontory from which he brought a specimen of rock. He saw a bear on the point. While taking a sounding their rope broke and they lost the weight. After dinner, which we had late in the afternoon, Jackson and I went over to the Lake and took three pictures. Elliott took a ride over to the Mountains. Jo Clark brought in a blacktail deer today. We are living now on meat and coffee and tea with sugar. José went out this evening after game. When we eat, each man takes his plate, cup, spoon, and knife and fork, helps himself, and squats somewhere with it. When we are through eating, we deposit the dishes on one pile. Steve went along the Lake this afternoon and built a fire and left a note according to Jim's orders.[13]

WEDNESDAY, AUGUST 16

I spent this morning about Camp reading and packing specimens. Jackson and I built a fire and made a cup of tea and roasted each a piece of deer. José brought in a blacktail deer.

After eating our lunch we went over to the Lake. He took a number of photographs and we started back to camp. On getting there we found {the supply train had arrived [with] Jim, Charlie, Duncan, Huse, Jo Smith, Flint, Loucks, and John Raymond. Jim was eagerly welcomed, not only for his own sake, but also for the sake of what he brought with him.} They had just finished eating. We went to work and took our meal having warm biscuits, the first in a long time. Jim went down [to Bottler's Ranch] in two days and a half. I got two letters from home . . . I also got two copies of *The Miner's Journal*, one . . . with a notice of myself as connected with the expedition. I also got a copy of the *Inquirer*.

After we were done eating, Lieut. Doane came in soon after, the Doctor and Mr. Schönborn arrived. Dick and Coxe did not come in for some time after. Charlie, Huse, and I went over to the Lake and enjoyed a fine sunset. We found Cam and Duncan fishing. Coming back we picketed our horses and built a fire in front of our fly. Charlie took Kelley's place in the fly. Smith and Kelley went out in the boat this morning and did not come in tonight.

THURSDAY, AUGUST 17

This morning I got my horse, saddled him, and started for the brimstone basin about 5 or 6 miles back on the side of the mountain.[14] I found them to be the remains of old springs, every one of which is now extinct. The white deposit extends up deep ravines and gullies in the side of the mountain. Over the white deposit is scattered, in places, broken down grey blue volcanic rock. In places there is also a deposit of sulphur. In a few places water escapes and runs down. It is impregnated with alum. There is also a sulphurous odor in these gullies.

I did not get in until evening. The Doctor and some of the rest of the party went up to the mountains and went up one which they called Mt. Stevenson [H] from which they brought specimens.[15] I got a number of specimens, also, spending the time after supper wrapping them up. Jackson and Turnbull went out photographing and did not get in until after dark.

FRIDAY, AUGUST 18

I got to work this morning packing specimens that the Doctor got on his trip over to the mountains. After I was through the Doctor and I went over to the Lake and got some specimens of rocks and agates and chalcedonies. Getting back to camp I resumed work on specimens. After I was through with them I put pieces of buckskin on the knees of my breeches and mended my overcoat which was torn in bringing up on the pack. Jim came in toward evening, bringing some rocks from the top of Mt. Doane [H], which is 10,250 feet high.[16] Jackson and Turnbull started for the falls this morning. Charlie left me some medicines. I packed all the specimens in a par fleche, and wrapped up medicines and got my things ready for starting in the morning. After picketing my horse, I built a fire in front of my bed, Jackson having taken the fly. I will sleep in the open air tonight.

SATURDAY, AUGUST 19

This morning we were up before daylight. After breakfast we packed the mules, Elliott, Cam, and I attending to one of them. We had quite a long train, and, striking across the prairie in which we were encamped, we soon entered the woods. After travelling awhile, the Doctor, Lieut., and I went along the sea shore. I got a number of specimens. Striking across through the woods, we came on the trail again, and following it, soon came to camp. {Our tents were pitched on some high bluffs some distance above the level of the lake, on a beautiful lawn, dotted with grand old spruce trees whose symmetry would have been an ornament to the finest park.}

Everybody was busily engaged in picking and eating gooseberries which grow very plentiful near camp. They are very large and there are a number of varieties. In coming along the shores of the Lake, we passed quite a good many raspberrie bushes. The berry resembles in size, appearance, and taste, our cultivated one. The bush, however, does not grow quite so high.

It began to rain soon after we got in camp. Toward evening, however, it cleared beautifully. I wrapped up the specimens we procured today. After dinner, Elliott and I took a walk to the top of the hill back of camp. The point on which we are now encamped is Steamboat Point [H], so called from some steam jets at its foot about a quarter of a mile from camp. The bay, just before us, is Mary's Bay [H], so named by Elliott, after some lady to whom he has promised to introduce me next winter.[17]

After we got back, the Doctor and I went back about a mile or two to some hot springs – the Doctor on horseback and I on foot. There are about four or five springs and a number of smaller holes and steam jets . . . on the side of a small hill [*Butte Springs*]. The ground around, for some distance, is quite bare, covered with red deposit and sulphur here and there. There is also a slight deposit of alum in a few places. The highest temperature was 192°, the lowest 110°. About 1/4 mile below, there are a few iron springs gushing from the side of the mountain, with a deposit of iron and silica, also some vegetative matter. Average temperature was 170. I got a bottle of water from the first mentioned springs.

I had a walk through the rain back to camp. I got some pine cones today of a different variety from any I have yet obtained. On the road today, Schönborn's sextant was damaged somehow, and when he found it out he was very angry indeed. Jim and Lieut. Doane were out this afternoon and brought in some specimens of clay formation, some of which were very curious in shape. They got them along the shore of the Lake. After picketing my horse, I fixed my bed at the foot of a large pine. Smith was to have come in tonight, but did not. Elliott lit a fire and says it was answered from Stevenson's Island.

Earthquake Camp Near Steamboat Point, 75 feet above Yellowstone Lake

SUNDAY, AUGUST 20

This morning about 1 o'clock we had quite an earthquake. The first schock [*sic*] lasted about 20 seconds and was followed by five or six shorter ones. Duncan, who was on guard, says that the trees were shaken and that the horses that were lying down sprang to their feet. Some birds in the tree near which I had my bed were wakened and flew out of its branches. Some of the men were not wakened at all. We had three shocks during the morning.[18]

The Doctor, Lieut. Doane, Mr. Schönborn, and Elliott, with one of the soldiers and John Raymond, started for the Grand Canyon this morning. After they had gone, Duncan, Henry Greve, and I went over to Steamboat Point. There are only one or two small springs here that contain any water. One of them is like a sieve through which there is a slight bubbling. There are a number of steam jets, however, from two of which there issue vast columns of steam with great force, making a good bit of noise. The resemblance to a steamboat letting off steam is perfect. It is constant also.

After taking a wash in the Lake I came back to Camp and spent the remainder of the morning in putting up some plants and airing those already put up. Jim and Cam started off this morning and did not get in until dinnertime. They visited a small lake and discovered a number of hot springs [*Turbid Lake and Turbid Hot Springs H*]. They also saw two deer and an elk. Just before they started Jim killed a rabbit. I spent the afternoon wrapping a few specimens and sleeping and reading. Late in the afternoon Duncan and I took a walk along the Lake, the waves of which were very high. After taking a wash we came back to camp and had not been in long before a soldier, one of Col. Barlow's escort, came . . . {riding into camp on a gallop, telling us that Indians were after Colonel Barlow, who had left us . . . to go to the head of the Snake River. After he became somewhat composed, we learned that Colonel Barlow's party had left their camp in the morning but a short time when they discovered that one of their pack mules, with all their cooking utensils, was missing. Two men [*Jack Baronett and one of the soldiers*] were sent back to hunt for the mule. On getting to the old camp they found a number of redskins prowling about it. They immediately turned about and hastened to join the rest of the party.

Reporting what they had seen, a soldier was despatched to us for help. We sent back our escort, and about seven o'clock in the evening they all came in together pretty badly scared.} [*We learned that*] an Indian dog came into their camp.[19] Our guard tonight will be doubled and Steve and I be on until 11 o'clock.

MONDAY, AUGUST 21

After I had turned in last night we were wakened and told that the Indian dog was in camp. I was wakened about 2 o'clock by Loucks coming and asking what time it was, so I did not get much sleep the whole night. Between 3 and 4 o'clock everyone was wakened for fear of an attack, as this is the time the Indians prefer. Three men were put on herd today. Smith and the Soldier came in this morning. They made thirty soundings, leaving only a few to be made. They camped on the shore a few miles from camp last night and fired some shots but they were not answered by us on account of the Indian scare.

I saddled my poney after breakfast and started to go to the little lake that Jim and Cam visited yesterday. I had gone about 2 miles when I saw what I supposed to be an Indian. As I had no gun I went back about a mile to the herd and got one of the soldiers to go back with me. Whatever it was it had disappeared. He saw tracks of a bear and supposed that was it. I concluded to go back to camp and get one of the boys to go along. It was dinner time when I got back. While Steve and I were on guard last night we had a slight quake.

After dinner Cam, Duncan and I started for [*Turbid*] Lake. On the way we came across a deer. Cam shot but missed him. After going through some pretty thick timber we got to the Lake. It is heart shaped. It is about 1/2 or 3/4 of a mile long and about 2/3 as wide. The water is very turbid and has an alum taste. We passed a number of springs and followed a valley through which a creek flows into the lake for about 3 or 4 miles until the creek forked. It was a beautiful valley getting quite wide as we progressed. We saw three elk but got none of them. Coming back we visited a mud spring. It is about 30 feet in diameter and is black, tasting strongly of alum. There are some pretty sulphur specimens near it, some of which I got. Turning our faces towards camp, after passing through some pretty bad timber and crossing the creek which flows from the Lake, we came near the herd which was in the woods. In front of the woods was an open prairie. We came across it on a lope and gave a scare to those on herd. They had forgotten we were out and thought we were Indians. I slept in the tent last night and will also tonight.

Capt. Heap and some men went back on the trail and this evening brought in their missing mule, [*finding it*] . . . {where they had lost him, the pack still in position. We concluded that the Indians must belong to the Sheepeaters, a tribe that is afraid of even the sight of a white man. They belong to the same class as the Diggers. When Utah was settled by the Mormons, the Ute, Bannack, and Snake Indians were driven out, and as the game disappeared they were obliged to separate into small bands. Some were driven to the mountains [*and*] having no ponies they are very poor, and live principally by stealing.}[20]

TUESDAY, AUGUST 22

We had another earthquake last night which woke those on guard. [*They*] say there were two very strong [*ones*], followed by lighter ones. Smith and Carrington went out in the boat about 4 o'clock to finish the soundings. They have had a splendid day for it, the Lake being very quiet.

Col. Barlow and party started for the falls this morning. After Col. Barlow's party left I started out with the botanical can over my shoulder and two tin boxes for specimens. I got quite a number and returned to camp just in time for dinner and found that the Doctor, Elliott, and Schönborn had got back. After dinner the Doctor, Jim, Schönborn, and myself went up to the Lake. On the way I got some mud from a white mud spring on the side of the hill near camp.[21] When we got to the Lake I got sulphur specimens from the springs, also alum deposits and some of the mud. These springs are along the edge of the creek running into the Lake. There is an abundant deposit of alum, sulphur and some iron. The mud is of a bluish color. In the stream, a little above the springs, there are some [*springs*] right in the midst of the creek. The banks about here are covered or composed of white sediment. Going around the Lake we came to some soda springs.

38. "Earthquake" Camp soon after the *Annie* was dismantled, August 23. U.S. Geological Survey, W. H. Jackson 106

There were four or five. There is a white deposit about them which contains salt, for the horses licked it with avidity. There are a lot of springs bubbling in the Lake itself and the turbidity of the water must be due to this. It has an alum taste.

On getting back to camp we found Jackson, Turnbull, and the Lieut., had got in. The boat was dismantled and will be left here at Earthquake Camp as we call it. I spent the remainder of the afternoon and part of the evening packing and labeling specimens and plants, most of which were collected by the Doctor on his trip to the falls. I moved my bedding out under a tree again. Tomorrow we will move towards the East fork of the Yellowstone River [*Lamar River*].

9
Pelican Valley, Baronett's Bridge, Bottler's Ranch, and Fort Ellis

WEDNESDAY, AUGUST 23

I got up early this morning and finished packing specimens. Charlie told me there was a Slight earthquake last night while he was on guard. Jackson took two views of the camp. Everything being packed we started bidding farewell to Yellowstone Lake. The boys all called goodbye as we struck into the woods. Our way at first lay up towards the little lake. Instead of passing along it however we turned to the left and entered Pelican Creek valley. On the way we saw two elk. Jo and José went after them but did not get either of them. Pelican Creek valley is quite wide where we entered it, the creek winding through it in a beautiful serpentine manner. It is full of ducks and geese, some of which were shot. Shooting at the ducks did not seem to frighten them at all. There are a number of springs along the banks, some hot and some cold. I got a specimen from one, which is evidently at times a geyser. We followed the valley . . . {going upward, the ascent being very gradual. The creek became narrower and narrower until, at last, we reached the divide between it and the water that runs into East Fork.}[1] We then struck across the country travelling until we reached a very beautiful small Lake [*Mirror Lake*][2] on which we camped about [*half*] past 4 o'clock. We saw a deer on Pelican Creek and the Lieut. shot a second one. We saw numbers of places where elk had lain and their tracks were fresh in every direction. Joe Clark shot some geese this afternoon.

I pitched my tent under a spruce tree in a very nice place. Jo Clark killed an elk and José came in with a deerskin (blacktail) having hung up the meat. Smith also killed an elk. For dinner we ate two quarters of deer. Everyone was ravenously hungry. {If ever there was a disgusted person, it was our

Panorama 9. Bottler's Ranch, Emigrant Gulch, Emigrant Peak, July 17–20 and August 27–28 cook; when after demolishing plate upon plate of venison, we still called, like Oliver Twist, for "more." It disappeared faster than he, with the help of two assistants, could supply it.}

The Doctor went out this afternoon and brought in some cones of the nut pine.[3] They are very large and fine. He also brought in a plant that he thinks is new and gave it to me. The rocks today that we passed over were all volcanic, mostly basaltic. We had easy travelling most of the way, very little timber and quite a number of fine open prairies. The grass and plants on the latter were quite dry showing signs of Fall. Charlie and I had a cup of tea together this evening. Our ride today was about 22 miles.

Lake [Mirror Lake] on the divide between Yellowstone Lake and East Fork of the Yellowstone River [Lamar River]

THURSDAY, AUGUST 24

I got up early this morning after a good night's sleep and packed the specimens I got yesterday and also put the plants in press – all before breakfast. After breakfast Jackson took two pictures of Camp. When all the packs were ready we all mounted and formed in line along the Lake and Jackson took two views of it. Before the second one was taken, Joe and José came in and were taken in it. They had gone out early for the deer and Elk they had killed. They stayed behind for Jackson to photograph separately.

Our way, most of the time, was through beautiful open prairies. I got some cones of the nut pine. We descended the side of a high mountain [*Mirror Plateau*]. It was so steep . . . {in some places . . . the animals seemed in danger of turning involuntary summersaults}.

At the bottom of the ravine we crossed a stream and went up on the other side. We soon got out of the timber and followed the west branch of the East Fork of the Yellowstone River over an open prairie, descending which for some distance. We camped on the banks of the stream. The Mountains are grand here. They are all volcanic and rise {in sharp peaks, white on the sides; huge masses of rock stand out in bold relief, resembling castles and fortresses. Our view of them was somewhat interfered with by the smoke from numerous fires which are now raging in their forests.}[4]

I pitched my bed under some willow bushes and as I lay upon it I can see in the distance a peak on the mountain which looks as though it had been cast in some huge jelly mold. The Doctor and some of the rest of the party went to the top of a peak near here and found it 11,950 feet high.[5]

I spent the afternoon collecting specimens along the Creek, Loucks and Henry helping me. I got some very pretty pieces of chalcedony and agate.

39. Mirror Lake Camp, August 24. National Park Service, Yellowstone National Park

There is a great abundance of petrified wood.[6] John Geiselman lost the little bay pony of the Doctor's this morning and had to walk in. He and Steve went back but could not find him. They also lost the mess kit of the men. We passed the Elk that Smith shot and when Jackson came along he photographed him. He and Turnbull came in this evening.

Camp on East Fork of the Yellowstone [Lamar] River[7]

FRIDAY, AUGUST 25

I spent this morning packing specimens and plants. The Doctor, Jackson, and Turnbull started up the East branch of the East Fork to photograph. Mr. Schönborn took an observation at noon. I was on guard last night from 10:30 P.M. to 1:30 A.M. Starr and Hamill of our escort were also on. Jo Clark, José, and Smith went back to hunt for the poney.

After dinner I saddled my poney and started to join Jackson. I had considerable trouble to get my poney to cross the creek. Succeeding, finally, I joined them at the cone of an extinct geyser or spring [*Soda Butte*]. It is similar to the deposit at the Hot Springs on Gardiner River. It contains

40. The Geological Survey with pack train, August 24, led by Doane, followed by Hayden, Stevenson, Schönborn, and Goodfellow. U.S. Geological Survey, W. H. Jackson 114

lime. The Cone is about 60 feet high and very regular.[8] Standing on a platform, I got a number of specimens. Just below on the edge of a small creek [*Soda Butte Creek*] there is quite a good sized spring of a lead color and quite an abundant escape of sulphuret[t]ed hydrogen. The water tastes of it and also has a slight alum taste, probably contains alum also.[9] There is a deposit of alum about it which I obtained.

Leaving here we had a good broad trail all the way. The first part of our course lay along the side of the mountain [*Druid Peak*]. As we were going along we saw somebody riding across the meadow below in the distance. I rode down the river's edge and found it was Col. Barlow. We had a talk across the River. His party had just come across from the Falls taking two days to do it. He wanted to know whether or not we had seen any Indians and said he would camp in our old place. They will scarcely join us before we get to [*Bottler's*] Ranche.[10]

41. The survey hunters, Jo Clark and José, August 24. U.S. Geological Survey, W. H. Jackson
113

Our way led through the open country, at times passing along the edge of the mountain, until we got near the Yellowstone River, where we came among a lot of huge boulders of granite that have either been deposited there by water or ice.[11] As we came nearer the River we passed hills of granite on one side, a basaltic Mountain on the other. We crossed the Yellowstone on a bridge owned by Jack Burnet [*Baronett*]. He has a log cabin on the shore above it. . . . {It is substantial and quite pretty, spanning the river just before it is joined by the East Fork, and immediately after its emergence from the Grand Canyon. . . . The bridge was built . . . in expectation of a rush to the gold diggings of Clarke's Fork. The rush, however, has not yet taken place as the indians have driven back the few who have ventured there. A few mines, however, have been opened with every promise of success.}[12]

Crossing a ridge just beyond [*the bridge*], we saw camp in the valley, in the same place where Barlow camped the time they got separated from us on the way up after leaving [*the*] hot Springs.

Dan got us supper after which we spread our beds, I putting mine next

42. Extinct Geyser (Soda Butte) on the Lamar River, August 25. National Gallery, v4, 306.tif

to Charlie in the fly for fear of rain as it has been cloudy this afternoon. We saw a herd of six antelope on the way. Jackson fired but missed. We also saw three polecats [skunks]. Jackson fired at them also but missed.

Camp Near Yellowstone [Baronett's] Bridge[13]

SATURDAY, AUGUST 26

This morning Jackson and I started with the pack mule back to the bridge and took an excellent picture of it. It was dark and cloudy, raining at times, and Jackson had to give a long exposure. We had rain in the night. Jackson also took another picture of granite boulders which are very thick near the bridge. It was not very successful however. We then started back to Camp and found José waiting to help pack the mule which being done we started on our way.

We had a good bit of rain and could not see the trail very distinctly in one place but we made a beeline for the mountains and thought we were following Jim's trail as he was taking a short cut while the Doctor intended to go to the springs. José struck off to the right after game. We travelled along through the rain when suddenly to our surprise away in front of us was the white mountain of hot springs [*Mammoth Hot Springs*] and we were in the canyon [*Lava Creek Canyon*] above it. How we got there we could not tell. We did not go up to the springs, however, but kept along Gardiner's

43. Baronett's Bridge, August 26. National Gallery, V2, 214.tif

River past the Camp where the Invalids were.[14] While there, talking to some of the men, who should we see but Charlie coming down the hill with the Doctor's Saddle bags on his horse full of specimens. The Doctor, Huse, Lieut., and Duncan had gone on. We soon followed and got into Camp on the Yellowstone River about 5 miles below the Springs at dusk, when we had a good supper of antelope, José having killed three and Jo Clark one. We had fish also, without any worms. Charlie and I put up the fly as it looked very much like rain. I packed some specimens for the Doctor that came from Hot Springs after which I turned in.

First creek north of Gardner's River, 50 feet above Yellowstone River[15]

SUNDAY, AUGUST 27

This morning we were on the way early. I collected specimens from the Devil's slide and from the hill near a small lake [*Aldridge Lake?*] where there was an abundance of chalcedonies. I overtook a man who was going from the Springs to see Charlie in order to get some medicine. Places that seemed rough when we came up, on going down, now seemed easy.

After going through the lower canyon [*Yankee Jim Canyon*], I overtook

Jackson and Turnbull, who had been photographing. We all went along together and did not get into Camp until between 4 and 5 o'clock. The Camp looked very large in the distance. . . . {Having been away six weeks, our pack train was now at an end. Could our animals have spoken, they no doubt would have expressed their satisfaction, for they all came in with sore backs, notwithstanding all our care.}[16] When we got in we had a good square meal {with fresh milk from the ranche,} after which I read my letters. I got two from mother, one from Clara, and one from Dr. Mills. I also got a paper with one of my letters in it. I spent the remainder of the afternoon wrapping up specimens.

Bottler's Ranch, 80 feet above Yellowstone River

MONDAY, AUGUST 28

This morning Elliott and I rose early, took breakfast at 4 A.M., and started to go to the top of Emigrant Peak. I rode Beaman's horse. We forded the Yellowstone and rode our horses to the elevation of about 8,000 feet and then dismounted and unsaddled, tying them to a tree. After we left our horses we had a very steep climb over a slide of volcanic rocks and over the snow, or rather ice, for such it is. After a tough climb through two gorges, I arrived near the summit and the rest of the way was easily gone over. Elliott reached the top long before I did. It was an elevation of [ ] feet.[17] We were told before we started that it could not be done, and indeed, by any other route than we took, it was impossible.

After Elliott had finished his sketching we commenced the descent, which we made very rapidly as we slid down over the rocks most of the way. Elliott would go ahead until he reached a corner, where he could be protected from the rocks. Then I would start and slide, the rocks rolling before and behind me all the time. When I reached Elliott, I waited and let him go on. We were not long in getting down. When we got to the foot of the slide we ate our lunch by the side of a moss lined stream of ice cold water. Gathering some of the moss we proceeded onward and regaining our horses started for camp. We flushed three flocks of prairie hens and saw two antelope besides a number of rabbits. On the way I was afraid Beaman's horse would give out before we got up.

We got back to Camp just after they were through dinner. After dinner I spent packing specimens and wrapping those I got this morning. The whole mountain is volcanic. I also got some pine cones. Jackson was printing this evening [so] I turned in the tent with Charlie.

Report No. 8: Hayden to Baird

BOTTLER'S RANCHE
EMIGRANT GULCH
YELLOW STONE VALLEY
AUGUST 28TH 1871

Dear Professor Baird:

Your letter was received yesterday on my return to my permanent camp. We have completed our survey of the Upper Yellow Stone. Our success has been complete. Our map is now complete of every stream emptying into the Lake or the River above this point. Henry Elliott with young Carrington returned in seven days with a wonderful sketch of the Lake. Every bay or indentation for 175 miles of Coast line was sketched and located with a Prismatic compass. He [*Elliott*] has also sketched all the mountains surrounding it so that a Birds-eye view may be made, showing the Lake and all its surroundings with all the soundings.[18] Several hundred soundings were taken, but no depth was found over 300 feet. Every peak and important geographical point has been carefully triangulated and fixed. Observations for Longitude and Latitude [*were*] taken. Two of Siemen's mercurial Barometers, and two aneroids – excellent Thermometers – have been constantly at work. We have secured the most important altitudes with accuracy. We have made beautiful charts of all the Hot Spring districts in the valley of the Yellow Stone and in the Gallatin, taken the temperatures and located them on the chart of over 600 Springs. Henry Elliott has sketched all the Craters, the Geysers in motion, the Mud Springs, etc. We have a splendid lot of specimens also. I enclose you some Photographs. We have about 400 negatives, 8 × 10 and stereoscopic. Tower Falls, Crystal Falls, Upper and Lower Falls of the Yellow Stone, Hot Springs, Craters, etc. The Lake has been well photographed. Any facts you can pick out of my letter or from the back of the pictures, you can publish.

I intend to leave Fort Ellis on the 4th of September and explore a belt to some point on the Union Pacific Railroad, near Fort Bridger.

In some modern Tertiary Beds at the Head of Jefferson Fork, I found the remains of an animal which I sent to Dr. Leidy [*who responded:*] "The jaw fragments are interesting and most probably indicate at least a new species. The teeth are like those of Anchitherium Palaeotherium, Titanotherium [Palaersyops?] etc., and are not generically distinct. Now the corresponding upper teeth are very different in all these genera. I suspect the specimens indicate a new Anchitherium, about twice the size of the A[*nchitherium*] bairdii of the White R[*iver*], Mauvaise Terres [*Bad Lands*]. I am sorry the same locality did not turn up other things."[19]

On the night of the 20th of August at one o'clock we had a severe shock of an earthquake on the shore of the Yellow Stone Lake. The men, encamped on a high Bluff about 80 feet above the Lake, on what is called Steamboat Point . . . were [raised] from sleep by a rumbling noise beneath us which shook us for a moment violently. The animals lying down in camp leaped to their feet and threatened a stampede. A couple of squirrels domiciled in a tree near our camp commenced chattering. The men on guard were much frightened, the pine trees swayed to and fro. The shock came from the north and moved to the south like a wave. There were several other slight shocks during the night and the next morning. For two more successive nights slight shocks occurred. The shock of the 20th was the most severe. It was felt by Col. Barlow's party 18 miles south on the Lake, and by another small party on the opposite side of the Lake. Shocks have been felt before which came from the direction of the Yellow Stone Lake and been felt at Emigrant Gulch 140 miles distant. If I think of any more items I will send them to you. . . .

Huse does not amount to much. I shall drop him at Chicago and that will end him so far as I am concerned. I intend to have a nice little fellow, Dr. Peale, of Philadelphia, spend the winter at Washington arranging our collections and making chemical analyses. He is one of my students, and a nephew of Mr. T[*itian*] R. Peale.[20] He is, I think, a young man of the right stamp. Henry Elliott is the biggest kind of a "Trump." He has done some great things on this trip. He started this morning, before daylight, ascended Emigrant Peak, which is a volcanic cone with almost vertical sides, 6,050 feet above our camp, and returned by noon. It is on the opposite side of the Yellow Stone, at least 5 miles to its base from here. I did not believe he could get back before dark.

Yours truly,
F. V. Hayden

TUESDAY, AUGUST 29

This morning we packed the wagons and started for Fort Ellis. Just before we left we went up to the Ranche and took a farewell drink of milk. The Doctor, Mr. Schönborn, Jim, Charlie, Elliott, Negley, Dawes, Jackson, and Dixon went around to the [Crow] Mission[21] with the two ambulances. The remainder of us came by the way we came up. We have camped in the place where we had such trouble making the road going up. We have with us a man with tuberculosis. I wrote some to Papa and enclosed it with two pictures Jackson gave me in an envelope, which I will send when we get to the post. I have Jackson's and Turnbull's letters to mail also. I began to get quite cold towards evening and we put up the fly for the invalid. I put my bed under a willow bush. We had but little trouble on the road today, with the exception of one hill where Loucks almost upset.

Trail Creek, near Gallatin and Yellowstone River divide

WEDNESDAY, AUGUST 30

I started ahead of the train this morning and went to the top of the mountain back of where we camped first on our way out, in order to get fossil plants. I passed José and Jo Clark and after I left them, I saw a doe, antelope, and two fawns. When the wagons came up I joined the train. We did not have very much trouble getting along. In one place, we were obliged to have some of the escort hang on the side, and in another, we had to attach ropes which the whole party manned.

Beaman went ahead and got the mail and picked out our camping ground. He met us just before we got to Fort Ellis. I got one letter which was from Dr. Mills. On getting into camp Adams and I put up our tent, after which we put up the cook fly. We then took a bath in the creek and changed underclothing. After dinner I commenced a letter to the *Press* which occupied all my time. Adams stayed over at the Post. The invalid slept in the tent with me.

Second Camp near Fort Ellis

THURSDAY, AUGUST 31

This morning I finished my letter to the Paper and wrote a letter to Dr. Mills. I went over to the Post and got an official envelope. It was Muster and Inspection day and everything was very clean and neat about the Fort. The men and officers were all dressed in their best. Jim came in from the mission at noon today. {There is a party of engineers [with] the Northern Pacific Railroad in camp here. They will go the route we took until they reach the valley of the Yellowstone, and will go down the river until they meet a party which is on the way up. They expect to be out until next January, and will take with them a strong escort of cavalry from the post.}[22]

I spent the afternoon in the tent reading and writing. . . . Duncan started for the Ranche below Virginia [*City*] for his poney.

FRIDAY, SEPTEMBER 1

I wrote a letter to Clara this morning and wrapped up the fossils that I got on the way over from the Ranche. The Doctor came in about noon and Elliott and Schönborn also. I spent all afternoon in Camp. Ed Flint was sick and I put a wet towel on his neck. Huse and Adams left this evening.

SATURDAY, SEPTEMBER 2

Smith and I packed specimens, taking up the whole morning. I got some nails and wire from the Quartermaster. Ed Flint was no better this morning and I got some medicine for him from the Hospital. He has tonsillitis. Jackson, Dixon, Negley, and Dawes came in at dinner time. It rained this afternoon and blew pretty hard. Turnbull came in towards evening. Ed Flint was taken over to the Hospital this evening. I was on guard last night.

Report No. 9: Hayden to Baird

FORT ELLIS, MONTANA T[ERRITORY]
SEPTEMBER 2D, 1871

Dear Professor Baird:

I enclose a few prints, nothing as good as we shall have, but some which will show a hint of the wonders of the Yellow Stone.

We have completed our survey and in a day or two will be ready to start down. Huse has gone to California. I paid him $250, which was much more than he earned. Three of my party have gone now, making 5 in all that have left.

I have sent you more notes, though I do not see them in any journal yet.

Yours Truly,

F. V. Hayden

[*Hayden also responded to a letter awaiting him at Fort Ellis from George Allen, the party's earlier botanist and diarist who was unable to continue with the party to the Yellowstone area.*]

FORT ELLIS, MONTANA TRY.
SEPTEMBER 2ND 1871

My Dear Professor Allen:

Your very kind letter of August 23d came last evening. We have just returned having completed our work to our entire satisfaction. We have had an uninterrupted series of successes, without a single pullback. Not an accident has happened to any member of our party – we made a most admirable survey of the Yellow Stone Basin, the Lake, all the Hot Springs. Mr. Jackson made most abundant pictures. Mr. Moran was filled with enthusiasm and has returned to devote himself to the painting of pictures of the Yellow Stone region. We also succeeded in getting good pictures of the tribes of Indians, the Crows and Nez Percés. Never have we had such success and received such a vast amount of material. I will now hasten home and endeavor to work it up and get it ready for publication.

We shall start now in a day or two with our party to explore another belt of country home to the Railroad near Fort Bridger. We shall pass down Bear River, past the celebrated Soda Springs, etc. No portion of the American continent is perhaps so rich in wonders as the Yellow Stone.

Adams and Huse have gone to California and intend to take the steamer on the 16th for New York, via Isthmus of Panama. Dixon intends to start soon. I think the remainder of the party will go through with me. We hope to get to the railroad on or before Oct. 1st, and then the labors of the season will close.

I was certain you would speak with enthusiasm of this great west. I feel sorry for the man who must leave the world without having his eyes fed with the grand vision. If I have aided you to the sight, I am glad.

. . . I am sorry that you were not able to see the wonderful things in the Yellow Stone but when reports come before the world, you will get a pretty clear conception of them.

All my party are well and speak of you with affection.

Yours most sincerely,

F. V. Hayden

44. Survey members with Fort Ellis officers and wives outside Hayden's tent, September 4. *Seated, left to right:* A. C. Peale, W. B. Logan, Mrs. G. F. Wright, Lt. Jerome, Mrs. Doane, C. Negley, J. W. Beaman; *standing, left to right:* A. J. Smith, Dr. A. B. Campbell, probably Anton Schönborn, C. Carrington, Lt. Doane, J. Stevenson, C. Dawes, G. B. Dixon. Courtesy of the Swann Gallery, Photographic Department.

SUNDAY, SEPTEMBER 3

Smith and I fixed the boxes of minerals this morning, it taking all our time. Jackson was over at the Post and photographed the Command mounted. I was in camp all afternoon reading. I also wrote a letter to Mother. Jackson made a second trip to the Post and photographed the officers.

MONDAY, SEPTEMBER 4

I spent all the morning fixing up my boxes of specimens. Jackson took pictures of Beaman, Negley, Dawes, Logan, Carrington, and Lieut. Jerome. Just before dinner Mrs. Doane and Mrs. Wright came over from the Post with Lieut. Doane and Dr. Campbell and Jackson took a group of all in camp, including them, before the Doctor's tent.[23] After dinner I went over to the Fort with Jackson, Dixon, and Negley to help take photographs. He took pictures of Mrs. Wright, Mrs. Doane and Lieut. Jerome. After we were through we went back to Camp and packed up so as to be able to leave tomorrow.

10

To the Jefferson Valley, the Beaverhead, Fort Hall, and Salt Lake City

TUESDAY, SEPTEMBER 5

I was up early and packed up my bedding etc. After breakfast we struck tents and packed. The wagons were all very full as we have turned in two and one of the Ambulances. After we were pretty nearly ready I took the Doctor's horse over to the Fort to him. Going back to Camp afterwards I found the train just starting out. I went back to the Post and bid goodbye to all and went up to the hospital and bid Dr. Campbell goodbye. The Ambulance went up to the hospital for Ed Flint.

When we got to Bozeman we stopped about a half an hour. I saw Jeff Stanford and some of the other men who were with Barlow. I also saw Nebraska Bill. Charlie introduced me to a Frank Kneass of Philadelphia who is in charge of a party of engineers of the Northern Pacific Rail Road here.[1] They are going out to stay until January. They will take an escort from Fort Ellis.

Leaving Bozeman we took a Northwesterly direction across the country going down the Gallatin Valley. Our way lay between wheat and oat fields in which the grain was stacked. We passed a number of ranches. The mountains away off to our right [*Gallatin Range*] were only dimly seen being covered with haze. We crossed the Gallatin, fording it, and soon after went into Camp having come 21 miles. We are near a place called Hamilton [*Manhattan*] having come 21 miles from Fort Ellis.[2] After dinner I gathered some shells from the creek near us. I also got some plants from the same creek. We fed our horses and then turned them out again on herd. The guard tonight will be doubled.

Camp on small creek near Hamilton [Manhattan]

Panorama 10. Beaverhead Rock and Bridge, September 9

WEDNESDAY, SEPTEMBER 6

I got up early and put the plants I got yesterday in press. We were on the road by 7 o'clock and passed through Hamilton, a town consisting of about a dozen houses. We went along the Gallatin River some little distance and passed Gallatin City [*near present Three Forks*][3] but did not go to it. We crossed a number of forks of the Madison. The rocks along the road today were all limestones. Along the Gallatin they were beautifully exposed in strata in the hills on the opposite side of the River. We passed a number of ranches with fields full of wheat almost ready to be brought in. We had some trouble with one of the wagons in crossing a creek, that kept us some little time as it had to be unloaded before we could get it out. After travelling 20.5 miles we camped near a ranche owned by a man named Allen.[4] We had milk and cream for dinner also fresh butter. Mr. Allen has twenty-five cows and keeps a dairy. We got a load of hay for our horses as the grass is not very good. After dinner I mended my old breeches and read in the newspaper. It was very warm today. We are on Willow Creek.

Allen's Ranch, Jefferson Valley

THURSDAY, SEPTEMBER 7

We were up early this morning and had our tent down first. Jackson photographed or rather took a ferrotype of Mr. Allen's ranche and gave it to him.[5] He was very much pleased with it. We got on the road by 8 o'clock. At first our road led up hill and then gradually down. The rocks at first were limestones, and after we got up, granites and gneisses, and on top of the [*latter*] a red quartzite. Jim got a piece of gold ore from someone that came from Red Mountain Mine near Bann[a]ck City.

After travelling 22.5 miles we went into Camp on South Boulder Creek, one of the tributaries of the Jefferson River. We are near a ranche. It has been windy and cloudy today making the travelling very pleasant. I spent the time after dinner in labeling and putting up the specimens I got today. This evening we all went to the ranch and each got a bundle of hay for [*the*] horse[*s*].

South Bowlder [Boulder] Creek, 5 feet above the stream

FRIDAY, SEPTEMBER 8

This morning I put up the flowers I got yesterday and helped pack the ambulance. We were on the way by 7:30 A.M. and soon got out of the hills down into Jefferson River Valley. Our way today led along the River up the

Valley. We crossed two branches of the Jefferson passing quite a number of ranches, some few of which were deserted. The valley is very beautiful, averaging about 5 miles in width; the river is lined with trees and bounded by beautiful meadows. The wheat through the valley is ready to take in. I got a few specimens of rocks. After going 20 miles we camped on Fish Creek. There is a post office here, and three or four houses.[6] Smith and some of the boys got a watermelon. I wrote a letter to Mother and spent the afternoon writing on a letter for the *Press*. Towards evening I put some flowers that the Doctor got, in press. I turned in early. We got a load of hay for the horses.

Fish Creek Stage Station

SATURDAY, SEPTEMBER 9

I was on guard last night from 11 P.M. until 2 A.M. when I woke John Raymond and turned in. I was up again at 5 o'clock and found it somewhat cold, the thermometer standing at 32 degrees. We were on the road by 7:30 A.M. and soon crossed the Jefferson on Parson's bridge. Some distance on we crossed the Beaver Head River at Twin Bridges. The Beaver Head unites with the Big Hole River and forms the Jefferson. The Beaver Head comes in from the left hand side.[7]

We had a very dusty ride for over 10 miles and after travelling 32 miles we again crossed the ~~Jefferson~~ Beaver Head and camped on the ground that Clark and Lewis wintered on in 1847 [*1805*].[8] Just before crossing the bridge we passed along Beaver Head rock which is composed of limestones. It is a point that has considerable resemblance to a beaver's head especially at a distance.

The mountains, on the [*opposite*] side of the Jefferson . . . [*are*] composed of granites in which are a number of auriferous quartz-ledges, so we were informed by a farmer whose ranche we passed. Indeed, we could see the mines from where we were and the roads leading up to them. There are a number of quartz mills situated at the foot of the mountain. One mine is down 300 feet and has been steadily paying for three years. There is one lode called the Clipper and another the Highland. The mountains on the side on which we were are evidently composed of granites also. Near our camp the rocks were limestones.

Beaverhead Rock, near the stage station[9]

45. Beaverhead Rock, September 9. National Gallery, v3, 309.tif

SUNDAY, SEPTEMBER 10

I woke to find it cold and ice in the water in the tent. We were on the road by 9:15 o'clock. The Doctor gave me a piece of sandstone that came from near the ranche [*where*] they make grindstones. The mountains on our ~~right~~ left were evidently granite as the pebbles in the streams coming from them were [*granite*] pebbles. Between us and the mountains were bluffs of recent drift formation. On our right, away off in the distance, were red porpherys, same as we saw on the road to Virginia City. We crossed the Black Tail Deer Creek and after a ride of 21 miles went into Camp on the Beaver Head River.

We passed a letter box this afternoon. It consisted of a tobacco box posted on a stick: as the stage passes, the Driver drops letters in it and the people to whom they are directed get them. They also put letters in for the driver to take with him. It is an institution quite common in the west, I believe.

I wrote some on my letter this afternoon. We fed the horses and turned them out on herd. Along the way today I saw quite a deposit of alkali.

One mile from Beaverhead River bridge at the Canyon

MONDAY, SEPTEMBER 11

This morning, early, the wind began to blow very strong, and when I got up, the fire Jackson built, felt very comfortable. I saddled as soon after breakfast as possible and started up the Black Tail Deer Creek Valley to determine the character of the rocks. The wind was blowing quite strong and my coat felt very comfortable. After a ride of 4 or 5 miles past an alternation of limestones and quartzites and a trap dyke, I turned back. On the way I passed an old hot spring deposit very much like that on Gardiner's River up the Yellowstone. There were the ruins of old basins like those at Gardiner's. The springs here were all extinct, however, all the water running down being cold.

Getting to Ryan's Ranche, I found the stage there and Woods of Barlow's party in it.[10] Leaving the ranche I started on after the train and soon crossed the Beaver Head on a toll bridge and entered the Beaver Head Cañon passing between high volcanic rocks, on either side of the road, standing out boldly. I very soon crossed the Beaver Head again and passed by a high bluff of shales, in the midst of which, about 100 feet from the road, there pours a cascade with rocks of hot spring formation. The water however is now cold. I went but a little further when I met Jackson and Dixon with the Pack mule coming back to photograph the entrance to the Cañon. I turned back with them. As soon as the Cañon was taken we started on to the Cascade. While they were photographing it I went to the top of the hill and followed the stream some little distance. I found the formation all around to be identical with that I saw up the Black Tail Deer Creek Valley and I think it must connect with it.

We soon started on again, on the lope . . . stopped and photographed some very high volcanic rocks which were so weathered as to stand out in sharp [spires] all along the side. . . . We continued our way, on the lope, for about 10 miles, passing several ranches, when we took a road leading to the right, proceeding . . . for some distance. On passing over a hill of limestone we saw Camp near us. We were considerably surprised as we expected to go 25 miles. We found we had come 15 miles.

The camp is in Horse Plain Creek Valley. There is a great deal of alkali scattered around, some of which I procured. After dinner I commenced work on the specimens I got and on those the Doctor got. He got some very pretty brecciated porphyries and a volcanic rock with amygdaloidal spaces filled with chalcedony. He also got some fossils. Along the road today there were a number of beds of red sandstone, and a red siliceous, probably Triassic, conglomerate. At the bridge, under the volcanic rock, there were beds of a white sandstone, probably modern.

Horse Plain Creek Valley[11]

TUESDAY, SEPTEMBER 12

On getting up, the thermometer stood at 26°F. After breakfast I put up some plants that the Doctor got yesterday. We got out of camp at 8 o'clock, the Doctor taking the mountains on the right while I went on the left. The rocks I found were limestones at first, afterwards passing into quartzites, and then again into limestones, and so on. The Doctor found a place where there were some hornblendic gneisses. . . . About noon we passed a party of miners who were going down the road. They were in a six horse wagon and had stopped for their dinner.

The Doctor came across a bed of clay slates, probably Cretaceous, in which there were a great many fossils, ferns, and scales of fish. I stayed behind with him collecting them. We got both pair of saddle bags full and then went on to camp.

There was an Indian teepee near our camp. The owner was a Bannock with his squaw and six children – four girls and two boys. The Bannocks and Shoshones are two tribes of the Snake Indians. The tent was made of canvass stretched over willow poles, the leaves of which were left on the tops. It was about 10 ft. They had a large quantity of meat (antelope and Rocky Mt. Sheep) drying. Charlie paid a visit to it after dinner. His squaw was cleaning the skin of a rocky mountain sheep. She had it on a willow pole against a tree. She was scraping the hair with a knife after which she scraped the rib bone. We bought four hams of antelope for $4.00. Turnbull, Elliott, and I carried them back to camp.

I spent the afternoon packing the fossils. This evening I commenced a letter to Mother and one to Ed Hubely. Jackson tried to photograph the Indian and the teepee but there was not light enough.[12] We came 20 miles today.

Sage Creek, under Bald Mountain

WEDNESDAY, SEPTEMBER 13

This morning the Indian, his squaw, and one of the children came in the camp. They had their faces all painted. The squaw brought down some antelope and traded it for some coffee and sugar.

We got out of camp at 7:30 o'clock. I went on one side and the Doctor on the other. The rocks were limestones and quartzites. After travelling a short distance we crossed a sort of a divide on which were quartzites and volcanic rocks, the latter being covered with a bright orange colored lichen. We met a herd of cattle of 2,000 head on their way from Texas to the North

46. Bannock family, September 12. National Park Service, Yellowstone National Park

where they will winter, letting them graze on the hills. They extended about 2 miles in length. They have been two years on the road.

I was with the Doctor all day and he was quite communicative, talking to me about Frazier Ford Curtin, the University, and my letters.[13] After the quartzites, which we passed on the divide, came limestones. It has been so hazy ever since we have been in the mountains that we are unable to see very far. I spent the afternoon writing on my letter for the *Press* and to Mother and Ed Hubely. Jim and the Doctor went off to the hills and brought back some fossils among which was the bud of a crinoid. We travelled 22 miles and camped on some little streams which run into Red Rock Creek, a branch of the Beaver Head. We passed the miners and after we were in camp they passed us. We were obliged to make our fires with buffalo chips as we had no wood.

Camp on a branch of Red Rock Creek

THURSDAY, SEPTEMBER 14

I was on guard, or rather on herd, from two o'clock this morning. Joe Smith was on at the same time. We made a fire of buffalo chips and willows and sat by it most of the time to keep warm as towards daybreak it was very cold. At daylight we drove the herd into camp. The thermometer stood at 19°. We got on the road by 7:45 o'clock and, after about a 5 mile ride over the hills, began to go up over the divide.[14] The rocks, until we got to the divide, were limestones, with the exception of one exposure of volcanic rock. In the hills, over which we passed, were boulders of quartzite among which a few chalcedons were scattered. After crossing the divide we began to go down very gradually along Medicine Lodge Creek. On the way we met a herd of cattle containing 800 head. As we got down we came across light volcanic rocks succeeding which was a rock about 50 or 60 feet in thickness, very much resembling a hot Spring deposit. We passed between a small canyon composed of it. Succeeding this were limestones. We camped on Medicine Lodge Creek close to the road having travelled [*16.05*] miles.

In the afternoon I got Henry Greve to help me and spent the time packing specimens. I also finished my letter to Mother and wrote to Ed Hubely. The Doctor took a trip to the hills and brought in some carboniferous fossils. After he came in he gave me a sort of lecture on my letter writing, betting me that I was too scientific.

Ed Flint rode the mare this afternoon. She started on the run [afterwards]. Jim got a hornet's nest and created [lots] of fun.

First camp on Medicine Lodge Creek

FRIDAY, SEPTEMBER 15

Immediately after breakfast I packed the fossils that the Doctor brought in last night. The train was on the way by 7:45 o'clock. Ed started off on the broncho on a run. The Doctor went back to a cañon while I went up on the hills to the right of camp. I found volcanic rock on the top while immediately underneath was a sandstone, very white probably modern. I then went down to the road again and met the Doctor and we rode along together. The rocks still continued the same, with the exception of some limestones occurring. We had not gone far before we came across basalt exactly like that in [*the*] Snake River basin.

We went a short distance and came across the wagons which were delayed on account of the bad rocky road. We crossed two volcanic hills the valley getting narrower and narrower and very rugged and with a regular layer of basalt of a porous kind at the top on both sides. The valley becoming a canyon, we turned to the right and commenced going up. After a long pull we reached the top and were on a wide level plain of basalt covered with a fine sand and dust and sage brush. Going across this a short distance we commenced to go down very gradually till we came out on the Snake River plain across which we made our way until we again reached the Medicine Lodge creek. Proceeding along it a short distance we camped.

Almost everyone went fishing and we soon had plenty for dinner. The Doctor caught twenty-one in one hole. The trout on this side of the mountains are small but have a delicious flavor. The stream on which we are camped has a great many beaver dams along it. I packed up some specimens this afternoon and this evening pressed some flowers that I and the Doctor got.

Second Camp on Medicine Lodge Creek

SATURDAY, SEPTEMBER 16

This morning we were out of camp early. After proceeding along the Medicine Lodge for some distance, we crossed it and made our way across the dusty sage-brush covered plain to Dry Creek. We passed some horses belonging to the men who passed us a few days ago. At Dry Creek there was a road turning to the left on which we started. We had gone but about 100 yards when a singletree on one of the wagons broke and we had to stop.[15] While mending it a man came up on the hunt after his horses. His mule was almost played out as he had come from Market Lake. He told us that the road we were on was very sandy and the right-hand road was also the nearest. We turned therefore and took it. Steve went back and got his horses for him. As most of our party had gone ahead we soon saw some of them trooping back to us as they discovered the change.

We had two or three short places of sand which were not very deep. We came on to the Stage road at Camas Creek about half a mile above where we camped on the way up. After a drive of about 5 miles we came to Desert Wells [*Hamer*] and found a bull train and a mule train here. Among them was a load of apples from California. Jackson and Turnbull invested and we enjoyed some of them. We pitched our tents in the midst of the sand. Just as we were done with dinner the bull teams started out. There were eight – six yoke teams and one seven yoke. The large wagons were heavily loaded and they moved out slowly. Another mule train came in also. I wrote to Ed Hubely (finishing my letter) and wrote some more to Mother.

Towards evening the horses came in and we watered them at the well with buckets, after which we went up to the ranche and each got a bundle of hay for our horses. While we were getting it another mule train came in and camped near us. I had to watch the hay for my poney, keeping Joe Clark's away from it. We came 22.75 miles. This evening Charlie and I went up to the Ranche to take our letters and had a talk with the man who keeps it. After we came back to camp we caught a kangaroo mouse in our tent. It has a long tail with hair at the end. It is of a reddish color with a white belly and a stripe on its side. Its hind legs are about twice the length of the fore legs.

Desert Wells Stage Station [Hamer], 6 ft. above the mouth of the well[16]

SUNDAY, SEPTEMBER 17

This morning we were up about 5 o'clock and had breakfast before sunrise. While the wagons were loading, I, with Dixon, Smith, and Carrington, hunted for arrowheads on the shore of what forms the Lake when there is water in it. I succeeded in getting but one, while Dixon got about a dozen. We left Smith and Carrington and followed the wagons. The road was very dusty. We caught up with the wagons at Market Lake, where 13 miles on, we watered and bought some hay, as we used the last of our oats this morning. Smith and Carrington came in before we left. Smith had quite a pocket full of arrowheads. Leaving Market Lake, after buying some bales of hay, we kept on our way, soon striking the [Snake] River in which were an abundance of ducks. After a march of [18.94] miles, we camped on the bank of the river. I spent the afternoon in writing. It was very windy all afternoon, as it was yesterday.

On bayou of Snake River, 3.5 miles from Market Lake

MONDAY, SEPTEMBER 18

Last night we heard the Coyotes howling about camp and on the opposite side of the river. We were wakened in the night by some firing which, this morning, we found was done by some freighters who camped near us. They killed a bear and we obtained its head. We were up early and on the way by 6:30. We passed a large drove of cattle that were feeding near their camp. Some distance further on we passed another small herd. After passing the stage ranche, where we traded a horse on the way up, we passed a deserted ranche. Procuring some logs from it we continued on our way. At Eagle Rock [Idaho Falls] we again crossed the Snake River on Taylor's Bridge. The river is at least 15 feet lower than it was when we went up.

After a ride of 31 miles we reached Blackfoot Fork and went into camp at evening. After supper, for which we had slapjacks, Negley, who had eaten a pretty good sized meal, was sitting on a log by the teamsters fire, by which I also was standing. The teamsters were making fun of him for eating so much and got him at last to run a race with me. He exerted himself and beat me in. The Doctor left us early this morning for the Fort [*Fort Hall*].

Camp at bridge over Blackfoot Fork
of Snake River [*today's city of Blackfoot*]

Report No. 10: Hayden to Baird

Dear Professor Baird:

I wrote you that we left Fort Ellis the morning of September 5th. We passed down the Gallatin Valley to the three Forks, thence by the Jefferson to its very sources, exploring many of its branches. If you look at Col. Raynolds' map, you will see that river was omitted. We had the opportunity of studying some most interesting ranges of mountains and some rich mines. The valleys of the Gallatin, Madison, and Jefferson Trib[*utarie*]s with all their little branches are now settled more or less with Ranchmen and farmers. Twelve (12) years ago I was exploring this region and there was not a settler in Montana Territory.

We crossed the Rocky Mountain "Divide" at the Head of Horse Plain Creek over into the Medicine Lodge Creek and followed it down into the Snake River Plain. This gives us a most interesting belt, parallel with the one we took going up in June last. If you look on the map, you will see that Medicine Lodge, Camas, and Godins Creeks, all sink. They are streams 50 to 75 miles long, 5 to 20 yards wide, and clear, swift flowing, with two kinds of trout in them, and more abundant trout I never saw. We caught 20 to 50 trout out of one hole. This was done many times. I caught 21 in one small hole without moving and yet these streams had no visible connection with any other drainage or with each other. The water passes off in a marsh in the plains, passes through the superficial gravel deposits into the great Basalt floor down into the Snake river. Eventually though they sink 30 to 50 miles from the Snake river.

We return from Fort Hall by way of Soda Springs, Bear Lake by Bear River, to Evanston on the Railroad, thence to Fort Bridger where our expedition will close. All is well with us. We are moving along pleasantly without accident or interruption. We perform a good day's work every day. We have not lost a day from storms or anything else since we left Ogden in June last.

Yours Truly,

F. V. Hayden

47. Survey camp at Fort Hall on return trip, September 19. U.S. Geological Survey, W. H. Jackson 119

TUESDAY, SEPTEMBER 19

I was on guard last night until 11 o'clock. We herded the stock and Joe Smith was on with me. I kept hold of Toby's lariat for fear of a stampede. The grass was somewhat scarce and they moved about considerably. Once, they started running but went only about a hundred yards before they stopped. At 11 o'clock I went into camp and wakened Al Smith and John Raymond and sent them out to relieve Joe.

This morning, after an early breakfast, we started for Fort Hall getting in about 9 o'clock after travelling 7.9 miles. Our tents are pitched on our old camping ground and it is very dirty. Jackson photographed the remainder of the boys and also took a picture of our tent, of the Topographical, and Y.M.C.A.[17] Charlie and I went down to the Post and secured a place to write. I got one letter from Clara and two from Mother which have made me very uneasy about Papa. There were enclosed two notes from Uncle Burd in regard to him, from which I fear Papa is very ill, indeed.[18] As he sends for a picture of myself and poney, and a print cannot be obtained, Jackson very kindly took a ferrotype for me.

Fort Hall, same spot as in June

WEDNESDAY, SEPTEMBER 20

Charlie and I sat up last night until 11 o'clock writing. I finished my letter to the *Press*, wrote to Dr. Mills, to Clara and also to Mrs. Turnbull. At 11

48. Tentmates at Fort Hall camp, September 19. *Left to right:* Jackson, Peale, Turnbull, and Dixon. U.S. Geological Survey, W. H. Jackson 500

o'clock, Charlie went on guard, so we came up to camp. We wrote in the Commissary office. I spent the morning packing some specimens so they can be shipped from Evanston when we arrive there. Jackson took another picture of Toby and myself. He also photographed the Doctor on his horse, and the alligator mess. I went down to the Commissary office again and commenced a letter for Jim to send to the *Chicago Tribune*.[19] It has been very warm ever since we have been here and also very windy.

THURSDAY, SEPTEMBER 21

Charlie and I were at the Commissary's office writing last night until nearly 12 o'clock. I finished my letter for Jim and mailed my pictures to Mother writing her a short note. We were on the road early, Logan and I going ahead to get fossils. We got a good many in the Jurassic limestones. Going back to the road we began to go up hill over a divide. We were overtaken by Turnbull who stayed behind for the mail. After a ride of 18.75 miles we got into camp. Capt. Putnam and Lieut. Wilson, with an ambulance, and four men, are with us. I spent the afternoon wrapping up specimens. The rocks today were principally limestones. We came down into a valley and are camped on the headwaters of the Port Neuf River. There is good grass for the horses. It has been windy ever since we have been in. The hills are covered with autumn [tinted] bushes.

Head-waters of Port Neuf River, at the Chimney

49. Camp at Three Springs (also called Twin Springs), September 22. Stevenson (*center left*) and Hayden flank Capt. Putnam. U.S. Geological Survey, W. H. Jackson 120

FRIDAY, SEPTEMBER 22

We left camp this morning by 6:30 o'clock. We had just light enough to see to eat our breakfast. Our road at first led through a very level plain, grass covered. When we got across the plain we came to low hills of basaltic rock over which we passed. We had a creek to cross which was somewhat miry. One wagon, after putting on four extra miles (making eight in all), got through all right, but the others were taken around to a safer place. The rocks today were limestones and quartzites. We are camped near some springs. There are deposits here of some extinct Springs probably hot. The basins of some are left, or rather their rims.[20] The hills in back are limestones. Jackson photographed the camp, also Jim and Capt. Putnam. I spent the afternoon writing. The Doctor was out all afternoon and came in with a lot of carboniferous fossils.[21] We came [*22.65*] miles today.

Twin Springs

SATURDAY, SEPTEMBER 23

We were up very early and I packed up the fossils that the Doctor got last night. After breakfast the Doctor went up towards the hills back of camp, sending me to examine the hills on the opposite side of the valley. After a long ride over a basaltic covered plain, I arrived at the mountains and found them to be of the same character as those on the side along which we came, *viz* carboniferous limestones. On the way back I saw a coyote. Going past what seemed to be two old volcanic craters I reached the road and hurried on after the train. I had not gone very far, when turning to the left (through a canyon) I was in Bear River Valley and proceeded up the stream until I reached Soda Springs and found camp in the midst of the village.[22] I was about two or three hours behind [*our wagon*] train.

After getting some dinner, Jackson, Turnbull, Dixon, and I started out for a walk. We first visited a spring some little distance below camp on the bank of Soda Spring Creek, not far above where it joins Bear River. The spring is about 2.5 ft. in diameter and the water flows from one side of it coating the surface of the ground with a deposit of iron. There was also a slight iron deposit tasting slightly of chloride of sodium. The water in the spring was not over three inches in depth and on tasting revealed a sharp pungent taste which was very agreeable, resembling Vichy water.[23] The escape of carbonic acid, although violent, was quite abundant. Elliott coming up with some lime juice and sugar, we regaled ourselves with soda water equal to that sold in our cities.

Leaving this spring we went up towards the mountains, passing on the way, a number of places that must a long time ago, have been the cones of springs. We also passed a number of pools of stagnant water with a strong alkaline taste. The whole surface over which we passed was once hot springs and there is now, in places, an abundant alkaline deposit, specimens of which I secured for analysis. I also got specimens of the hot spring deposit. We next went down to the river [*Bear River*] and found on its bank a boiling spring. It is slightly warm . . . and is on the bank of the river. It has formed a cone-like mound 8 or 10 feet [*two illegible words*] at the top of which, from an almost circular hole, the carbonic acid escapes with great violence. The escape of water is not very great. The depth of the spring is about 18 inches and the gas, in escaping, throws the water up about a foot. It foams and looks as though it were boiling. The basin of the spring is covered with an abundant deposit of bright red iron. The water is pungent in taste resembling very much that near our camp. It is not as strong, however, the carbonic acid gas escaping with such violence that the water does not take up so much of it. Near the spring are two small openings from which air and CO_2 gas (slightly warm) escape with a hissing noise. There are also near this a number of old cones. There is one also on the opposite side of the river. The point

50. Hooper's Spring at Soda Springs, September 24. U.S. Geological Survey, W. H. Jackson
122

on which these are all situated is formed of the deposit, some of which is of a rust color and very beautiful in texture, very much like coral. We then started back to camp.

Soda Springs, on the public square, 20 feet above the Bear River

SUNDAY, SEPTEMBER 24

This morning I was on guard until 2 o'clock. I felt somewhat sick all the time. I think it was the result of drinking too much of the spring water.

After breakfast, Jackson, Dixon, and myself started on a trip to visit the hot springs. We went to the boiling one first, secured a bottle of the water while Jackson took a photograph. Leaving this place we went up to the edge of the hill back of the white deposit and proceeding along the edge of the hill until we came to the Mormon town which is to the North East of the gentile town in which we are encamped. Here there are two large oblong mounds about 30 or 40 feet in height, about 20 in width, and probably 60 in length. On top of these are [warm] springs strongly impregnated with CO_2. About a hundred yards from these mounds is a cold spring on the bank of what is called Soda Creek. It has had a pavilion erected over it by Mr. Hooper, delegate to Congress from Utah.[24] The spring is about 3 feet in diameter and has had the sod banked about to form a rim. It is lined with [iron]. There are three small holes outside of the same character. The water is delightful in taste and the escape of CO_2 is quite considerable. I secured a bottle of it for examination.

Having secured photographs we went up Pemb[rury] Pass, about 4 or 5 miles, to an old soda spring basin. At some time in the past this has been very extensive. There are the remains of the old basins still left, some 10 feet and over in depth. The rims in many places are still left in very perfect condition. In some of the old basins there are the remains of plants left, with an encrustation on them, bound together by the cement. The inhabitants call it petrified sage brush.[25] The whole deposit occupies an [*area*] about a quarter of a mile square. In the centre of it there is a stream of water flowing filled with beautiful green vegetation. After taking several photographs of the extinct basins we started back for camp, getting in at supper time. The Doctor was out all day with Capt. Putnam, and Lieut. [*Wilson*] and got a great many specimens.

[*Peale wrote no more journal entries for eleven days. It is possible that he returned home for this period either to visit his very ill father or to attend his funeral. During these eleven days the survey left Soda Springs, proceeded up the Bear River, and passed through the towns of Bennington, Montpelier, Ovid, Paris, St. Charles, and Fish Haven – the last just three miles north of the Idaho-Utah border on Bear Lake. They continued in Utah Territory through Laketown, Randolph, and Woodruff, reaching Evanston, Wyoming Territory (six miles from the Utah border), on the morning of September 29. The following day the party traveled on UPRR cars some thirty-four miles east to Fort Bridger. There the survey officially disbanded on Monday, October 2.[26]*]

[*Hayden and Peale, however, continued westward as a twosome, traveling by train and on foot. Although their time together remains largely unaccounted for, they were searching for Tertiary fossils and investigating geological features primarily along the railroad cuts between Fort Bridger and Weber City, Utah Territory.[27]*]

[*Peale's next journal entry finds the two on the Union Pacific Railroad line, in or near the town of Echo, and heading west toward Weber City (present-day Peterson), Utah.*]

THURSDAY, OCTOBER 5

We did not hear the freight train in the night and therefore did not get away as we expected. After breakfast I went to the store and got my box, carrying it over to the depot. I got a bill of lading for it. I learned that the freight train had not gone through at all.

The Doctor and I started on foot for Weber. I had to wear my overcoat in order to take it. We carried our saddle bags in our hands. Following the wagon road for a short distance the rocks were conglomerates, the same as those in Echo Canyon, of a brick red color. In many places on the sides of the hills they have been curiously weathered and fashioned into almost perfect towers. We soon left the wagon road and took the railroad leading into Weber Canyon. We rested a few moments under the 1,000 mile tree, the red conglomerates rising high on each side of the gorge. The River has cut through the end of the range leaving a high hill on one side while, seemingly, it would have been a great deal easier to have flowed around it. Immediately succeeding the conglomerates come limestones, which, from some fossils we found, we determined to be Jurassic. We here left the railroad again and crossed Lost Creek. The railroad goes through quite a cut of limestones most of them of a bluish color. They continued for about half a mile when we came to red sandstones which contained a percent[age] of lime. At Weber Quarry there were a number of men taking out the stone. It was of a light red brick-red color and very fine grained like we found at Fort Hall. We crossed a number of [bridges]. Succeeding these were sandstones, some dark and others light, until [eventually] we came to Tunnel #3 which is cut through limestone of light blue color. Between here and the next tunnel were whitish quartzites. The Tunnel #4 is cut through limestone which at the western end is of a dark blue color and very hard. From here to Weber, quartzites and limestones alternated. At Weber [the limestones] are carboniferous.

The Doctor got considerably ahead of me in walking as I have a sore heel. I took to the railroad and on getting to the station I found him waiting.

We went to a house and had a good wash after which we took dinner or rather supper. Our landlady brought us some peaches and she and the Doctor and the owner of the house had quite a discussion in regard to Mormon affairs. The owner of the house used to be a Mormon. The passenger train passed us this afternoon with two carloads of soldiers for Salt Lake. We walked 16 miles today and as a consequence I am pretty tired.

Weber City [*Peterson*]

Friday, October 6

The Doctor had a bed made on the lounge while I slept on a settee last night with my overcoat for a quilt. We got up at 5:15 A.M. and had breakfast at half past. Just as we finished at 6 o'clock we heard the freight train coming, so paying the bill, the Doctor and I hurried to the station and got in the caboose. At 8 o'clock we arrived at Ogden and immediately went to the depot of the Utah Central Rail Road and got tickets for Salt Lake City.

We found quite a crowd waiting. This being the week of the semi-annual conference of the Mormons, we procured excursion tickets. The train was crowded. The people seem to be of the lowest class and exhibit very little intelligence in their faces. It is especially noticeable in the females.

After a couple hours ride through a well cultivated country, the Lake lying to our right with the mountains beyond, we arrived at Salt Lake City. I was surprised to find such a large place. It is very pretty. The streets are very wide and lined with trees. On each side of the street there is a stream of water. The Wahsatch mountains are seen in the distance.

Afterword

As Ferdinand Hayden and Albert Peale explored railroad cuts west of Evanston, Wyoming Territory, William Henry Jackson (at Hayden's request) was taking a side trip of his own in the opposite direction. With "Charlie" Turnbull serving as his assistant, the two traveled to Nebraska, where Jackson photographed tribal members and their dwellings at Pawnee villages (on the Loup Fork) and the Omaha Reservation on the Missouri River.[1]

Once back in Washington, Hayden devoted his considerable energies to publicizing the results of the expedition, writing his official report, and making arrangements for the distribution of the survey's collected specimens. Even before the survey ended, he had written Joseph Leidy that the party had accumulated an "immense amount" of material for investigation – "more than ever before in the same length of time." Indeed it had. Forty-five large boxes containing more than one thousand specimens of minerals (including specimens from the hot springs), more than six hundred specimens of rocks, large numbers of mammal and bird skins, eggs, and other items had been sent during the expedition to the Smithsonian. A complete set of the collection would be kept and displayed there, and duplicate specimens would be distributed to selected colleges and universities.[2]

In November, George Allen received a letter in Oberlin from Albert Peale that described other kinds of post-survey activities:

WASHINGTON, D.C., NOV. 27TH, 1871

My Dear Professor:

Having a little leisure time this evening I think I could not employ it more pleasantly than in writing you. I have been wishing to do so for some time but have been so busy that I found it impossible until now.

I am very comfortably fixed here in the same building with Jackson who is very busy printing. He has two rooms.[3] Beaman is also in the city but I have not seen him since I have been here. I have been at work the last two weeks unpacking our specimens and today have been getting out those from the geysers. They have all come very well preserved. As soon as I can command the time I will try and send you some. The Doctor has a large room in the Smithsonian in which I am to arrange all his specimens. As soon as I get them in some order I will go to work in the laboratory analyzing – which will keep me all winter.

I wish you could have been with us on our trip to the Lake and the geysers for I know you would have enjoyed it very much.

If it is convenient and will not give you too much trouble I would like you to send me anything you may have observed in regard to the mines at Helena in Montana.

Adams, Turnbull and Dixon are all in Philadelphia. Quite a large number of the Survey were at the Doctor's wedding and we had a very pleasant time.[4] It seems very odd indeed to think of the Dr. as actually married. He is boarding in Washington and will remain here until after his report is written which will take some time I suppose.

Jackson wishes to be remembered to you. Elliott is here in Washington painting some sketches of the geysers and hot springs.[5] I expect to get to work analyzing in a week or two and I have material enough to keep me busy for a long time.

Hoping to hear from you soon, I am,

Yours Truly,

A. C. Peale[6]

In December, Allen received another letter from a member of the survey team, James Stevenson. Neither Peale nor Stevenson, however, informed him of Anton Schönborn's death by suicide on October 14 – just ten days after his return from Fort Bridger. No public explanation for his suicide was made, although he reportedly left a note in his boardinghouse room before cutting his throat. One might infer, however, that depression and alcohol contributed to his decision to end his life. One newspaper account of his suicide described Schönborn as an "immoderate drinker," and in his last *Philadelphia Inquirer* report, Robert Adams recollected many of Schönborn's positive characteristics but also referred to a "morbid disposition."[7]

Schönborn's death was a devastating blow to Hayden and the work of the survey, for Schönborn had agreed to return to Washington and to create the first topographical maps of the Yellowstone area as well as of areas he had surveyed in Idaho, Montana, and Wyoming Territories. These maps were to be based on the instrument readings and field notes he had carefully recorded in two field notebooks. Fortunately, these notebooks were recovered, and Hayden subsequently convinced officials at the Coast and Geodetic Survey in Washington that by using them they could prepare coherent maps of the areas the survey had just explored.[8]

To make matters worse, soon after the Barlow-Heap party returned to its Chicago headquarters, the great Chicago fire destroyed most of its specimens, all but twelve of its photographic prints, and all its negatives. Fortunately, both Barlow and Heap had retained their field journals, and Heap still had his topographical notes and a reasonably completed map. Soon an uneasy partnership based on mutual losses developed, as the Hayden and Barlow parties began to share their respective scientific findings through letters. Barlow, for instance, asked to see Hayden's outline of Yellowstone Lake's shoreline and confirmed that the two parties' maps of the geyser basins "compare very well."[9]

Neither party, however, seemed willing to acknowledge publicly the other's assistance, despite the fact that both surveys undoubtedly incorporated some of each other's findings into their reports and maps. For instance, in a letter dated February 2, 1872, Barlow expressed concern about their differing elevations. Hayden's seemed "very low," he wrote, "for instance . . . Emigrant Peak which we thought was 12,000 [feet] you state as 10,628. I, of course, adopt your measurements as mine were all lost in the fire."

Hayden's elevation of Emigrant Peak turned out to be far closer to today's measurement (10,960 feet) than Barlow's figure. Later, for his official report, Barlow lopped off some one thousand feet from the figure he reported to Hayden, listing Emigrant's elevation as "close to 11,000 feet above sea level."[10] Hayden must have felt strongly about his Emigrant calculation because it was one of only several mountain elevations that he included on his official map. Barlow provided no mountain elevations at all on his official map.

In the end, Barlow produced the superior map. If Schönborn had lived to complete his work, Hayden might, at the least, have avoided some of the elevation errors that appeared in his report. One of Hayden's later topographers, Henry Gannett, reported that the party's mistaken elevations came from a "faulty method of computation," which led to errors of as much as several hundreds of feet.[11] It is even conceivable that Schönborn was responsible for these miscalculations.

Whatever the problem, Hayden decided not to produce the colored geological maps that Interior Secretary Delano had instructed him to create. Hayden explained that the survey's "journey homeward" was so rapid that he could not do more than work out the geological features along the route itself. Moreover, he pointed out, the geology of the area was "exceedingly complicated" and still largely unknown, especially along the Rocky Mountain divide. "None of our published maps convey any idea of the almost innumerable ranges," he declared; "from longitude 100° to 118°, a distance of over five hundred miles, there is a range of mountains, on an average, every ten to twenty miles." It would require a vast amount of labor, he reported, to "explore, analyze, and locate on a suitable scale, these hundreds of ranges . . . each one of which is worthy of a name."[12]

Hayden recognized at the conclusion of the survey that the party's work in Idaho, Montana, and Wyoming Territories was only the beginning of a long process – thus the designation of his report as "preliminary." He learned a valuable lesson from it as well: for his second Yellowstone Survey, he hired not one but four experienced topographers.

In the end, Hayden more than fulfilled his promise to supply geological details and a "fine set of maps" of the areas he explored in 1871.[13] During the summers of 1872 and 1878 his survey continued its work in Idaho, Montana, and Wyoming Territories, and after the 1878 survey concluded, he began preparing what became the massive two-volume twelfth (and final) *Report of Progress of the Exploration in Wyoming and Idaho for the Year 1878*, published five years later. It included not only many highly detailed maps and illustrations within each volume but an accompanying packet holding a dazzling array of large, folded geological maps of the area, several in color. Also included were three striking panoramas of the Teton and Wind River ranges by the survey's last topographer-artist, William Henry Holmes.

Despite the 1871 survey's incomplete findings and the loss of its topographer, Hayden threw himself into the task of making his Fifth Report both positive and quickly available to the public and to Congress. Funding for his upcoming 1872 survey was, after all, still dependent on congressional approval.

Hayden had a great deal to be positive about. With characteristic enthusiasm, he hastily began to put together his official report, editing his detailed (and now-missing) field notes and determining what illustrations to use (drawing heavily on the work of Henry Elliott). Hayden also cajoled his consulting scientists, who had been busy analyzing survey specimens, to submit their reports in a timely fashion.

Rather than omit descriptions of some of the great Yellowstone geysers in eruption (which his party had not observed or photographed), Hayden included Nathaniel Langford's written descriptions of the erupting Giant, Giantess, and Beehive geysers, which appeared the year before in *Scribner's Monthly*. Hayden even illustrated the Giant and Beehive eruptions with two of the article's engravings, done by Moran the previous year, *before* Moran participated in the Hayden Survey.

Several survey members wrote up their own observations for the report. Especially noteworthy, yet long overlooked, are the reports of Albert Peale and Cyrus Thomas. Thomas's seventy-four-page account, "Agricultural Resources of the Territories," described areas in the northern part of the Salt Lake Basin, the Snake River Plain, and parts of Montana Territory. Thomas emphasized the surprising amount of available fertile land, but more important, he made one of the earliest recommendations for a planned system of irrigating arid regions, and he was the first to plea for the protection of timber resources from exploitation.[14] (Hayden also included a letter by George Allen to Thomas describing the effect of irrigation on California's Santa Clara Valley, an area Allen had visited after he left the survey in July.)

Peale's forty-page report, "On Minerals, Rocks, Thermal Springs, etc.," was the first study of Yellowstone's thermal features. It laid the groundwork for his later mammoth treatise (of almost four hundred pages) on the subject, which constituted nearly the entire second volume of Hayden's Twelfth Report.

In the midst of preparing this report, Hayden was suddenly faced with quite a different matter. Late in October he received a letter from Jay Cooke's office manager relaying a suggestion that Congress "pass a bill reserving the Great Geyser Basin as a public park forever."[15] In amazingly short order, Hayden dedicated all his energy to making this idea become a reality.

Hayden and Langford led the campaign to set aside the Valley of the Upper Yellowstone as a national park. Hayden saturated congressmen with Jackson's most dramatic photographs of thermal features, waterfalls, and mountains. He also displayed some of Moran's watercolors and published illustrations, along with Yellowstone geological specimens, at the Smithsonian and in the Capitol rotunda.[16]

With the help of Hayden's influential political friends (especially "Annie" Dawes's powerful father, Congressman Henry L. Dawes), the Yellowstone Park Bill passed both houses of Congress in record time. It was signed into law by President Ulysses S. Grant on March 1, 1872 (see appendix 4). Thus, Yellowstone became the world's first national park as well as the first reserved American wild land to be placed under federal management. Although Hayden was only one of several people who claimed to have originated the idea for the park, there is no question that he was the park's first and most enthusiastic advocate.[17]

Hayden was, in some respects, acting in accordance with railroad interests. At the same time, he was assuring Congress that because of its altitude, weather, and geography, the entire Yellowstone area could never serve any "useful" purpose – whether for mining, ranching, or farming. Consequently, he concluded, setting it aside as a national reservation would incur "no pecuniary loss to the Government."[18]

More important, Hayden believed in the value of "setting aside the area as a pleasure ground for the benefit and enjoyment of the people," and he warned that if the bill failed to become law soon, "persons are now waiting for the spring to open to enter in and take possession of these remarkable curiosities, to make merchandise of these beautiful specimens, to fence in these rare wonders, so as to charge visitors a fee, as is now done at Niagara Falls, for the sight of that which ought to be as free as the air or water."[19]

The designation of "pleasure ground for the benefit and enjoyment of the people" suggests that Yellowstone's thermal features, wildlife, and spectacular scenery were to be preserved more for the enlightenment and entertainment of park visitors than for ecological purposes. Environmental concepts would come later as America's western wilderness began to diminish. Nevertheless, "pleasure ground" did not signify an amusement park. The pleasure ground envisioned by Hayden and Northern Pacific interests was to be similar to those that prosperous Americans had long visited in Europe for health, recreational, and scenic reasons. Mammoth Hot Springs had the same health benefits, for instance, as spas in England, Germany, and Switzerland. Moreover, Mammoth, as well as the rest of Yellowstone, provided the kind of sublime scenery (snow-covered mountains, picturesque waterfalls, lakes, and deep woods) that Americans associated with European resorts.

Whereas Hayden's report emphasized the intrinsic importance of making the "remarkable" Yellowstone area available to Americans, commercial interests supported the exploration of the area, and the park bill itself, for more straightforward economic reasons: "to attract people and their money to Yellowstone as a tourist resort." This included not only travel by railroad but also the building and management of future palatial park hotels, also carried out by the railroads. Such investment and promotion would attract countless tourists (both American and European) who sought to be among the first to travel to the scenic West and to experience Yellowstone's wonderland.[20]

Thomas Moran's painting, *The Grand Cañon of the Yellowstone*, only added greater incentives to visit Yellowstone. Not completed until two months after the Yellowstone bill had been signed by President Grant, this painting laid to rest any doubts the public may have had about the sublimity of Yellowstone scenery, or about Moran's artistry. A few days before the unveiling, Moran wrote Hayden that the Northern Pacific's president, vice-president, and a number of directors had visited him to view the painting and were "decidedly enthusiastic about it."[21]

On Thursday evening, May 2, 1872, at a private unveiling party (apparently funded by *Scribner's*) held in New York, Northern Pacific officials, the press, literati, artists, and Hayden himself gathered to view Moran's great painting in Leavitt's Art Rooms in Clinton Hall.[22] Two months earlier Moran had written Hayden that he was "casting all his claims to being an Artist, into this one picture of the Great Cañon, and [*I*] am willing to abide the judgment upon it."[23]

Those at the reception judged the painting to be "magnificent" and "splendid," and it was soon exhibited at the Smithsonian. Congress later purchased it for ten thousand dollars, and for years it was displayed in the Capitol rotunda. Moreover, Moran's other Yellowstone paintings and engravings received such acclaim that the editor of *Scribner's*, Richard Watson Gilden, a fellow Philadelphian and Moran's good friend, suggested to Hayden, "You ought to call one of the three Tetons 'Mount Moran.' "[24] Although Moran's name does not now grace one of the "three" Tetons, Hayden named a massive mountain about fifteen miles north of the Grand Teton "Mount Moran." Moran's mountain name remains, whereas attempts to rename the Grand Teton after Hayden failed, despite the fact that "Mount Hayden" appeared in articles and on maps until 1876. By this time Hayden recognized that his supposed namesake would always be locally called the "Grand Teton," and he restored its earlier name in his Twelfth Report.[25]

In 1872 Hayden received another congressional appropriation, enabling him to return to Yellowstone and also to explore areas in Jackson Hole and the western side of the Tetons. This time the newly appointed (unpaid) first superintendent of the park, Nathaniel Langford, returned with Hayden as a guest of his party.[26]

Many members of the 1871 survey party returned with Hayden, including Stevenson, Peale, Jackson, and Carrington. Moran, however, was absent this second time, for he was busy painting oil and watercolor scenes from the year before. Also absent was the survey artist, Henry Elliott, who was off in Alaska, where he would devote his energies as an artist and environmentalist to preserving an increasingly threatened population of Alaskan fur seals. George Allen's health would continue to deteriorate until his death in 1877.

Hayden's original boundaries for the park encompassed about 3,344 square miles. Since then its boundaries have been somewhat extended, so that today it covers about 3,472 square miles.[27] Management of this vast area has never been easy. Civilians first administered the park, but in 1886 federal troops had to be called in to stop poaching and rampant vandalism. Finally, in 1916, Congress created the National Park Service to regulate and conserve Yellowstone as well as several new national parks.

As for Jay Cooke and the Northern Pacific, the Panic of 1873 delayed completion of their transcontinental route and the hoped-for rail link to Yellowstone Park. The depression also delayed a more dramatic plan. Included in Hayden's 1872 official report was a report entitled "Means of Access to the Yellowstone National Park by Railroads." Two rail routes were proposed, approaching the park from the southwest via the Union Pacific and from the north by the Northern Pacific, thus linking the two lines. The proposal took this rail line through the park itself, past such points of interest as Lewis Lake, the Lower Falls, and the Geyser Basins.[28]

Not until 1883 would the Northern Pacific route be completed across Montana, with a spur connecting Livingston first to Cinnabar and, in 1903, to Gardiner – today's north entrance to the park. The plan to run train tracks through the park itself never materialized. No one in 1872, least of all Hayden and Congress, envisioned the millions of visitors who would come to the park. Nor could they predict the impact that two twentieth-century inventions, the automobile and the recreational vehicle, would have on the park. Today one can't help but wonder, while trying to negotiate a vehicle along Yellowstone's deteriorating roads or idling in long lines of summer traffic awaiting road repairs, whether train travel through the park might not have been a good idea after all.

Nevertheless, what Hayden and his 1871 party saw and experienced in Yellowstone was rare and precious, and would become even more so with time. Hayden wanted others to see and experience it as well. Railroads would eventually make that possible. In fact, they could have done so even without the creation of the park. It turns out that Yellowstone National Park was created just in the nick of time.

In his report to the Committee on Public Lands, Hayden prophesied, "If this bill fails to become a law this session, the vandals who are now waiting to enter into this wonder-land will, in a single season, despoil, beyond recovery, these remarkable curiosities, which have required all the cunning skill of nature thousands of years to prepare."[29] Hayden was right. On March 9, 1872, Matthew McGuirk filed a claim ("not to exceed 160 acres") for the area where the subterranean runoff from Mammoth Hot Springs empties into the Gardner River. McGuirk had begun to develop the area in August 1871 as "McGuirk's Medicinal Springs," a place for "miraculous" cures. Unknown to McGuirk, the land had been withdrawn from the public domain only eight days before he filed his claim, when President Grant signed the Yellowstone Park Bill into law. McGuirk's claim was denied.[30]

The creation of the world's first national park had come none too soon.

Abbreviations

AHC	American Heritage Center, Laramie WY
ANS	Academy of Natural Sciences, Philadelphia
APS	American Philosophical Society, Philadelphia
CPS	College of Physicians and Surgeons, Philadelphia
C.PL	Committee on Public Lands
DAB	*Dictionary of American Biography*, ed. Allen Johnson (New York: Scribner's, 1956)
LC	Library of Congress, Washington DC
NA	National Archives, Washington DC
NYPL	New York Public Library, New York City
OCA	Oberlin College Archives, Oberlin OH
RG	Record Group
SIA	Smithsonian Institution Archives, Washington DC
USGS	United States Geological Survey, Denver
YRL	Yellowstone Research Library, Mammoth Hot Springs WY

Appendix 1

Biographies of 1871 Survey Members

Robert Adams (1846–1906), a native of Philadelphia, prepared for college at the Philadelphia Classical Institute and graduated from the University of Pennsylvania in 1869. When Adams was not engaged in Hayden's summer expeditions (1869–75), he studied and later practiced law under one of Philadelphia's most prominent attorneys, George W. Biddle. Adams became a distinguished congressman, served as minister to Brazil, and was the author of the congressional resolution of April 25, 1898, declaring war against Spain. See *DAB*.

George Allen (1812–77) was born in Mansfield, Massachusetts, and as a youth studied under Boston's Lowell Mason, the pioneer of public music instruction. Allen later enrolled as a student at Western Reserve College in Hudson, Ohio, but soon discovered that his liberal views on reform and religion were out of place there and transferred to Oberlin College, also in Ohio, during the 1836–37 academic year. After graduating in 1838, Allen remained at Oberlin for thirty-seven years. He served the college in a number of capacities: as a teacher of music (both the violin and piano) and a professor of sacred music (1838–64), as principal of the college's Preparatory Department (1842–46), as professor of geology and natural history (1848–71), and as secretary and treasurer of the college (1863–65). He established the ongoing Oberlin Musical Union (the second oldest choral society in America) and was also a writer of hymns.

Allen had a deep interest in and knowledge of natural history and did geological fieldwork in the East as well as in Ohio, where he worked on state geological surveys under John Strong Newberry. In 1864 he traveled to Jamaica, where he collected many specimens for his own personal natural history cabinet, which he later sold to the college for three hundred dollars.

Although a retiring man, he was a popular teacher, and he was "rarely without a group of children or young people about him, whom he was either teaching to play their instruments, to study natural history, or . . . instructing in the Christian life" ("In Memoriam"). He shrank from public occasions, and eventually a nervous condition forced him to restrict his teaching duties. This affliction was undoubtedly influenced by his perception that his work as a musician and scientist was undervalued (in both salary and status) in comparison with the better-rewarded Oberlin teachers of religion and theology. For years the Allens took in a houseful of college students as boarders to help defray the expenses of raising five children.

In 1841 Allen married Caroline Mary Rudd, one of the first three women in the United States to receive a college degree when she graduated from Oberlin (the first coeducational college in the United States) the same year. "Biography" by Brian Williams, George Allen Papers, 30/67, OCA; "In Memoriam," *Oberlin Review*, Jan. 9, 1878, p. 98.

John Warren Beaman (1845–1903) was born in North Hadley, Massachusetts. During the Civil War he entered the army at age eighteen and served in the Red River Expedition with the Massachusetts Artillery. He subsequently completed a three-year course at the Troy Polytechnic Institute in Civil and Mining Engineering and soon afterward began work with Hayden's 1870 survey in Wyoming Territory. After the 1871 Yellowstone Survey Beaman was scheduled to teach natural science and civil engineering at the Red Wing Collegiate Institute in Red Wing, Minnesota, although his name does not appear on the list of faculty members. Beaman and his wife probably visited Henry Elliott in the Pribilof Islands for a good part of 1872. Much of Beaman's later life was spent in government service, in which he worked as an engineer and superintendent of public building construction. Lois M. Fawcett to J. V. Howell, May 16, 1960, RG 1638, Box 34, file: "Beaman," AHC.

Edward Campbell Carrington (1851–1917) was born in Fincastle, Virginia, and came to Washington DC as a child, receiving his early education there. He graduated from Columbia College and became a lawyer, specializing in criminal law. Henry Elliott recalled in 1917 that "in June, 1871, 'Cam' Carrington left Washington with me and joined Hayden's Geological Survey party at Omaha . . . [he] was the most amiable courteous fellow that ever lived and he was a great favorite in the Camp." His "much older" brother, Ed, had been a member of Hayden's 1869 survey. His obituary (*Washington Times*, July 19, 1917) described him as "one of Washington's most prominent criminal lawyers." Elliott reported that Campbell's father, General Edward C. Carrington, was an "old school Virginian" who had served as district attorney in Washington during Lincoln's and Andrew Johnson's administrations. Carrington Island, a tiny island located northeast of Bluff Point on Yellowstone Lake's West Thumb, was named by the 1871 party for Campbell Carrington, probably to commemorate his work with Elliott on taking lake soundings. Fryxell to Howell, March 21, 1955, RG 1638, Box 34, "Carrington Family," AHC; Whittlesey 1988b, 33.

Henry Elliott (1846–1930) was born in Lakewood, Ohio, the oldest of Franklin and Sophia Elliott's five children. Franklin Elliott ran a successful seed and nursery business in Ohio and became a lifelong friend and associate of horticulturist Jared Kirkland (one of Hayden's professors at Cleveland Medical College), who later served as a consultant for the U.S. Department of Agriculture. In 1862, when Henry was a sickly sixteen-year-old, his father, determined to encourage Henry's natural talents for sketching and painting, arranged with the secretary of the Smithsonian Institution, Joseph Henry, for him to stay at the institution to sketch and study natural history. Elliott studied and participated in several expeditions in the next few years. In 1864 he joined a survey for the Russian-American Telegraph line across the Bering Strait. Other adventures ensued, including a 725-mile canoe trip from the Yukon to Victoria, British Columbia.

From 1867 to 1871 Elliott worked for the Hayden surveys and improved his skill in sketching landscape panoramas. In 1872 he obtained an appointment as assistant treasury agent for the Pribilof Islands (then newly acquired by the United States from Russia) and supervised the Alaska Commercial Company's management of the fur seal herd there. He became a leading authority on the increasingly endangered Alaskan fur seal and devoted much of his life to defending and protecting it by testifying before Congress and helping draft legislation that regulated seal hunting. Elliott sketched and painted hundreds of scenes of seal herds in the Pribilofs as well as in other parts of Alaska.

According to an exhibition catalog of his work, his watercolors are "more than documentary, and they put forth a claim for aesthetic recognition . . . showing a mastery of the medium, an awareness of composition, and a delight in lighting effects and atmosphere that suggest exposure to the work of contemporary luminists." In this, he may have been influenced by Moran's watercolor sketches during the Yellowstone expedition. Elliott wrote and illustrated numerous articles about Alaska and Alaskan seals for *Harper's*, *Scribner's*, and other leading magazines and wrote two books with many of his illustrations, *Our Arctic Province: Alaska and the Seal Islands* (1887) and *The Seal Islands of Alaska* (1881 and 1976), as well as *Biographical Sketches of Authors on Russian America* (1915). Shalkop 1982; Busch 1985, 119–22.

F. L. Goodfellow: Goodfellow Creek in Teton County, Idaho, was named for him by Hayden in 1872.

Ferdinand Vandeveer Hayden (1829–87) was born in Westfield, Massachusetts. When he was about twelve years old, after his mother's divorce and remarriage, he was sent to Rochester, Ohio, a small farming community about forty miles southwest of Cleveland. There he was raised by one of his father's sisters on a family farm. At sixteen, Hayden entered nearby Oberlin College, graduating with an A.B. degree in 1850. For the next year and a half, he continued his studies in the college's theological department (but did not graduate), while often teaching in district schools.

In the fall of 1851, probably through the influence of Professor George Allen of Oberlin, Hayden's interest in natural history and geology led him to study these disciplines by enrolling at Cleveland Medical School. During his time in Cleveland, Hayden worked with geologist John Strong Newberry and horticulturist Jared Kirkland. Later he enrolled in the Albany Medical School in Albany, New York, where he received his medical degree in 1854. In Albany, Hayden renewed an acquaintance with paleontologist James Hall, whom he had met at Newberry's home in 1851. Hall was the "leading spirit" of the New York Geological Survey, and in 1853 he arranged a fossil-collecting trip to the White River Bad Lands (in modern South Dakota) for Hayden, and Hall's assistant, paleontologist Fielding Bradford Meek. Thanks to Meek's and Hayden's fossil discoveries and their collaborations with Philadelphia zoologist Joseph Leidy, dinosaur science formally began during this period in North America.

Hayden continued his western explorations for another thirty years (except when he served as a Union Army surgeon during the Civil War). From 1866 to 1872 he was an adjunct professor of geology and mineralogy at the University of Pennsylvania. In 1867 he was named head of the U.S. Geological and Geographical Survey of the Territories. Hayden received congressional appropriations for his western surveys from 1869 to 1879, during which time his surveys examined and mapped some 420,000 square miles across the western Great Plains and Rocky Mountains. In 1879 all government surveys were consolidated under the U.S. Geological Survey, and after a bitter battle for the directorship, Hayden lost to fellow geologist Clarence King. Hayden continued to do geological work (largely in Montana), however, with A. C. Peale under the auspices of the new organization. Because of failing health, he was forced to resign in 1886, and he died the following year in Philadelphia.

More than forty living and fossil taxa have been named for Hayden; besides Hayden Valley in Yellowstone, his name is attached to a number of land formations (glaciers, mountains, buttes) as well as two towns. Peale 1891, 1892, *Bulletin of the Philosophical Society*, Box 50, file: "Hayden" – MS, memoir, and biography by Peale, AHC; Haines 1977, 2:438–39; Goetzmann 1966; Merrill 1924, esp. 513–27; Norell, Gaffney, and Dingus 1995, 7; Sterling et al., 1997, 335–38; White 1971, 132–35. For a book-length biography, see Foster 1994.

Stephen D. Hovey served with the Hayden summer surveys from 1871 to 1878. Although he was probably employed in other work during the spring, fall, and winter seasons, he appears to have been responsible for the year-round care of at least some of the survey's horses and mules. His many letters to Hayden concerning the care and health of the animals are postmarked Cheyenne. Microfilm 623, reel 8, NA.

William Henry Jackson (1843–1942), the official photographer of the Hayden expeditions from 1870 to 1879, became one of the most important landscape photographers of the American West. The earliest photographic record of the Yellowstone territory, his work during the 1871 survey was a major factor in persuading Congress the following year to preserve the area as America's first national park. After 1878 Jackson settled in Denver and set up his own photography studio. During this time *Harper's Weekly* commissioned him to make regular photographic reports of many western areas, and he also produced a number of paintings that illustrated his western experiences. In 1898 he moved to Detroit to become part owner of the Detroit Publishing Company, which specialized in the production of colored prints; at the same time, he continued to work in the field as a photographer. He later moved to Washington and finally to New York, where he died at the age of ninety-nine. Jackson often returned to the scenes he photographed on Hayden's expeditions. Perhaps his most noteworthy visit was to the Yellowstone area at the age of ninety-eight when he helped celebrate the creation of the

Jackson Hole National Monument. Jackson's two autobiographies, *Pioneer Photographer* (1929) and *Time Exposure* (1940), provide many interesting details about his work and life, although given his age at the time he wrote them, his memory cannot always be counted on. For a more recent biography of Jackson and an excellent analysis of his photography, see Hales 1988.

Thomas Moran (1837–1926) was born in Bolton, Lancashire, England, and emigrated with his family to Philadelphia in 1844. At sixteen he was apprenticed to a local wood engraving firm, but three years later his talents in painting led him to become an unofficial pupil of James Hamilton, a successful Philadelphia painter. In 1862 and 1866–67 Moran studied painting in Europe, especially the works of J. M. W. Turner in England. In 1870 he worked as an engraver at *Scribner's*. There he prepared engraved illustrations for Langford's two-part article on Yellowstone, based on a few crude drawings by two members of the Washburn party.

Moran's Yellowstone's work in 1871, and his later paintings (both oil and watercolor) of the area, firmly established him as a landscape artist. So associated was he with Yellowstone images that in 1872 he began signing his work with the initials TYM for "Thomas Yellowstone Moran." But Moran traveled and painted landscape scenes throughout the American West: the Yosemite Valley in 1872 and southern Utah and Arizona with Major John Powell in 1873. In 1874 he penetrated the wilderness of central Colorado in search of the Mountain of the Holy Cross. His work was, and is, seen as the definitive treatment of these scenic wonders.

Moran produced some very large canvases. Most notable are his oil paintings *Grand Cañon of the Yellowstone* and *Chasm of the Colorado*. He also did smaller paintings (both in watercolor and oil), capitalizing on a market that he and William Henry Jackson had helped create, and illustrated numerous articles for popular magazines and journals. In 1876 a folio edition of Moran's western landscapes (mostly of Yellowstone) was reproduced in color by L. Prang and Company of Boston as a series of chromolithographs. Today most of his original paintings – more than eight hundred items – are owned by the Gilcrease Museum in Tulsa, Oklahoma.

Moran's work is characterized by art historian Joni Kinsey as topographically and geologically accurate: "like a surveyor, however, Moran was attempting a visual appropriation; by compiling a series of views into a single image, he was imparting a sense of place" (Kinsey 1992, 57–58). See Fryxell 1958; Wilkins 1966; and Clark 1980.

Albert C. Peale (1849–1914) was born in Hecksherville, Pennsylvania, and was the son of Charles Willson Peale (1821–71) and Harriet Friel Peale (b. 1830). His great-grandfather, Charles Willson Peale (1741–1827), was the illustrious portrait painter of Revolutionary times; his grandfather, Rubens Peale (1784–1865), was manager of the historic Peale Museum in Philadelphia; and his great-uncle, Titian R. Peale, was naturalist on the Major Long expedition to Colorado and the Wilkes expedition to the South Pacific.

Albert Peale rarely made himself conspicuous, even though he lived a far more adventurous life than most of his family. As was common in the nineteenth century, Peale, like Hayden, entered on a career in natural science and geology by taking the scientific courses required for a medical degree, which he received from the University of Pennsylvania in 1871. He probably first met Hayden while taking Hayden's course in geology at the university, and their long-lasting friendship began developing during the 1871 Yellowstone expedition.

Peale served on Hayden's surveys from 1871 to 1879 and continued to work with Hayden under the auspices of the U.S. Geological Survey from 1883 until Hayden's death in 1887. The staunch professional and personal friendship between the two men was enriched by the friendship of their wives. In fact, their wives accompanied them at least twice while they did summer geological work together in Montana. Peale married a minister's daughter, Emily Wiswell, in 1875, and like the Haydens, the Peales had no children.

From 1898 until his death Peale was in charge of the paleobotanical collections of the Smithsonian. As a field geologist, Peale published his writings mainly in Hayden's annual reports. Probably his most important contribution was his monograph on the thermal springs of Yellowstone, which filled nearly four hundred pages of volume 2 of Hayden's Twelfth Report (published in 1883).

Peale's name has been attached to several geological features located in widely separated localities, including Peale Island, the most southerly island in Yellowstone Lake; Mount Peale, the highest peak in the La Sal Mountains in eastern Utah, near the Colorado border; and the Peale Mountains in eastern Caribou County, Idaho. Fryxell 1962; Merrill 1924, 513–23, 587.

Anton Schönborn (1829–1871) was one of fourteen children. His father, an "apotheker" in Saxony, was married and divorced several times. Anton, as well as several of his siblings, emigrated to the United States and assisted an older brother, August, an architectural draftsman in Washington DC. August worked on a number of prominent Washington buildings, including the Capitol and the White House. In 1858–59 Anton served as an illustrator at the Smithsonian Institution. Like Hayden, he was a member of the Smithsonian's tightly knit "Megatherium Club," a group of young scientists who lived in the Smithsonian's towers and took their meals in the basement. Their club name was a coined Greek word roughly meaning "great wild animals," signifying the group's hearty appetite for drinking, eating, and singing.

In 1853 Schönborn joined the North Pacific Exploring Expedition, a coastal expedition to the Bering Sea, where he may have served as a meteorologist. Later he worked with Hayden on the Warren expedition (1856) and the Raynolds expedition (1859–60). After the Civil War he worked for the topographical engineers and surveyed western forts, painting quite detailed watercolors of them. He also painted other subjects at this time, primarily landscapes.

Soon after Schönborn concluded his topographical work for the 1871 survey, he committed suicide in his Omaha rooming house. In his pocket was a train ticket for Washington, where he was to work up his topographical notes into maps for Hayden's official report. Fellow survey member Robert Adams reported this "melencholy" news to the *Philadelphia Inquirer*, saying: "He was a talented gentleman in his profession, a German by birth, a graduate of one of the leading universities; he possessed that morbid disposition so common to his countrymen and took his own life by cutting his throat. . . . Kind, gentle, humorous, he was often the life of the camp."

A conical mountain identified as "Bald Mountain of Shonborn" is pictured in a panorama done by Elliott near the mouth of the Big Horn River in Montana (see Elliott 1872, plate LV). No official record has yet been found of a mountain in this area with this name. Many of Schönborn's watercolor drawings of western forts are in the permanent collection of the Amon Carter Museum in Fort Worth, Texas. A published Schönborn painting, "Canyon of Rapid Creek," pictures Hayden in the midst of collecting geological specimens (see Viola 1987, 142). In a July 1996 conversation Jackson Hole historian Bill Resor identified two landscape paintings as Schönborn's that appear in Hayden's Twelfth Report. Both were probably done when Schönborn participated in the 1859–60 Raynolds expedition. Robert Adams, ["Botanicus"]: "Homeward Bound," *Philadelphia Inquirer*, Oct. 24, 1871; Schönborn to Hayden, Dec. 28, 1870, RG 57, microfilm 623, reel 2, Office of the Archivist of the Architect of the National Capitol, NA; Stenzel n.d.

James Stevenson (1840–88) was born in Maysville, Kentucky and ran away from home at the age of sixteen. He met Hayden when they served together on the Warren expedition (1856). During the Civil War Stevenson served in the Thirteenth New York Regiment, and in 1866 he accompanied Hayden to the Badlands of Dakota.

Stevenson served as Hayden's executive officer from the survey's inception until 1879. He possessed extraordinary skill at managing finances, but he also organized, trained, and led survey detachments that moved safely through large expanses of western wilderness.

While managing Hayden's surveys, Stevenson became interested in observing the customs and dialects of Native Americans, and he spent his winters among the Blackfoot and Sioux tribes. This experience provided him with a knowledge of their languages and customs and prepared him for his later work as an ethnologist.

After 1879 he worked in the service of the Bureau of Ethnology, based at the Smithsonian. He explored ancient ruins in Arizona and New Mexico; investigated the languages and customs of the Navajo, Zuni, Hopi, and other tribes; and made extensive collections of artifacts and art work of the region, both ancient and modern. Stevenson worked in partnership with his wife, Matilda Coxe Stevenson, and their joint fieldwork was, after his death, described by her in numerous published articles. "James Stevenson," *Science*, Aug. 10, 1888, 63–64, RG 1638, Box 50, file: "Stevenson, James," AHC; Haines 1977, 2:439; W. H. Holmes, "In Memoriam, Matilda Coxe Stevenson and James Stevenson," *American Anthropologist* 18 (1916), 552–59; Parezo 1993, chap. 2.

Cyrus Thomas (1825–1910) was born in Kingsport, Tennessee. After receiving a doctor of philosophy degree at Gettysburg College, he began work as a lawyer and Lutheran minister. From 1865 to 1869 Thomas was minister of the Evangelical Lutheran Church in DeSoto, Illinois. Enthusiastic about natural history, he read widely on the subject and it soon became his primary vocation. By 1858 he was the principal founder of the Illinois Natural History Society. Perhaps because of Thomas's connection with Congressman John Logan (Thomas's first wife, Dorothy, was Logan's sister), Hayden appointed Thomas to his 1869 survey team as botanist and entomologist, and he served with the Hayden surveys until 1873. His yearly findings were often included as articles in Hayden's official reports.

Although he was an accomplished scientist, Thomas and his work are largely underrated because of his association with the theory that "the rain follows the plow," a belief commonly held throughout the West at the time. Advocates of this theory believed that rain was in some way increased with the settlement of the West and the extension of farming, so that as the population increased, so would the amount of moisture.

Thomas became professor of natural history at Southern Illinois Normal (1873–75) and served as Hayden's office manager in Washington during the summers of 1873 and 1874 while the survey was working in the West. He became Illinois state entomologist (1874–79) and a member of the U.S. Entomological Commission (1877–79), which tried to cope with the grasshopper plagues. From 1882 until his death he was based at the Smithsonian as archaeologist for the U.S. Bureau of Ethnology. A recognized authority on ethnology, he wrote a number of books on American Indians and early inhabitants of Central America. Bartlett 1962, 17–18, 21; Cassidy 1991, 139; Foster 1995, 247; misc. papers, including obituary from the *Washington Post*, June 27, 1910, RG 1638, Box 35, file: "Thomas, Cyrus," AHC.

Charles Turnbull (1847–1918), son of a prominent Philadelphia doctor, Laurence Turnbull, was born in Philadelphia. He received his medical degree from the University of Pennsylvania in 1871, as well as both an A.M. and Ph.D. from the university. After his work on the Hayden Survey, for which he served as physician and general assistant, Turnbull studied for two years in the ophthalmic and aural departments at the Imperial General Hospital of Vienna and then served as an intern at a London hospital. After his return to Philadelphia he practiced ophthalmology and otology, was chief of the aural department of Jefferson Medical College, and served as a fellow of the American Academy of Medicine. A recognized authority in his field, he authored numerous articles for medical journals with special reference to diseases of children. A longtime friend of Albert Peale's, Turnbull was also Emma Hayden's personal physician for many years after the death of her husband. *DAB*; J. V. Howell to Frank Updike, Nov. 5, 1959, RG 1638 Box 37, file: "Howell 1958," AHC.

Appendix 2

Peale's Journal: May 21 to July 3, 1871

Except for Peale's first entry of May 21, which is from Peale's journal, deposited at the Yellowstone Research Library, the remaining entries in this appendix are all from Peale's journal notebook, deposited at the USGS Field Records Library in Denver. Peale's entry dates within paragraphs have been italicized.

SUNDAY, MAY 21

We left the depot in West Philadelphia last night at 10 P.M. We had our berth made up and retired soon. Chester Dawes of Pittsfield, Mass., who was with me, slept very soundly all night although I (probably from being unaccustomed to riding in a sleeping car), did not rest very well. I was awake when we passed through Lancaster and Harrisburg, and also when we crossed the Susquehanna River. I awoke at 4 A.M. and found that we were beginning to get into the Mountains. I lay in the berth looking out of the window, enjoying the scenery until nearly 6 o'clock when I rose and performed my morning ablutions. At 6:40 A.M., we arrived at Altoona, our breakfast station. Immediately on stopping I went to the telegraph office in the hotel to send word to Clifford Negley of Pittsburgh (one of our party) to meet us and go on with us. There being no operator there I went to the R[ailroad] Company's office but met with the same success. I therefore concluded to take my breakfast (which, by the bye, I bolted) and wrote a telegram to throw off at Cresson.

OGDEN, UTAH TERRITORY: JUNE 3 TO 10

Ogden is situated in the Salt Lake basin, to the east of which, upon the hills at the foot of the Wahsatch Mountains, we encamped. The Mountains are cut up into sections by numerous cañons, the principal one being Ogden Cañon. I took a trip up this as typical of the others. The rocks at the mouth are composed of a red syenite in which the only veins to be seen are of quartz and feldspar, the feldspar being of the variety of orthoclase. The syenite passed into quartzites which extend for some distance and are succeeded by a silicious slate which itself passed into a cherty limestone. There are three kilns in operation which produce from this limestone a good quality of lime which has been used by the Union Pacific Railroad in building its engine house. Farther up the Cañon than I was able to go there is said to be [a] ledge of silver that promises to pay well. A piece of one that was handed me and alleged to be from the same, on examination yielded both [*silver and*] copper, the percentage of which however I did not determine. I obtained specimens of the various rocks I passed in going up the Cañon.

We left Ogden *June 10th*, proceeding northward through the Salt Lake basin. Ten miles from Ogden, we came to the hot springs. They are very numerous, scattered along the base of a hill fronting towards the West. The average temperature of the water was about 129°F. The temperature of the air at the time of observation being 83°F. The highest temperature was in one of the smaller springs, 2nd from South, being 136°F., while the lowest was at about the distance of 100 ft., further west being 109°F. The principal springs was circular and from 12–15 ft. in diameter and 4 or 5 ft. in depth, its temperature being 128°F. In all of them there was Bubbling at intervals, caused by the evolution of CO_2. At no time while under observation was it very considerable. The analyses of the water gave the following result: (1) A considerable area around the springs is covered with a sediment composed mostly of sesquioxide of iron, giving the soil a rusty appearance while in patches, here and there, as well as on the edges of rocks in the springs, themselves, there occurs a white deposit, the analysis of which gives (2) [ ]. The analysis of the red deposit gave (3) [ ]. [*At the bottom of the page Peale has written, "1, 2, 3 See appendix."*]

On *Monday June 12th* we left our Camp 11 miles from Ogden and followed the Salt Lake valley until near Brigham City, the same range of Mountains, the Wahsatch, being on our right when we [reached] Box Elder Cañon. The rocks along this part of the road were Quartzite. After 1[6] miles of traveling we reached Box Elder Park, 1,000 ft. above the Level of Salt Lake. The Park is almost circular, being about 2 miles in diameter and surrounded with hills. There is here a Danish settlement called Copenhagen. Leaving here the next day, the *13th*, we [*one blank line*]. The only rock for miles is a blue cherty limestone identical with that found in Ogden Cañon. I saw one kiln where it had been burned, producing good lime and heard of another. After almost 13 miles ride, we entered Cache valley and encamped. Just before stopping we left the Limestone behind us and met with a Limestone of a gray appearance and containing more silica. *Wednesday the 14th* we left our camp at Wellesville and continued along the Cache valley. It is about 54 miles in length and will probably average 7 miles in width, a great deal of it being under cultivation, presenting a beautiful appearance. The soil contains [*one blank line*]. The rock is principally limestone with, here and there, quartzites. *Thursday 15.* Still in Cache valley, the character of the rock remaining about the same. Passed one isolated mountain, the rock of which is a recent conglomerate. This occurs below Franklin to the right at the foot of the Mountains. Leaving Franklin we passed a butte to the left, the basis of which is a blue limestone. This stands as monument, the surrounding rock having been swept away on all side. *June 16th* we continued on our way, soon passing over Bear River where I found the character of the rocks changed, being chloritic and probably in contact with igneous rocks. The next day [*June 17th*] the rocks continued of the same character until about 5 miles above where we came across a calcareous quartzite, the lime, however, being small in quantity. Three miles above Oxford on top of the Mountain, I came across a mine which has been opened by W. J. Cooper of Oxford. The ore seems to be [rich] in silver, the ledge is 7 ft. wide Dip west, [Trend] North and South. They have gone down about 30 feet. Assay [ ]. 6 miles above Oxford we passed between two high buttes, one on the left being composed of a ferruginous sandstone, very red on the outside, rising above the road [*illegible interlineation*]. The one on the left is [ ] [higher] composed of a silicious limestone. It forms a natural gateway. Leaving here we were in Marsh Creek Valley. Some distance on we passed to the right some beds of a white calcareous sandstone. The road soon ascended to the top of the terrace of drift formation, riding over which for about 14 miles we again descended and encamped alongside of Marsh Creek. *June 18th*: Soon after leaving camp we came to an igneous rock, probably trap, over which we passed, arriving at Port Neuf River after 9 miles ride. We now followed the River on the right bank. All along the left bank the Igneous rock is in columnar form, reminding one of giants causeway. We were passing over a Modern formation, probably Drift. Encamped 6 miles from where we crossed the river. From here we still had the igneous rocks along the river until we reached the mouth of the Cañon. On the left the rocks in the Hills consisted of alternations of quartzites and limestones which succeeded each other at short intervals. We arrived at Fort Hall on *June 21st*. On *the 22nd* I made a visit to some warm springs which are about 3 miles to the south east of the Fort. I found 5 springs gushing out at the foot of the Mountains in a little valley running east and west. The temperature of the warmest was 87°F. It was about a foot in diameter and about 8–9 inches deep. The next two to the south east were of the same temperature, *viz* 77°F., only one of them being defined as a spring, being about 3 ft. in diameter and one foot in depth. In the other the water gushed right from the hill. The remaining two were not defined as springs. Their temperature was 69°F. They were most eastern. The specific gravity of the water was 1003, the analysis showing carbonate of lime and a little alumina, probably as sulphate. It is beautifully clear and there is a deposit which has formed around moss and [c] of carbonate of lime. It is not very abundant, however. About a mile to the East of Fort Hall, the Dr. and I came to a number of hills composed principally of a very fine grained red sandstone of an excellent quality for building purposes. The rocks that succeed these and lie upon them are limestones in which the Dr. found some very rare fossils.

FRIDAY, JUNE 23

We left Fort Hall about noon today and commenced our journey across Snake River Valley. No rocks to be seen, nothing but beds of sand. Encamped on Blackfoot Fork.

SATURDAY, JUNE 24

Still in Snake River Valley. The igneous rocks cropping out at times. We camped at Taylor's bridge on banks of Snake River. The river here passes through Basaltic rock, forming a small gorge and is broken with rapids. On both banks the columns of basalt rise above the water about 10 ft. We caught sight of the Trois Tetons in the distance, enveloped in clouds.

SUNDAY, JUNE 25

We followed the River for a short distance to day when we left it to the right, keeping our way across the plains, they being very level. We encamped on Market Lake. Far away to the North East we caught a glimpse of Mt. Madison, its top enveloped in clouds while nearer to us we could see what appeared to be the crater of an old volcanoe.

MONDAY, JUNE 26

Our route still lay across the Snake River Valley. At times we passed over exposed igneous rocks of the same character we have seen before. Encamped at Kamas [*Camas*] Creek.

TUESDAY, JUNE 27

Our route lay over sandy hills and plains along Dry Creek and encamped above "Hole in the Rock" on a bed of Basalt. The creek at this point flows through a deep cañon cut in the rock and is quite picturesque.

In company with Mr. Stevenson and Dr. Turnbull visited a cave about 2 miles from camp. We found the spot marked by a pile of stones. The entrance is formed by what seems to me a falling in of the Basaltic crust, for the roof of the cave is formed of it and seems to have separated from the floor beneath, much in the manner of pie crust! Entering to the N.W., we found 3 chambers, each about 23 ft. in height and about 200 ft. in diameter, they being almost circular. They are separated by piles of rocks over which we had to scramble with candles in hand. After proceeding as far as possible we retraced our steps when just as we were about leaving we discovered a hole just large enough to admit a man, leading back to the S.E. Entering this we discovered 4 chambers separated by piles of rock in the same manner as those described above. Instead of being circular, however, they are oblong, each being about 300 ft. in length and 150 in width, the height of each being about 20 ft. Each succeeding chamber is lower than the preceding. The roof is arched and, with the walls, formed of basalt. The floor of the cave is formed layers of sand and clay looking as though deposited by water. The cave has probably been formed by a stream flowing beneath the bed of lava. From the roof in places I obtained small stalactites. Wednesday, *June 28th*: For a short distance we passed across Snake River valley until the mountains were reached when we entered Beaver Cañon and commenced to ascend to the Mountains. On our way across the igneous rocks still present themselves. Near the mouth of the Cañon I obtained some specimens that seem as though they had cooled in thin layers. It looks somewhat like schistose rock. We encamped in Pleasant Valley. In the Cañon near camp I procured some rocks which seem to have disseminated through them some crystalline substance, probably feldspar.

THURSDAY, JUNE 29

Our way today was still up in the Mountains and over the divide. After passing the summit I obtained specimens. Again, they were trach[y]tic and basaltic as before. The more recent rocks along the road were conglomerates. *Friday, June 30th*: We did not move camp today. We paid a visit to the Mountains to the S.E. of camp. I found the more recent rock near the base to be limestone with conglomerates while the older ones were limestone with sandstone above.

SATURDAY, JULY 1

Our route lay along the valley, still high up in the Mountains, through Pliocene formations composed of white limestones and sandstone capped with conglomerates. Here and there we passed volcanic outbursts from which I obtained specimens of phonolite. I got some Pliocene limestones and sandstones (another Lake basin). *July 2nd*: We traveled but little over 7 miles today, our way being through Wild Cat Cañon. The rocks are hornblendic granites and gneissic, seeming to be capped with igneous rock. I obtained quite a variety of [porphyritic] rocks, some of them exceedingly beautiful. In one place I passed a vein of mica and feldspar with crystals quite distinct. I also picked up a large piece of copper ore which lay alongside of the road, having evidently rolled from the mountains. We encamped on Blacktail deer Creek in another old Lake basin. *July 3rd*: The first part of our course was over recent formation. We ascended a hill(?) when we soon descended into the head of a Cañon. At first the rocks were Pliocene white sandstones and limestones as we have had before. The main rocks of the cañon, which is called the "Devil's Pathway," were gneissic, becoming granitoid on top of which even the igneous rocks, in some places basalt, in others porphyries. Passing through the Cañon we emerged again into an old lake basin.

Appendix 3

George Allen's Report to Cyrus Thomas

This account appears in George Allen's journal entry of July 8.

As Prof. Thomas requested me on parting at Virginia, to make what observations and inquiries I could regarding agricultural features of the country between Virginia [*City*] and Fort Ellis, I place here in my memorandum book such facts as I have thus far learned:

The hills forming the divide between Alder Creek at Virginia and the valley of the Madison by stage road, are high and broad presenting a succession of carving slopes of the most magnificent proportions. Their surfaces are to a considerable extent covered with drift boulders and their summits usually capped with basalt. The depressed lines or water channels which bound and separate the several hills are small and for the most part dry, indicating that the amount of water flowing in them is very limited even in the season of greatest fall and hence that the amount of land capable of being brought under cultivation by irrigation must also necessarily be very small.

Madison Valley, where the stage road first strikes, is quite broad – say 3 to 5 miles – is flanked by high mountains especially on the East. A succession of splendid terraces, almost perfectly horizontal and miles in length lead gently down from the mountains to the river on either side. The soil was of coarse gravel near the hills but became finer as the immediate river channel was approached. Several large cañons were observed on the opposite side and it was evident that on that side at least the facilities for irrigation were almost unlimited. The valley far to the South presented the same broad and beautifully terraced appearance; but some 8 to 10 miles below, at the junction of Meadow Creek the river enters a narrow canyon with precipitous sides. Meadow Creek Valley is one of the most beautifully grassed valleys that I have seen in these parts and well deserves its name. It contains about ten sections of splendid Meadowland traversed by brooklets which united form the "Meadow Creek." The hill sides and terraces are susceptible of cultivation by irrigation. The valley has been settled some seven years (first by Mr. Spaulding from Michigan) and now has fourteen families almost within hailing distance. There is also a quartz mill in the vicinity, and placer mining is carried on to considerable extent.

Leaving Meadow Creek Valley the divide over which we passed to Hot Spring Valley was scarcely different from that which separated Virginia City from Madison Valley. Broad hills, roughly paved with stones and mostly dried up brook channels.

In Hot Spring Valley the water seemed more abundant but the valley was comparatively narrow and unimportant, though at favorable points a few ranches existed. Gold mining was observed in the hills.

On descending again into Madison valley we found it still considerably contracted, but several ranches were observed and the means of extensive irrigation were evident. A considerable stream came in from a canyon on the East (Porphry Creek?) and another smaller one from a valley up which the road proceeds on leaving the river. Several enclosed and beautifully green fields of wheat were seen in the valleys already mentioned. As from illness I was obliged to ride in the ambulance most of the time yesterday and today it was impossible for me to make any inquiry of settlers after leaving Meadow Creek.

Appendix 4

Hayden's Yellowstone Report to the Committee on the Public Lands and the Yellowstone Park Bill

This report is a synopsis of Hayden's draft report on Yellowstone which the Committee on the Public Lands approved and passed along with Chairman Mark Dunnel's signature. It appears along with the park bill "The Yellowstone Park" as House Report 764, 42d Congress, 2d session, February 27, 1872. After its passage by Congress, President Grant signed the bill on March 1, 1872.

The bill now before Congress has for its object the withdrawal from settlement, occupancy, or sale, under the laws of the United States, a tract of land fifty-five by sixty-five miles, about the sources of the Yellowstone and Missouri Rivers, and dedicates and sets it apart as a great national park or pleasure-ground for the benefit and enjoyment of the people. The entire area comprised within the limits of the reservation contemplated in this bill is not susceptible of cultivation with any degree of certainty, and the winters would be too severe for stock-raising. Whenever the altitude of the mountain districts exceeds 6,000 feet above tide-water, their settlement becomes problematical unless there are valuable mines to attract people. The entire area within the limits of the proposed reservation is over 6,000 feet in altitude, and the Yellowstone Lake, which occupies an area fifteen by twenty-two miles, or three hundred and thirty square miles, is 7,427 feet. The ranges of mountains that hem the valleys in on every side rise to the height of 10,000 to 12,000 feet, and are covered with snow all the year. These mountains are all of volcanic origin, and it is not probable that any mines or minerals of value will ever be found there. During the months of June, July, and August the climate is pure and most invigorating, with scarcely any rain or storms of any kind, but the thermometer frequently sinks as low as 26°. There is frost every month of the year. This whole region was, in comparatively modern geological times, the scene of the most wonderful volcanic activity of any portion of our country. The hot springs and geysers represent the last stages – the vents or escape-pipes – of these remarkable volcanic manifestations of the internal forces. All these springs are adorned with decorations more beautiful than human art ever conceived, and which have required thousands of years for the cunning hand of nature to form. Persons are now waiting for the spring to open to enter in and take possession of these remarkable curiosities, to make merchandise of these beautiful specimens, to fence in these rare wonders, so as to charge visitors a fee, as is now done at Niagara Falls, for the sight of that which ought to be as free as the air or water.

In a few years this region will be a place of resort for all classes of people from all portions of the world. The geysers of Iceland, which have been objects of interest for the scientific men and travelers of the entire world, sink into insignificance in comparison with the hot springs of the Yellowstone and Fire-Hole Basins. As a place of resort for invalids, it will not be excelled by any portion of the world. If this bill fails to become a law this session, the vandals who are now waiting to enter into this wonder-land will, in a single season, despoil, beyond recovery, these remarkable curiosities, which have required all the cunning skill of nature thousands of years to prepare.

We have already shown that no portion of this tract can ever be made available for agricultural or mining purposes. Even if the altitude and the climate would permit the country to be made available, not over fifty square miles of the entire area could ever be settled. The valleys are all narrow, hemmed in by high volcanic mountains like gigantic walls.

The withdrawal of this tract, therefore, from sale or settlement takes nothing from the value of the public domain, and is no pecuniary loss to the Government, but will be regarded by the entire civilized world as a step of progress and an honor to Congress and the nation.

THE YELLOWSTONE ACT S. 392

AN ACT to set apart a certain tract of land lying near the head-waters of the Yellowstone River as a public park.

Be it enacted by the Senate and House of Representatives of the United States of America in Congress assembled, That the tract of land in the Territories of Montana and Wyoming, lying near the head-waters of the Yellowstone River, and described as follows, to wit, commencing at the junction of

Gardiner's River with the Yellowstone River, and running east to the meridian passing ten miles to the eastward of the most eastern point of Yellowstone Lake; thence south along said meridian to the parallel of latitude passing ten miles south of the most southern point of Yellowstone Lake; thence west along said parallel to the meridian passing fifteen miles west of the most western point of Madison Lake; thence north along said meridian to the latitude of the junction of the Yellowstone and Gardiner's Rivers; thence east to the place of beginning, is hereby reserved and withdrawn from settlement, occupancy, or sale under the laws of the United States, and dedicated and set apart as a public park or pleasuring-ground for the benefit and enjoyment of the people; and all persons who shall locate or settle upon or occupy the same, or any part thereof, except as hereinafter provided, shall be considered trespassers and removed therefrom.

Sec. 2. That said public park shall be under the exclusive control of the Secretary of the Interior, whose duty it shall be, as soon as practicable, to make and publish such rules and regulations as he may deem necessary or proper for the care and management of the same. Such regulations shall provide for the preservation, from injury or spoliation, of all timber, mineral deposits, natural curiosities, or wonders within said park, and their retention in their natural condition. The Secretary may, in his discretion, grant leases for building purposes for terms not exceeding ten years, of small parcels of ground, at such places in said park as shall require the erection of buildings for the accommodation of visitors; all of the proceeds of said leases, and all other revenues that may be derived from any source connected with said park, to be expended under his direction in the management of the same, and the construction of roads and bridle paths, therein. He shall provide against the wanton destruction of the fish and game found within said park, and against their capture or destruction for the purposes of merchandise or profit. He shall also cause all persons trespassing upon the same after the passage of this act to be removed therefrom, and generally shall be authorized to take all such measures as shall be necessary or proper to fully carry out the objects and purposes of this act.

Notes

INTRODUCTION

1. Manning 1967, 216.

2. Mike Foster's *Strange Genius* (1994) remains the only full-length biography of Ferdinand Hayden and is the most complete and detailed source of information about him. The entry for Hayden in the *Biographical Dictionary of American and Canadian Naturalists and Environmentalists* (Sterling et al., 1997), 355–58, provides key information about Hayden's scientific accomplishments. For specific references, see Foster 1994, cover leaf; Cassidy 1991, 3; Sterling et al. 1997, 356; and Rabbitt 1989, 6, 109.

3. Hayden's philosophy of government survey work appears in his official reports and in his 1877 *Sketch of the Origin and Progress of the United States Geological and Geographical Survey of the Territories*. More can be found in several untitled documents that appear to be drafts of letters or articles, all written in Hayden's hand (Hayden Survey Papers, microfilm 623, reel 5, NA). Hayden's ability to popularize science and geology is best revealed in his official reports, which have been aptly described as "a kind of scientific exposition through travelog" (Foster 1994, 116).

4. Hayden to Allen, Sept. 2, 1871, OCA. Hayden often used this phrase or the phrase "The Great West." He used the latter as a book title in 1880, and the phrase appeared in many other Hayden articles and books, including his volume *Sun Pictures* (1870), where he writes, "Never in the history of our country has the term, 'The Great West' possessed so much significance as at the present time . . . farms and villages with sites of future cities dotted over the plains and mountain slopes as they stretch westward to the setting sun" (Hales 1988, 310 n.9).

5. Lamar 1977, 992–93.

6. Eleven men (one-third of the Frémont party) perished when they became stranded in the virtually impenetrable San Juan Mountains during winter storms (Viola 1987, 107–9).

7. Viola 1987, 111, 119, 140.

8. All four of these leaders were contenders for the directorship of the USGS in 1879. On this bitterly fought contest, see Bartlett 1962; Foster 1994, 305–22; Manning 1967, 30–59; Rabbitt 1979; and Wilkins and Hinkley 1988.

9. Waldman 1985, 157.

10. See Bonney and Bonney 1970 for more about the 1871 Sioux attack on Baker's escort and the great number of Indian losses. Five years later the Battle of the Little Bighorn took place.

11. Lamar 1977, 136.

12. Allen Journal, Aug. 8, 1871.

13. Janetski 1987, 86.

14. Schullery 1997, 8, 16; see esp. pp. 1–30, "Ancient Yellowstone."

15. Bartlett 1962, 36.

16. Colter's time in Yellowstone came about after his release from participation in the Lewis and Clark Expedition during its return route. Colter made a winter journey for the Missouri Fur Company instead, in order to obtain furs from Indian traders. His route is shown on William Clark's manuscript map (1806–11) in the Coe Collection (303–IV) at Yale University's Beinecke Library. Haines 1977, 1:35–38; Aubrey Haines, personal communication, Aug. 7, 1998.

17. Haines 1977, 1:43.

18. Haines 1977, 1:52.

19. Hayden 1872a, 7.

20. Raynolds 1868, 2–3.

21. Haines 1996, 45.

22. The area Henderson explored is near a mine site that the Noranda Mine Corporation owned in 1996 and planned to mine. That summer, President Clinton preserved the area by offering Noranda federal property worth $65 million elsewhere.

23. Haines 1974, 37–38.

24. The story of the 1869 Cook, Folsom, Peterson expedition can be found in *The Valley of the Upper Yellowstone* (Haines 1965). Haines incorporates the explorers' reconstructed diaries, recollections, and newspaper accounts into one smooth narrative. Published accounts by members of the 1870 Washburn expedition include the excellent factual report drawn up by Lieutenant Gustavus Doane (who commanded the party's military escort), published in 1871 by the Government Printing Office and republished in Bonney and Bonney 1970. Nathaniel Pitt Langford contributed two articles about the expedition to *Scribner's Monthly* (published in the May and June 1871 issues). Thirty-five years later Langford published his "journal" of the expedition, *The Discovery of Yellowstone Park, 1870.* The most popular Yellowstone expedition account, it is akin to a raconteur's tale and suggests that Langford greatly

revised, if not rewrote, whatever might have been in his now-missing journal. The leader of the 1870 expedition, General Henry Washburn, afterward wrote two short articles that were published in the *Helena Daily Herald* on Sept. 27 and 28, 1870. The journal of survey member Cornelius Hedges appears in *Contributions to the Historical Society of Montana* 5 (1904). Warren Gillette's detailed journal (deposited at the Montana Historical Society) was published by the *Montana: The Magazine of Western History* (summer 1972). There are two unpublished journals from the Washburn expedition: one kept by Samuel T. Hauser and deposited in the Coe Collection at Yale University Library, and Washburn's long-missing journal, recently discovered (see "The Diary of Henry Dana Washburn for the 1870 Exploration of the Yellowstone Wilderness," by Lee Parsons, a paper presented at the Fourth Biennial Scientific Conference on the Greater Yellowstone Ecosystem, "People and Place: The Human Experience in Greater Yellowstone," Mammoth Hot Springs WY, Oct. 12–15, 1997).

25. Kinsey 1989, 123.

26. Kinsey 1992, 46; Haines 1977, 1:105–6, 137, 140, 142.

27. Haines 1977, 1:137–40.

28. *Scribner's Monthly* 2 (May–June 1871), 1–17, 114–28.

29. Haines 1977, 1:142, 349 n.126.

30. Hayden 1872a, 8.

31. Gustavus Doane's military career began when he joined the Union forces during the Civil War. The Piegan attack occurred early in the morning of Jan. 23, 1870, when temperatures dipped to 40 degrees below zero. Doane, under orders from Colonel Eugene M. Baker, commander of troops at Fort Ellis, led four companies of the Second Cavalry against the unsuspecting Piegans. Still referred to as the "Piegan Massacre," the attack resulted in the deaths of 173 villagers, including 90 women and 33 children. After the attack Doane and his troops destroyed the tribe's lodges and provisions and took 140 women and children prisoner. When Baker learned of a smallpox epidemic among the Indians, he ordered the release of the captured women and children but provided them with no food, shelter, or aid of any kind. According to the Bonneys (p. 22), Doane claimed (incorrectly) that the Piegan raid was "the greatest slaughter of Indians ever made by U.S. troops." Doane later participated in the Sioux War (1876–77) and the Nez Perce War (1877). Hayden to Gen. Sheridan, May 27, 1871, microfilm 623, reel 14, NA. On Doane's role in these conflicts, see Burlingame 1942, 219–26 (on "the Piegan War of 1870"), and Bonney and Bonney 1970, 22–26, 51–87.

32. Foster 1994, 202–3; Haines 1974, 99–100, 177 n.221.

33. Also missing in Hayden's orders are any references to the known thermal features in the area. Because Delano's directive was issued May 1, 1871, its omission

of such features can be explained if Hayden had not yet determined whether to include the Yellowstone Basin at that time. It also calls into question the widely held belief that it was Langford's January lecture on Yellowstone that inspired Hayden to go to Yellowstone. Although Jackson's recollections are frequently flawed, he may have been right when he recalled in *Time Exposure* that "even after Langford had published his story in *Scribner's Magazine* [in two installments, the first in May, the second in June] – the doubting Thomases demanded still further proof! And it was Hayden, spurred partly by the Langford article, who determined to satisfy them." This recollection, if true, provides a good explanation why Hayden did not communicate his survey destination earlier. Haines 1974, 99–100, 177 n. 221; Jackson 1940, 196; Foster 1994, 202–6. Foster discusses Hayden's lack of a clear survey objective but does not point out the omissions in Delano's instructions.

34. Haines 1974, 99–100, 177 n.221.

35. For a carefully documented account of the ties between Northern Pacific Railroad interests and Yellowstone, see Kinsey 1989, chap. 4. Haines contends that General Sheridan "put a crimp on" Hayden's commitment to do work for the Northern Pacific by ordering the Barlow party to share Hayden's army escort, and that Hayden was "not at liberty to return to Ogden by the Snake River route." It is doubtful whether the Barlow-Heap party affected Hayden's return route, for Hayden determined this route on the basis of his long-held desire to explore major river systems in western Montana. Barlow's party left for Chicago from Bozeman after completing its survey of Yellowstone. Kinsey 1989, 184–85; Haines 1977, 1:153.

36. Nettleton to Hayden, June 7, 1871, microfilm 623, reel 2, NA; Kinsey 1989, 181–84.

37. The description of the wagons and ambulances is from a Hayden letter to Delano, June 8, 1871, RG 48, Dept. of the Interior, NA. Hayden's first quotation is from his letter to Leidy, June 8, 1871, MSS 2/0304-01, CPS; his second quotation is from Hayden to Baird, May 29, 1871, RG 52, SIA; Hayden's last quotation is from his letter to George Allen, Apr. 13, 1871, OCA.

38. All eminent authorities, these scientists received no government compensation for their work. Hayden acknowledged them by name in his Fifth Report as George Henry Horn (1840–97), entomologist (specializing in Coleoptera); Philip Reese Uhler (1835–1913), entomologist (specializing in Hemiptera); Thomas C. Porter (1822–1910), botanist; Edward Drinker Cope (1840–97), zoologist and paleontologist; Joseph Leidy (1823–91), naturalist and anatomist; and Leo Lesquereux (1806–89), paleobotanist. Hayden failed to mention the services of his former field partner, paleontologist Fielding Bradford Meek (1817–76), who examined fossil shells collected on the 1871 survey and wrote a short piece about them for Hayden's official report. Hayden 1872a, 9, 373–77; see *DAB* for individual biographies.

39. Adams and Peale also contributed articles to the same newspapers during Hayden's 1872 Yellowstone Survey. Adams's articles have been characterized as "superficial and unimaginative," whereas Peale's published responses have been called "vivid, full, and authoritative." Peale's journal writings have also been described as "the single example of the scientist's private response to the wonders of Yellowstone" and "a mixture of aesthetic delight, youthful enthusiasm, and geological observation." Hardwick 1977, 180, 187–90.

40. Barlow to Hayden, June 3, 1871, microfilm 623, reel 2, NA; Hayden to Baird, June 4, 1871, RG 52, SIA.

41. Hayden 1877, 6. Barometric calculations were made by means of a siphon barometer with an assumed base of 30 inches for the barometer at sea level. Henry Gannett, "Geographical Fieldwork of the Yellowstone Park Division," Hayden 1883, 2:459. The list of instruments used on the 1871 Hayden Survey is from J. W. Beaman's meteorological report in Hayden 1872a, 501–2. Barlow's instruments are listed in Barlow and Heap 1872, 3.

42. Jackson 1940, 189.

43. For Jackson's list of the materials and chemicals needed for wet-plate work (both stereo and whole plate), see Hales 1988, 41. The wet-plate method of photography produced a glass negative from which multiple paper prints could be made. In *Pioneer Photographer*, 77–78, Jackson describes how he transported his photographic equipment on Hayden's early surveys: "When we were on the march, the members of the expedition, all mounted, roamed far and wide, coming back to the wagons, only at the end of the day when camp had been made. With my camera and my working equipment, I had to follow the mounted party in all its wanderings. . . . Most of my supplies were carried in an ambulance . . . but I was given a crop-eared mule to carry my working kit. . . . From the quartermaster I obtained a pair of parfleches. . . . They are large folding envelopes of rawhide . . . laced up in front with leather thongs and . . . with loops at the back to hang from the crossbars of the packsaddle. In one of these I carried my dark box with the bath holder; in the other a box of equal size containing my camera, glass plates, and chemicals for the day's work. On top, in the space between the boxes, was placed the tripod and a small keg of water to be used for plate washing when I was away from a water supply. When fast riding was the order, the whole pack was lashed securely with a cinch rope." Rather than use the 5 × 8 half-plate camera from his 1869 and 1870 photographs, Jackson bought new 6.5 × 9 and 8 × 10 cameras but apparently sometimes chose to use the lenses from his older 5 × 8 camera. As a result, "much more appeared on the ground glass of the camera . . . [and] space grew deeper, more profoundly recessive." Hales 1988, 98.

44. Baird to Hayden, June 2, 1871, microfilm 623, reel 2, NA.

45. Hayden claimed to have followed the "rigid law of priority, and first given names to geographical localities according to what they've been generally known as among the people of the country, whether whites or Indians." If no such descriptive name was identified with a place, then Hayden considered "the names of eminent men who have identified themselves with the great cause, either in the fields of science or legislation." In fact, many of the names bestowed by the Hayden party on the Yellowstone landscape were those of relatives and sweethearts, of army officers, and of members of the survey party. Hayden 1872a, 8.

46. Hayden to Henry, Sept. 4, 1871, RG 26, SIA.

47. Hayden to Delano, July 18, 1871, RG 48, NA; notes from participation in a seminar with field trips led by Ralph Ehrenberg and Bill Resor, "From Terra Incognita to Topographical Maps," Snake River Institute, Jackson WY, July 9–11, 1993.

48. Haines 1977, 1:120–21.

49. Peale 1892, 478; see also Foster 1994, 109, 184–98.

50. See Goetzmann 1966, 498, and White 1991, 132.

THE DIARISTS

1. From a lecture, "Geology and Religion," presented to Oberlin College seniors, Mar. 31, 1870 (George Allen Papers, OCA). Some of his lecture notes describe how Allen resolved the conflict between religion and new geological theories.

2. This descriptive nickname for Hayden has often been misquoted. Mike Foster writes several paragraphs about its misuse over time (Foster 1995, 60–61).

PROLOGUE

1. For a biography of Thomas and other survey members, see appendix 1.

2. Thomas Hastings Robinson (1828–1906) was pastor of the Market Square Church of Harrisburg PA from 1854 to 1885.

3. Probably Enoch Noyes Bartlett (1813–97), a classmate and (for a brief time) faculty colleague of Allen's at Oberlin College. From 1874 to 1887 Bartlett was a real estate and mining agent in Colorado Springs (OCA, Necrology Records, 28/2, Box 1). Alfred Wheat, a student in Oberlin's preparatory department in the 1860s, was a friend of the Allen family. He later spent a year at Harvard as a museum assistant and was appointed to the Ohio Geological Survey by geologist John Strong Newberry. Wheat became interested in natural science and specimen collecting when he was a sickly boy, and he eventually opened a free museum in his family's home. Like Allen's cabinet at the college, Wheat's museum featured specimens in natural history, geology, and anthropology. When Wheat died in 1875, the bulk of his museum was purchased by Carleton College. Bigglestone 1983, 164; O. C. Brown, n.d., "The Life and Character of Mrs. C. C. Wheat of Oberlin, Ohio," OCA, 28/1, Box 282.

4. Spencer Baird (1823–87), "the greatest Midas in the history of American natural history" (Foster 1994, 53), was then assistant secretary of the Smithsonian Institution in Washington DC. Baird and Hayden's friendship began in 1853 when Baird arranged for Hayden's first western fieldwork assignment in the White Mountain Badlands (then in Nebraska Territory, today in South Dakota). Sharing a professional commitment to the study of natural history, the two men worked together to develop the collections at the Smithsonian, the official repository for all collections brought back by government expeditions.

Baird was appointed the Smithsonian's assistant secretary when he was twenty-seven. A precocious youth, he had enrolled at Dickinson College, in Carlisle PA, at age thirteen, and then attended medical school at seventeen. His real interests had long been in ornithology and natural history, however. In 1840 he began a collaboration with John James Audubon after identifying two new species of flycatchers. At twenty-two he returned to Dickinson to become professor of natural history and later chemistry; early in his career he developed new and highly successful methods of field study in botany and zoology. Between 1855 and 1860 Baird, along with three assistants, produced four zoological volumes for the Pacific Railroad Surveys, encompassing "all the known species of animals, birds, and fishes in the West" (Goetzmann 1966, 323). These volumes were based on specimens sent back from the survey. Baird added some seventy new species to those portrayed by Audubon scarcely a decade before. In 1878 he became secretary of the Smithsonian. Foster 1994, 53, 56–71; Goetzmann 1966, 323; Conaway 1995; for a recent biography, see Rivinus and Youssef 1992.

5. John "Black Jack" Logan (1826–1928) and James Negley (1826–1901) both served as Union major generals during the Civil War. Logan, during his first year in Congress, worked with the Smithsonian's assistant secretary, Spencer Baird, forming an unofficial liaison between the scientific and political branches of the government. In 1866–67 their idea for a national survey of the territories resulted in Congress's establishment of the United States Geological and Geographical Survey of the Territories, better known as the Hayden Survey. After the Civil War Logan and Hayden lived in the same Washington DC boardinghouse. In 1871 Logan was a U.S. senator (Republican) from Illinois, and Negley was a Republican congressman from Pennsylvania, elected in 1868, 1870, 1872, and 1884.

Henry Dawes (1816–1903) was a powerful Republican congressman from Massachusetts (1857–75). He served as chair of the Appropriations Committee in 1869 and chair of the Ways and Means Committee in 1871. From 1875 to 1892 he was a U.S. senator, and during some of this time he served as chair of the Committee on Indian Affairs. One of his major goals was to assimilate Indians into American society. To that end he was author of the controversial Dawes Severalty Act of 1887 and (after his retirement from the Senate) chair of the equally disputable Dawes Commission to place the Five Civilized Tribes in Oklahoma under the provisions of the Dawes Act.

Logan's nephew, William Logan, served as secretary of the 1871 survey; and the sons of Negley and Dawes, Clifford Negley and Chester Dawes, served as general assistants. Stucker 1967, 44; Lamar 1977, 290; Howell to Fryxell, Dec. 16, 1954, RG 1638 Box 37, file: "Howell, J. V., 1954," AHC; Cassidy 1991, 176.

6. Wilcox and Stephens was a large dry goods establishment in Omaha, located at 239 Farnham Street (*Omaha City Directory*).

1. FROM OMAHA TO CHEYENNE AND OGDEN

1. Loess: see Glossary of Geological Terms and Fossil Shells.

2. George Francis Train (1829–1904) was a flamboyant Boston merchant who initiated diverse reforms, including promoting Columbus NE as the national capital because it was located in the geographic center of the country.

3. Long's Peak (elevation 14,256 feet) is located north of Denver in what is now Rocky Mountain National Park. Sighting this peak from the distance Allen reports would be unlikely today because of air pollution.

4. Fort Russell was established in the summer of 1867 east of a construction camp for UPRR workers. Intended to protect workers and citizens, the fort is now the Francis E. Warren Air Force Base. Hayden picked up supplies for the expedition there, including wagons, pack supplies, horses, mules, and cooking utensils. Frazer 1965, 184–85.

5. Clarence King (1842–1901), geologist, mining engineer, and writer, graduated from Yale in 1862 and after the Civil War embarked on ambitious geological surveys in California and Nevada. When the Hayden party encountered King's survey team in Cheyenne, King was in the midst of a ten-year governmental survey of a one-hundred-mile continental cross section of the fortieth parallel. King's objectives and leadership styles differed from Hayden's, and the two found themselves competing for federally funded survey work. In 1878 Congress combined all the western surveys into one survey under King's direction. See Bartlett 1962, 123–219; Rabbitt 1989; Nelson and Rabbitt 1982, 19–35; and Foster 1994, 283–323.

6. General Thomas Duncan (d. 1887).

7. This paragraph was moved from its placement in Allen's journal entry for May 29. Sherman was a train inspection point when Allen's train stopped there. Later, after the relocation of the Union Pacific Railroad tracks three miles to the southeast, it deteriorated into a ghost town. Today only a graveyard marks the site of Sherman, which can be found seventeen miles southeast of Laramie on Interstate 80, then two miles south on Ames Road. Urbanek 1988, 181; Burt 1991, 62.

8. Allen began a new paragraph at this point, writing, "Coal is mined at Carbon." He then left ten blank lines, probably hoping to supply more information later.

9. Located close to the southwest corner of Wyoming, Echo Canyon drains southwest and ends near the mouth of Echo Creek at the Weber River. The canyon had been a principal Indian and trapper trail and later a pioneer road. Interstate 80 passes through the canyon today. Van Cott 1990, 124.

10. Allen may have meant the "Middle Kingdom" — somewhere between heaven and hell.

11. From Ogden the party switched train lines and took the Utah Central Railroad to Salt Lake City. This thirty-seven-mile line was completed in January 1870 and was built and managed as a Mormon cooperative with Brigham Young as its president. Arrington 1985, 349–50. The Townsend House was located at West Temple on the corner of First South.

2. SALT LAKE CITY AND OGDEN

1. The tabernacle was completed in 1870 and is still in use.

2. Brigham Young (1801–77), second president of the Mormon church, supervised the Mormon migration to Salt Lake in 1847, founded Salt Lake City, and colonized Utah. Although he hoped for a long period of isolation for his people, the gold rush of 1849 and the completion of the Union Pacific Railroad in the late 1860s brought the new Zion into direct competition with non-Mormon (Gentile) interests. Perhaps the foremost social pragmatist of his time, Young displayed brilliance as a city planner and agricultural innovator, instituting Mormon mercantile cooperatives as well as systems of agricultural irrigation. He inspired large Mormon groups to occupy potentially fertile valleys throughout the intermountain country, while his missionaries brought a constant stream of immigrants to the settlements. Young's practice and advocacy of polygamy was attracting much national notice at the time of the Hayden Survey. See Arrington 1985.

3. Construction on the temple began in 1853; it was not completed until 1893.

4. The Beehive House, built in 1854, was Young's primary home and office.

5. This museum opened in 1869 and was run by John W. Young. It was located at South Temple between East and West Temple.

6. Allen may have meant the Channel Islands, located off the coast of Santa Barbara CA.

7. Camels were introduced to the American West in 1856 by a congressional directive designed to facilitate the shipping of supplies to isolated military forts in desert areas. The Civil War interrupted the experiment, and soon afterward the completion of the first transcontinental railroad provided transportation. For a fascinating

account of this experiment, see Faulk 1976. I'm indebted to William Bigglestone, who alerted me to the significance of Allen's comment and to Faulk's book.

8. Water from the city's medicinal and thermal springs was pumped to a large bath house, built in 1850, located in the northern part of the city.

9. It is unclear whether these were Ute or Paiute Indians. Large numbers of Utes (or Utahs) had inhabited the central Utah valley long before Mormon settlements began in 1847. Nomadic hunters, the Utes resisted efforts to be taught farming and Mormon values, but they generally complied with a Brigham Young ruling that outlawed begging. Payment for desired items was required, whether in labor, grain, animal skins, or whatever came to hand. Allen was in error about Chief Kanosh, who was not a Ute but the leader of a band of Paiutes who farmed and hunted in the area of present-day Kanosh (Millard County) when pioneers first settled the area. He is buried in the Kanosh cemetery. Arrington 1985, 210–22; Wharton and Wharton 1993, 38–40, 221.

10. Thills are the two long shafts between which an animal is fastened when pulling a wagon.

11. Jackson married Mary ("Mollie") Greer, of Warren OH, in 1869. At the time of the survey she accompanied her husband to Ogden, where she remained until the party headed north. She then returned to Omaha to manage Jackson's photography business until his return in the fall. She died in February 1872, shortly after delivering the couple's first child, a daughter, who died soon after her mother. Jackson 1940, 204–5.

12. Estimates of the number of Young's wives range from nineteen to twenty-seven; he had fifty-seven children. The federal government, long opposed to polygamous practices in Utah, would arrest Young in October 1871 on cohabitation charges, but he was never brought to trial.

13. Aneroid (nonliquid) barometers were and are widely used as portable instruments because of their small size and convenience. They indicate atmospheric pressure by the relative bulges of a thin elastic metal disk covering a partially evacuated chamber. After the aneroids arrived at Fort Ellis, they were used for taking elevations on the road as well as in the mountains. Meteorologist J. W. Beaman reported that they were "worthless" unless checked against mercurial barometers. He faulted the sluggish return of the index to the correct reading after use at elevations of several thousand feet, but he also pointed out that "their structure is so delicate as to render them liable to permanent injury by a sudden fall, or by the constant jolting to which they are subject when carried on horseback" (Hayden 1872a, 502).

14. A wall tent has frames on three sides, and by overlapping the front canvas, one can enclose the entire interior. A fly tent consists of a single long piece of canvas

stretched over center poles but open at the front and back. Both kinds of tents are staked to the ground.

15. Charles Ambrose Reynolds (d. 1896) had served as a lieutenant colonel in the Civil War.

16. Hayden is referring to the scientists who had agreed to write reports based on specimens sent to them (relayed through the Smithsonian) during the course of the expedition.

17. See geological glossary for a list of the kinds of shells Allen collected. All were freshwater shells, and most were live or found among more "recent" Tertiary or early Cretaceous rocks. These specimens were important to Hayden's work because they helped identify the differing ages of landforms, especially in the period from the Upper Cretaceous to the Lower Tertiary epochs. Meek, in his report to Hayden, found the fossil shells sent to him difficult to identify, especially Carboniferous forms, saying, "The specimens [are] generally in a fragmentary condition, and imbedded in a very hard matrix that renders it almost impossible to work them out" (Hayden 1872a, 376).

18. Allen added a question mark after "rarely."

19. Aperient powders acted as a mild laxative.

20. Baird submitted portions of his letters from Hayden to *Harper's Weekly*. They appeared in the issues of June 17, July 8, Sept. 2, 9, and 16, Oct. 7, and Nov. 11. Hayden sometimes enclosed a few of Jackson's photographs with his reports for Baird, as well as western newspaper accounts ("slips") of the expedition.

21. The expedition was delayed a day, probably because of the missing animals.

22. Hayden is referring to the fact that Jackson could develop negatives on the scene (Jackson 1940, 198).

23. Professor Thomas Porter complained about the manner in which the plants were preserved and packed. He wrote Hayden that the package from Ogden contained some plants that "were badly molded. There was also too much crowding. I know the difficulties that must be overcome in the field, but an expert will manage to conquer most of them." Porter to Hayden, Feb. 21, 1872, Hayden Survey Papers, microfilm 623, reel 2, NA.

3. To Fort Hall and the Divide

1. Joseph and Charles Woodmansee were merchants and freighters in Salt Lake City and Ogden (Madsen and Madsen 1980, 25).

2. The Shoshones (or Snakes) lived mostly in central Wyoming and southern Idaho at the time of the survey. Known for their large horse herds, they were frequently besieged by rival tribes, especially the Blackfeet. Relations between the Shos-

hones and the early white fur traders were relatively amicable. White settlers, however, arriving in the 1840s, brought new trouble. The settlers killed Shoshone game, pastured off their land, and often harassed the Shoshones—who sometimes retaliated. Drastic reprisals continued on both sides until 1868, when a federal treaty with the Shoshones established a reservation adjacent to the first Fort Hall ID. Lamar 1977, 1107–8.

3. Allen added question marks after "schists" and "limestones."

4. Copenhagen, located eight miles to the east, is now named Mantua. Originally called Box Elder, Brigham City was named in 1867 to honor Brigham Young. Van Cott 1990, 50.

5. A popular rendezvous site for mountain men and Native Americans in the nineteenth century, Cache Valley was named by beaver trappers who cached pelts and supplies there in the early 1820s. Hayden reported that Cache Valley was about seven miles wide and sixty miles in length and populated with at least ten thousand people when the survey passed through it (Hayden 1872a, 22).

6. Wellsville, eight miles southwest of Logan, was named for Daniel H. Wells, pioneer settler and second counselor to Brigham Young. Hyrum received its name as part of an unfulfilled plan to build another city nearby to be named Joseph after the Mormon prophet Joseph Smith (Hyrum and Joseph Smith were brothers). Providence was three miles south of Logan. Settlers in 1859 had named it Spring Creek but the postal service would not accept the name. Van Cott 1990, 393, 196, 304.

7. Smithfield was originally settled in 1859 as Summit Creek. Soon afterward the name was changed to honor John Glover Smith, who served the area as the first Mormon bishop. Mendon, seven miles northwest of Wellsville, was first known as North Settlement. Hyde Park, five miles north of Logan, was settled in 1860 and named for William Hyde, first presiding Mormon church elder and bishop in the area. Van Cott 1990, 247, 345.

8. When the federal government began to assert its power over Utah, Mormon church authorities decentralized the water system, "devolving the building of canals and dams into the hands of the local bishop or community committee. Farmers then came together, paid a tithe (in the form of their own labor) on the water system, and elected from among them a water master to supervise the work." Worster 1985, 78 (quotation); Paul 1988, 74–75.

9. At the time of the survey Peale reported that farmers had become so discouraged with insect infestation that stock raising had become the principal dependence of the inhabitants. Indeed, the Hayden party found the ground at the southern end of the valley "covered" with grasshoppers. Later, while in the central and northern portions of the valley, Peale reported that they found the locust and brown cricket

or grasshopper "so thickly scattered that the sage bushes and tufts of grass were literally black." Peale, *Press*, June 29, July 14, 1871.

10. Richmond was settled in 1859, and several claims are made for the origin of the name (Van Cott 1990, 315). Franklin was named for Franklin Richards, a prominent Mormon leader. Settled in 1860, on the site of a Shoshone-Bannock winter campground, Franklin was thought to be in Cache County UT. Surveyed in 1868, the Idaho territorial line was found to be south of Franklin, thus making Franklin the first permanent white settlement in Idaho. In the meantime, Shoshones in the area, resenting intrusion on their land, attacked overland mail coaches and paraded in the street of Franklin threatening the settlers. In January 1863 a force of California volunteers retaliated by mounting a dawn attack on the Indians in their camp a few miles above Franklin. Twenty-three soldiers were killed and forty-four wounded. A Mormon civilian counted the Shoshone losses at four hundred dead, at least two-thirds of them women and children. Boone 1988, 143; Lamar 1977, 1108.

11. In the early 1860s a small station and a toll bridge were built here by a William Jackson and named Bridgeport. A townsite was established in 1883, known as Brownsville, and in 1895 a post office was established as Harpster, named for Abraham Harpster, an early settler in the area. Boone 1988, 171.

12. Carpenter's Station was on Marsh Creek. The survey had linked up with the well-used old stage road that ran five hundred miles from Corinne UT (four miles west of Brigham City) to Helena, Montana Territory. By 1870 more than eighteen million pounds of freight had entered Montana by this route. Wells, Fargo & Company ran daily stages, making the trip in four days. Freight cost fifteen cents a pound; first-class fare for passengers was sixty-six dollars. There was also a daily line of post freight and express wagons (which traveled night and day) that could make the trip in nine days. Cramton 1932, 21.

13. The party had reached the southern boundary of the great basaltic overflow in the valley of the Port Neuf and Snake Rivers, now called the Snake River Basin or the Snake River Plain.

14. This ridge is probably what Hayden refers to in his official report as a "high ridge, rising 1,500 to 2,000 feet above the river" (at the lower end of the Port Neuf Canyon). At one point "the river cuts a channel through the ridges at right angles for five or six miles, exposing at least 10,000 feet of quartzite." Hayden was unable to determine the age of these stratified rocks but believed there was evidence of "two great periods of outflow of melted material, forming horizontal belts" (see Hayden 1872a, 24–25).

15. This was the Fort Hall Reservation, established in 1867 for Shoshone and Bannock Indians who had long lived and hunted in this territory. Peale observed, "It is well that [the Indians] are fed and clothed by 'Uncle Sam' for if they were

expected to subsist upon the country they would fare badly indeed." Fort Hall II was built in 1870 next to the reservation with more than a dozen buildings and a parade ground. Camp Lander (1865) had been a temporary camp before the new fort was built and was located near the Ross Fork stage station.

16. Allen inserted a question mark after "volcanic."

17. The busy stage stop and trading post of Ross Fork served freighters and travelers who used a shorter route to Montana through Port Neuf Canyon. In 1870 it established a post office, and in 1911 its name was changed to Fort Hall. Loohse and Holmer 1990, 2–3; Peale, *Press*, July 14, 1871; Boone 1988, 321.

18. During and after the nineteenth century Bannock and Shoshone histories were closely interwoven. Because the two tribes shared the Snake River Plain homeland, intermarried, and usually acted in concert, Allen's identifications are suspect. "Snakes" was the name by which the Shoshones were generally known. The Shoshone-Bannock had few sharp boundaries between their cultures and dialects; their language was related to that of the Utes (Utahs). In historic times the Bannocks (a branch of the Northern Paiutes) inhabited the southeastern corner of Idaho and lived off buffalo herds in that area. Nomads, the Bannocks owned horses, lived in skin tipis, and depended on vanishing buffalo herds for their meat and skins. As these herds moved eastward, the Bannocks established the two-hundred-mile Bannock Trail (used also by other tribes), which crossed the Rockies and opened up areas in what is now the eastern and northern portions of Yellowstone Park. The old Fort Hall was established in 1849 about three miles above the Hudson's Bay Company's trading post (1834) by the same name. Ensuing white immigration into the heart of Shoshone-Bannock country impoverished pasture land and brought new diseases; in 1853 the tribes were decimated by smallpox. In retaliation warriors became the "scourge" of the overland trails until 1863, when a Shoshone-Bannock wintering campground was attacked by U.S. soldiers near Franklin (see note 10). By 1869 most of the Bannocks had been rounded up and placed on the Fort Hall Reservation, located eight miles south of present Blackfoot on Ross Fork. Some Bannocks, however, continued their migrations for buffalo. After the Bannock War of 1878, however, the Bannocks were confined to the reservation—their guns and horses confiscated—and their tribe was merged with the Shoshones by the commissioner of Indian Affairs. Frazer 1965, 44; Haines 1977, 1:22; Lamar 1977, 71–72.

19. This military fort (1870–83) was located adjacent to the Fort Hall Reservation, which it was intended to control. Captain James E. Putnam, of the Twelfth U.S. Infantry, had commanded the post since its establishment. Fort officers frequently invited some of the visiting survey members for dinner in their dining quarters, and these occasions sometimes included heavy drinking. Although Allen (a teetotaler)

lightened up on his disapproval of alcohol during his trip, he preferred absenting himself from such gatherings. Frazer 1965, 45.

20. Allen sketched a layout of the fort's buildings at this point in his journal.

21. The survey was relying on a number of maps, including one from the 1859–60 Raynolds expedition on which Schönborn and Hayden served (see introduction). Because Raynolds's official clock (a chronometer) was off by eighty seconds, the longitude of the expedition's published maps was incorrect. The Three Buttes — like the Tetons and other important landmarks for early travelers — were placed on Raynolds's map considerably to the west of their actual locations. Hayden was especially unhappy about his party's dependence on inaccurate maps, complaining: "We found all the maps, official and otherwise, utterly inadequate to travel by." Ehrenberg and Resor, "From Terra Incognita to Topographical Maps"; Hayden to Delano, July 18, 1871, RG 11, NA.

22. Hayden is referring to the wet and dry bulbs of a sling psychrometer. The wet bulb is ventilated to cause evaporation, and the dry bulb measures atmospheric moisture. After the psychrometer has been rapidly spun in the air, the difference between the readings of the two bulbs indicates the relative humidity when referred to a standard table. Hayden's readings indicated "*very* dry air." Haines, personal communication, Aug. 1998.

23. Albert Bierstadt (1830–92), German-American landscape painter, did not join the survey, although the NPRR tried to arrange for him, along with artist Thomas Moran, to be a guest of the expedition. A. B. Nettleton to Hayden, June 7, 1871, microfilm 623, NA.

24. This campsite was probably a stage stop near present-day Blackfoot ID. The "stream" was called Blackfoot Creek by Hayden and is now named the Blackfoot River. Because it emptied into the Snake River, "fork" was sometimes added to its name.

25. Matt Taylor, a freighter, built Idaho's earliest toll bridge here in 1864–65. Spanning the Snake River, it replaced a ferry operating upstream near a bald eagle's nest in a juniper tree on a small rock island. The settlement that developed around the bridge was known first as Eagle Rock and later as Taylor's Bridge and is today Idaho Falls. Boone 1988, 191; Marker 1980, 5.

26. Allen based his belief in the volcanic origins of the Tetons on a theory developed by Hayden while passing through Jackson Hole with the Raynolds expedition in June 1860. Hayden revised his opinion in 1872 when he visited the area as part of his second Yellowstone expedition. The Tetons are a fault block mountain range of metamorphics carved from a segment of the earth's crust that has been uplifted along a fault. See Raynolds 1868, 94; Love and Reed 1976, 37.

27. Allen's despondency over Oberlin College was partly explained later by his granddaughter, who claimed he had been dismissed from the faculty, not "retired," as official records indicate. She recollected, "My father [George Allen's son] said that [Allen] had grown too timid to teach and that it was necessary to drop some of the faculty to make ends meet." There is considerable evidence that Allen suffered from periodic depressions and "nervous disease." Mary Cochran to W. F. Bohn, Dec. 5, 1937, 3/1/2, Box 4, OCA.

28. Although a "Mt. Madison" appears in this area on Raynolds's map, as well as other maps of the period, there are no lofty mountains in the area today named Madison. Allen was not the only survey member to remark on this mountain. Hayden referred to it in his 1871 official report as "one of the finest peaks in the northern ranges of the Rocky Mountains," and he placed it on the expedition's official map in the far southwestern corner of Yellowstone National Park. Peale also described Mt. Madison for the *Press*, saying, "On the 25th, we had a view from our camp of Mt. Madison, its summit wreathed with airy clouds, standing like a sentinel over three Territories . . . Wyoming, Idaho, and Montana." Given the clearer atmosphere in 1871, some believe the party may have been looking at Mt. Sheridan (elevation 10,308 feet), located southwest of Yellowstone Lake. Frank Bradley, geologist for Hayden's 1872 survey of the Tetons and Yellowstone Park, tried unsuccessfully to locate this mountain and concluded that Mt. Sheridan "may have been the peak to which the name Mt. Madison of the old maps intended to apply." But Bradley also worried that the location of that peak "was so many miles distant from the position" of present Mt. Sheridan that he "could not consider the identification certain." Other, later topographers believed present-day Mt. Holmes had been called Mt. Madison before 1878 because of its location near the head of the Madison River. Henry Gannett named Mt. Holmes in 1878 for geologist-artist William Henry Holmes, who served on Hayden surveys from 1872 to 1878. Holmes accompanied Gannett on a climb of the mountain's southern summit in 1878 and noted, "This peak, or what we suppose to be this peak, has been spoken of occasionally by visitors as Mount Madison, but on what authority or for what reason it is not known."

Thanks to Rod Drewien, from the Hornacher Wildlife Institute at the University of Idaho (Moscow), it is now possible to conclude that the mountain once referred to as "Madison" is either today's Sawtell Peak (elevation 9,866 feet) or Mt. Jefferson (elevation 10,196 feet), adjacent mountains in the Centennial Range. Drewien traced portions of the 1860 Raynolds party route as well as the 1871 Hayden route by plane, car, and foot over a period of five months. Based on his observations from Pierre's Hole, Drewien believes the mountain labeled "Mt. Madison" on Raynolds's map and described by Raynolds in his journal entry for June 19, 1860, as a "lofty snow clad peak . . . which Bridger declares to be at the head of the middle fork of the

Jefferson" is undoubtedly today's Sawtell Peak. From this direction Drewien describes Sawtell as "the most noticeable and distinctive peak because of its cone shape." On the other hand, Drewien reports that from the more distant perspective of Market Lake (Hayden's location eleven years later), "Mt. Jefferson is more prominent" than Sawtell. Hayden 1872a, 28; Hayden 1873b, 252; Peale, *Press*, June 14, 1871; "Manuscript by Wm. Taggart," RG 1638, Box 20, p. 5, AHC; Whittlesey 1988b, 105, 107; Haines 1996, 119; Rod Drewien, letter to editor, Feb. 27, 1997.

29. The Snake River Plain is a giant lava field that sweeps in an arc over eighteen thousand square miles of southern Idaho. Considered worthless for farmland, it was referred to by early trappers as a "burnt-up piece of land." The plain was built up by countless floods of basaltic lava (along with some gravel and sand deposited in lakes and streams that had occupied the region between volcanic eruptions). The porosity and permeability of these basaltic rocks is very high and accounts for the ten-thousand-square-mile aquifer in southern Idaho, made up of vast amounts of water in lava beds. Water stored in the aquifer can now be recovered to support farming, ranching, and recreation, as well as to serve as a power source. Idaho Water Resources n.d.; Madsen and Madsen 1980, 5.

30. Allen is referring to the dramatic eruption of Mount Laki at Skapta (near the southern coast of Iceland) in 1783. Until the early twentieth century, geologists believed that the lava flow from Laki, covering 218 square miles, was "the largest volume of lava . . . issued at one outflow in modern times" (*Encyclopaedia Britannica*, 11th ed., s.v. "Iceland").

31. Hayden described Market Lake as "a kind of sink, probably produced by the spring overflow of [the] Snake River, and is entirely dry the greater portion of the year." For hundreds of years buffalo roamed the flats in this area, and it became a favorite hunting and camping ground for Native Americans. Early trappers and travelers commented on the great abundance of game, especially buffalo, and called the area "Jervey's Market." In 1868 a small community settled here, established a post office (1868–1910), and named itself for the lake. It is now a wildlife management area. Hayden 1872a, 29; Boone 1988, 242; Madsen and Madsen 1980, 7.

32. A stage station, Hole in the Rock, was probably named for this cave, which was located about a mile west of the station. Peale described the cave in his letter to the *Press*, saying it consisted of three circular chambers about two hundred feet in diameter. In the first "we found the bones of a number of animals, among which were the skulls of buffalo that we knew to have been killed by the Indians from the forehead being crushed in, which is done for the purpose of extracting the brains to use in tanning the hide." Hayden also described the cave in his report: "The bottoms of the caverns show unmistakable evidence of having once formed a river bed. . . . Underneath this basaltic crust, streams of water have worn in the past, and may be

now, wearing out their channels toward [the] Snake River. . . . Such rivers as [the] Camas, Medicine Lodge, Goodins [Godin], and many others disappear in the plains and find their way, from ten to thirty miles, to [the] Snake River, underneath this basaltic floor." These rivers could disappear for quite a period of time. Explorers named the Godin River and its valley in 1823, returned to the area several years later, and were unable to find the river, so they renamed the features "Lost River" and "Lost River Valley." Today the Big Lost River Valley is above Arco, and the Little Lost River Valley is above Howe. Rod Drewien, letter to editor, Nov. 26, 1996; Boone 1988, 157, 182; Hayden 1872a, 29–30; Peale, *Press*, July 14, 1871.

33. The party crossed the continental divide at Pleasant Valley Pass (elevation 6,928 feet), now known as Monida. Today Interstate 15 follows the general route of the old stage road. Cyrus Thomas reported that the stage road from Corinne to Helena crossed the range in this valley (Hayden 1872a, 224).

34. Hayden was beginning to recruit hunters and trappers who were familiar with Montana Territory and the Yellowstone area.

35. From 1871 to 1873 this stage stop also had a short-lived post office, Junction Ranch. Cheney 1984, 15.

36. Peale confirms (in his *Press* account of July 29, 1871) that Moran joined the party at the continental divide, near today's Monida MT, and not at Virginia City or Fort Ellis, as is often reported in secondary accounts. He writes: "While in camp, just after having crossed the summit of the Rocky Mts., we were joined by Mr. Thomas Moran, one of our Philadelphia artists, who goes with us as a guest. He will obtain a number of sketches which will, no doubt, be made public in some beautiful pictures on his return." Moran traveled west by train from Philadelphia to Corinne UT and then took a series of stagecoaches to Junction Ranch.

4. TO VIRGINIA CITY AND FORT ELLIS

1. This shortcut began just north of Junction Station and cut diagonally northeast. Called the Virginia City Road, it started being used in 1863. Johnson 1987, 1–3; Metlin 1932.

2. Portions of text inserted between braces are from Peale's *Press* report dated July 15 and published July 29.

3. This was called Wildcat Canyon at the time of the survey and is now known as Price Canyon.

4. Dr. Charles Karsner Mills (1845–1931) received his Ph.D. from the University of Pennsylvania in 1871, the same year Peale received his medical degree. The two were close friends, and in 1873 Mills married Peale's sister, Clara. A distinguished neurologist, Mills taught at the university from 1877 to 1915 (see *DAB*).

5. There was a stage station here also known as Black-tail Creek Station.

6. Allen's judgment is confirmed: Stinking Water Creek is now called the Ruby River. Its early name was probably derived from the odor of hot sulfur springs (Puller Springs) located about three miles below the junction of the Sweetwater and Ruby Rivers. Although the springs were (and still are) part of the Maloney brothers' ranch, Jim Puller developed parts of the area (1879–1906), building a dance hall, saloon, hotel, and post office. Cheney 1984, 217.

7. This narrow ravine is known today as Sweet Water Canyon; at the time of the survey it was referred to as the Devil's Pathway.

8. Allen's wife, Caroline Mary Rudd, was among the first three women to receive a bachelor of arts degree in the United States, graduating from Oberlin (the first coeducational college) in 1843. Rosa, Allen's daughter, was a student at Oberlin at the time of the survey.

9. Chinese immigrants were initially drawn to California after the discovery of gold in 1848. Later many moved to other parts of the West and worked mines or built the transcontinental railroads. By 1880 about 105,000 Chinese emigrants lived in the United States, most in California but 1,765 lived in Montana that year. Lamar 1977, 205–8.

10. Originally part of Idaho Territory and named Varina City (for Jefferson Davis's wife), Virginia City was organized in June 1863, less than a month after gold was discovered in nearby Alder Gulch. Allen's estimate of the town's population during the height of the boom may be low; Jane Brown Gillett (1993, 37) claims that in the fall of 1863 ten thousand people lived in the town (which included a Chinatown) while another twenty-five thousand lived in tiny communities that were strung along an eleven-mile stretch of the gulch. Most of these settlements have now disappeared, except for a restored Nevada City, once the second largest town in the area.

Approximately $30 million worth of gold was taken from Alder Gulch in the first three years. Miners began to leave the area in droves after gold was discovered at Last Chance Creek (modern Helena) in 1864, and by 1871 Virginia City's population had dropped to 867. The town was the territorial capital from 1865 to 1875. Many of the "temporary" buildings Allen speaks of remain today, thanks to the dry climate and the work of preservationists, with the result that both Virginia City and Nevada City have been acquired by the Montana Historical Society on behalf of the state of Montana. See Gillett 1993; Cramton 1932, 21–22.

11. The order of events in this paragraph has been altered from the original to provide an accurate chronology of the party's first activities in Virginia City.

12. "E. W." was undoubtedly Emily Wiswell, the daughter of a Philadelphia clergyman whom Peale married in 1875. Clara (b. 1851) was Peale's sister.

13. Allen's son, Frederick DeForest Allen (1844–97), graduated from Oberlin in

1863. A distinguished classical scholar, he received a Ph.D. in philosophy from the University of Leipzig in 1870, then taught Greek and classical philology at Harvard until his death. See *DAB*.

14. Placer gold is found in a free state after gold-bearing rock has been worn away by weather or glaciers or artificially washed away. By 1871 miners had begun to use hydraulic techniques to wash gold from the Alder Gulch gravels. Van West 1986, 193.

There is no official record of William Isaac Marshall (1840–1906) at Oberlin College. Marshall arrived in Montana Territory in July 1866 and resided in Virginia City until 1875. Reportedly, he acquired photographs taken by photographer Joshua Crissman during Hayden's 1871 and 1872 Yellowstone surveys. These, along with Marshall's own park photographs, were later sold for use in stereopticons. After moving to the East in the late 1870s, Marshall wrote and illustrated articles and delivered lectures on Yellowstone. He often returned to the park in summer and gave some of the earliest interpretive tours of the area. Whittlesey n.d., "Proper Presentation of the Park," 10–19.

15. "Pilgrim" was a commonly used western term referring to a new resident of an area.

16. Sidney Edgerton (1818–1900), a lawyer and Republican congressman from Ohio (1858–62), helped establish Montana Territory and became its first territorial governor in 1864. Benjamin Franklin Potts (1836–87) was born in Ohio, practiced law, and served as a Union brigadier general. A Republican, he served as governor of the territory from 1870 to 1883. See *DAB*.

17. Coleman Sellers (1827–1907) was a cousin of Peale's.

18. Judge William Y. Lovell, an early Montana pioneer, was probate judge of Madison County as of 1866. He died in Front Royal VA in 1894. Brian Shovers, Montana Historical Society reference librarian, letter to editor, July 15, 1997.

19. The party was heading for Fort Ellis (near Bozeman MT), where a wagon road connected Bozeman with Fort Benton.

20. George Kelly ("Dummy") was the driver of this ambulance.

21. Frank Deimling (d. 1887) had come to Virginia City with other soldiers under orders from President Ulysses Grant to protect miners from a threatened Indian uprising. When soldiers were no longer needed, Deimling stayed on and served for a time as secretary to Governor Potts and later was appointed postmaster.

22. The Meadow Creek Valley settlement had a post office from 1869 to 1883 and again from 1886 to 1908. Lutz 1986, 14.

23. The party was near the mining town of Sterling on Hot Springs Creek (three miles west of present Norris MT). More than five hundred people lived there in the

1860s, but by 1871 the area had been mined out and few people remained. Cheney 1984, 254.

24. Allen is probably attempting to use the Spanish name for these wheels, *arrastra*.

25. Located three hundred feet north (downstream) of the present Madison River bridge on the Bozeman-Norris Road, this bridge was built in 1870 by a Mr. Hayward and was in use until 1888. All that remains of it today are piers that can be seen along the river's edge. Madison County History Association 1982, 843–44; DeLacy map 1870.

26. Allen may have been confused about the name of the creek, for he later wrote "Willow" under "Got Beaver Wood on Elk Creek." According to maps of his day, a Willow Creek ran west of Elk Creek, in the area of the hot spring. On the other hand, he may have been identifying the wood as coming from a willow tree. Following this interlineation, Allen wrote a section he entitled "Observations on agricultural features of the country between Virginia [City] and Fort Ellis." This was recorded for Cyrus Thomas, who had left the party earlier, and it appears in appendix 3. Thomas later incorporated some of Allen's descriptions into his long published report, "Agricultural Resources of the Territories," which appeared as a separate section in Hayden's official report (Hayden 1872a, see esp. 260–61).

27. In his *Press* article Peale said he had been given a letter of introduction to Mr. Lown by "Mr. H. Blake," an attorney in Virginia City. Lown's mine, Red Bluff Lode, had been worked about six months. Peale wrote later that the ore was "principally a bright red jasper with particles of metallic gold disseminated throughout and plainly visible" (Hayden 1872a, 172).

28. The rivers at this junction are the Madison, Gallatin, and Jefferson. Both the Gallatin and the Madison were named in 1805 by members of the Lewis and Clark expedition for members of President Thomas Jefferson's cabinet: Albert Gallatin, secretary of the treasury, and James Madison, secretary of state and later president.

29. Bozeman, established in 1864, was named for John Bozeman, who guided the first train of immigrants into the Gallatin Valley. As the county seat of the valley, Bozeman grew as the need for food in the nearby Bannock and Alder Gulch mining camps brought about the development of ranches and farms in the area. Hayden notes in his report that "Bozeman is a pretty town with about five hundred inhabitants . . . surrounded on every side with well-cultivated and productive farms. It is most probable that within a short period the Northern Pacific Rail Road will pass down this valley, and then its beauty and resources will become apparent." Fort Ellis was built in 1867 to protect settlers and miners in the area from hostile Indians. Three to five companies were usually stationed there—both infantry and cavalry.

The fort was located on the west bank of the East Gallatin River, three miles east of Bozeman; it was abandoned in 1886. A plaque on Old Frontage Road now marks the fort's location. Hayden 1872a, 44; Cheney 1984, 31; Frazer 1965, 80; Cronin and Vick 1992, 30.

30. Allen added a question mark after "privilege." He did not know the government would retain its Preemption Act until 1891. This act allowed homesteaders to gain title to an additional 160 acres of land at the end of a six-month residence (instead of the usual five-year residency for the first 160 acres), by paying $1.25 an acre for it. They could then borrow on their title for additional improvements. As settlers moved into drier portions of the West, 160 acres proved too small for the extensive type of farming required there. Later, by making use of the Preemption Act and the Timber Culture Act (TCA) of 1873, homesteaders could acquire up to 480 acres of public land. The TCA required setting out trees on 40 acres (later reduced to 10) and maintaining them for ten years. My thanks to Karen Merrill, who familiarized me with the Preemption and Timber Culture Acts; Lamar 1977, 509, 639.

31. This section appears in Allen's fieldbook entry for the following day: July 11, 1871.

32. Allen refers to Deuteronomy 3:27, in which the Lord spoke to Moses, saying, "Get thee up into the top of Pisgah, and lift up thine eyes westward, and northward, and southward, and eastward, and behold it with thine eyes: for thou shalt not go over this Jordan."

33. Spring Canyon is about three miles east of the Fort Ellis site. Second Lieutenant Lovell H. Jerome and Captain Seneca Hughes Norton were among the officers in charge of the Second Cavalry, stationed at Fort Ellis. Both men had been trained at West Point. Dr. Archibald Barrington Campbell (d. 1878) was the post surgeon. Bonney and Bonney 1970, 28-29; Heitman 1903.

34. Edward Ball was captain of the Second Cavalry and temporarily in charge of Fort Ellis during the absence of Colonel E. M. Baker. Wives of officers lived with their husbands at most military forts.

35. Allen continued to keep his journal until he arrived back in Oberlin. His later entries reveal that he joined Thomas in Helena, and the two traveled together from there by stage to Corinne UT and then by train to California, where they both investigated and reported on irrigation systems. Thomas visited "suburbs of San Francisco, Oakland, and Sacramento," and Allen visited the San Jose Valley in the Santa Clara district. Allen's letter to Thomas, describing that valley's irrigation and vineyards and orchards, is included in Thomas's report, "Agricultural Resources of the Territories," published in Hayden's official report. Allen Journal, 1871; Hayden 1872a, 207-71.

36. Mystic Lake, located about twelve miles southeast of the Fort Ellis site, is the

source of the East Gallatin River. The party measured it as about "one fourth of a mile wide and three fourths of a mile long." Hayden claimed the group named the lake during this visit "on account of its great beauty, and being partially hidden." U.S. Department of the Interior, Geological Survey 1973, 44; Hayden 1872a, 47–48.

37. Thomas Moran's Yellowstone diary provides an unusually detailed entry describing his visit to Mystic Lake, in contrast to his later sketchy entries. Not mentioning Peale, he writes that after exploring the lake area the "party started back for camp excepting Jackson, Dixon, and myself, we having concluded to remain over until the next day for the purpose of photographing & sketching in the vicinity. . . . For the first time in my life I slept out in the open air." Moran Journal, 1871, YRL.

38. First Lieutenant Frank C. Grugan, along with Captain George L. Tyler, would head Hayden's military escort of forty men (of Company F, Second Cavalry) from Fort Ellis into Yellowstone territory (Peale, *Press*, July 29). Doane would not join the survey team until Aug. 8.

39. It is curious that Peale refers to his father only twice in his 1871 journal but frequently mentions writing his mother, Harriet Friel Peale (b. 1830). Harriet Peale lived in Philadelphia with Peale's sister, Clara. I thank historian Mike Foster, who alerted me to the custom at this time of sons writing travel letters to their mothers and not their fathers.

40. Captain David Porter Heap, a graduate of West Point, was decorated for gallantry during the Civil War and later served with the Corps of Engineers for the Department of Dakota. A specialist in astronomical observations, he was second in command of the Barlow expedition. Heitman 1903, 518.

Barlow and Heap brought with them three assistants: W. H. Wood (draftsman), H. G. Prout (assistant topographer and recorder), and Thomas J. Hine (photographer). Jackson later recalled that he knew Hine well and was aware of his "fine reputation as a landscape artist." Barlow's party had traveled by train from Chicago to Ogden and Corinne and then transferred to a Montana stage line that arrived four days later at Fort Ellis. While at the fort Barlow increased his party to eleven by hiring three civilian packers, two laborers, and one cook. Twelve riding animals were provided along with eleven pack animals. Although the Barlow party would sometimes share the large army escort accompanying the Hayden Survey, a six-man guard was also assigned specifically to it. Barlow's rank at the time of the expedition was captain. Hayden calls Barlow "colonel," probably referring to Barlow's honorary advancement to brevet lieutenant colonel on Mar. 13, 1865, for gallantry during the Civil War. Peale's more elevated title of "general" may indicate that he thought Barlow behaved in an imperious manner. Barlow and Heap 1872, 3–5; Heitman 1903, 19; Jackson 1929, 109.

5. FROM FORT ELLIS TO BOTTLER'S RANCH

1. Joe Clark was hired as a hunter and "José" as a hunter and expedition guide. Attempts to discover José's last name have been unsuccessful. Because of his familiarity with the Yellowstone area, José performed a very important role as a guide on the survey and deserves greater recognition. José may have been the "Mexican" who later hunted for the Crow Agency (then located ten miles east of present-day Livingston) and was killed by Sioux Indians in October 1873 just six hundred yards from the mission's school. Topping 1883, 99.

2. Material from the Philadelphia *Press* for this chapter appeared in the Aug. 11 issue. Peale dated his report July 23.

3. Barlow's party was held over because of a delay in the delivery of its baggage from Virginia City. Barlow and Heap 1872, 5.

4. The party was taking the route the Washburn expedition took the year before, following the valley of Trail Creek, which connects with today's Paradise Valley on the Yellowstone River. Offering spectacular scenery, the party's route can be followed approximately by car today by driving east from Bozeman on U.S. Highway 10 for eight and a half miles and then turning south on the Trail Creek Cutoff, a gravel road between U.S. 10 and 89. Bonney and Bonney 1970, 218.

5. Bottler's Ranch had been a hospitable way station for hunters, miners, and explorers since 1868, when Dutch brothers Frederick and Philip Bottler and a half-brother, Henry Henselbecker, took land in the Yellowstone Valley opposite Emigrant Peak. An active gold mining camp was then located across the river from the ranch at Emigrant Gulch (near present-day Chico Hot Springs). The miners provided a ready market for the brothers' vegetables, wheat, potatoes, meat, and fresh dairy products, all available at the ranch. The site of Bottler's Ranch is four miles south of Emigrant Post Office, on the west side of the river, and Highway 89, at the 27 mile marker. Bonney and Bonney 1970, 227-32; Haines 1977, 1:81. "Bottler" was spelled inconsistently for a number of years, but gradually the spelling became standardized as it appears in this note.

6. Blowflies had deposited their eggs on the antelope carcass.

7. The first of three Crow agencies was located on the south bank of the Yellowstone River ten miles east of Livingston, about four miles east of the Shield's River on today's Mission Creek. Its site is still evident from char, nails, glass, and the remains of building foundations. In his journal entry for July 16 Moran comments on this visit, writing: "Left camp on Trail Creek in company with Stephenson [*sic*], Jackson & Dummy for the Crow Agency. Stayed at the agency all night. We were each presented with a buffalo robe by Major Pease [Special Agent Fellows D. Pease]." Bonney and Bonney 1970, 42, 224; Haines, personal communication, Aug. 1998; Moran Journal, 1871; Topping 1883, 86.

8. This group sketched and photographed along its way through Yankee Jim Canyon and the next day at the Devil's Slide. The main party passed it on July 21, but the two groups met up later at Mammoth Hot Springs. Joshua Crissman was born July 29, 1833, in Madison OH and died in Los Angeles on Sept. 18, 1922. Crissman established photographic studios in several early western towns, and Jackson had already worked with him in Corinne during the summer of 1869. By 1871 Crissman was working in and around Bozeman, and he joined the Hayden expedition as a guest photographer at Fort Ellis and began working alongside Hine and Jackson. Many years later Jackson recalled that when they were busy photographing Yellowstone's Lower Falls at Artist Point, Crissman's camera was blown off a rock into the canyon. Because Jackson had an extra camera with him, he outfitted Crissman with it, along with other necessary equipment, so he might continue his work with the party. In 1872 Crissman was already in the park taking photographs when Hayden's second Yellowstone expedition arrived, and he joined the survey while it was there. Crissman continued to visit the park during summers through 1875. Many, if not all, of Crissman's Yellowstone photos were purchased by W. I. Marshall (see chap. 4, n.14), who sold them under his own name and used them for his illustrated lectures. Jackson 1929, 114–15; Hales 1988, 119, 313 n.40; Whittlesey in press. I am grateful to Steven B. Jackson, head of the Research and Collections Division and curator of Art and Photography at the Museum of the Rockies, Montana State University, for his carefully researched biographical information on Crissman.

9. The odometer wagon was a kind of go-cart made with two ambulance wagon wheels attached to a pair of long shafts about three feet apart. The shafts projected backward, forming handles so that the cart could be lifted off the ground. The odometer was placed on one of the wheels, and its revolutions determined mileage. The device frequently had to be lifted over fallen timber, and Peale complained that "it is no easy task to manage this arrangement; . . . often it becomes wedged between two trees, requiring the utmost strength to extricate it" (Peale, *Press*, Oct. 19, 1871).

10. Charles ("Charlie") Turnbull, another medical doctor on the survey team (besides Hayden, Peale, and Dixon), was in charge of the permanent camp at Bottler's Ranch. This group would periodically relay mail (from Fort Ellis) as well as food and supplies to Hayden's camps along the shores of Yellowstone Lake.

11. Hayden's party named this canyon Butter Keg Canyon, apparently for the butter cask Peale refers to in the next paragraph. But this name did not hold. Instead, a few years later it was named Yankee Jim Canyon, for James George, who was then operating a twenty-seven-mile toll road through the canyon, the only access to the park from the Lower Yellowstone. Bonney and Bonney 1970, 464–65.

12. One of the oldest place-names in Yellowstone, the Gardner River was probably named by fur trapper Johnson Gardner in the 1830s. It was called Warm Spring

Creek in the 1860s, but in 1870 the Washburn party reinstated the river's earlier name, misspelling it *Gardiner* (probably because Jim Bridger mispronounced the word). The name stayed that way until 1959, when it was officially changed back to its 1830s spelling. Whittlesey 1988b, 61.

13. Peale elaborates on this description in his account for Hayden's official report, saying, "The whole mass looked like some grand cascade that had been suddenly arrested in its descent and frozen" (Hayden 1872a, 174).

14. Peale's estimate doubles the actual height of the Liberty Cap, but it was corrected later in his *Press* report. This thirty-seven-foot phallus-like hot spring cone reminded Hayden of the peasant caps worn during the French Revolution, hence its name. Locally, it apparently was known by a cruder name that did not find its way into print. Both Hayden and Peale believed the formation to be an extinct geyser, but geologists now think it was once a flowing hot spring that became sealed off by travertine that accumulated at its top. It is estimated to be twenty-five hundred years old. Whittlesey 1988b, 87; Haines 1996, 63.

15. Hayden says more about this group: "Around these springs are gathered . . . a number of invalids, with cutaneous diseases, and they were most emphatic in their favorable expressions in regard to the sanitary effects. The most remarkable effect seems to be on persons afflicted with syphilitic diseases of long standing." This 160–acre spa had been claimed right before the Hayden party arrived, on July 5, 1871, by Harry Horr and James McCartney. They named the area Mammoth Hot Springs, for its size, that September. Hayden 1872a, 65; Haines 1996, 167–68. Questions about when McCartney and Horr began developing this area have plagued historians for some time. Retired park historian Aubrey Haines published the photograph of the Horr-McCartney bathhouses near Liberty Cap (see photo 30) and identified it as an 1871 Jackson photograph in volume 1 of his *Yellowstone Story* (1977). The negative used for Haines's photo is deposited at the Yellowstone Park Museum and is labeled "NPS 66–308." In the summer of 1998, Haines began to wonder whether this negative was misdated. He based this concern on several kinds of doubts, including whether Horr and McCartney could have had on-hand – as early as 1871 – the necessary tools to construct plank bath houses. By September, Haines believed that the negative had been taken at a later date, perhaps even by a photographer other than Jackson. He expressed his regret that he had "misled" me "and many other readers" by publishing this print.

Evidence, however, now seems to confirm the negative's 1871 date. Peale recollected the presence of bath huts at Mammoth in Hayden's Twelfth Report (1883, vol. 2, p. 37), saying: "In 1871, when we first visited [the springs], we found that several cabins had been erected, and that two men from Bozeman, Mont., had entered a claim to the springs. . . ."

Evidence from 1871 concurs: an article by "Semi-Occasional" (dateline, "Bozeman, July 7, 1871") appeared in the Helena *Rocky Mountain Weekly Gazette* on July 24, 1871, making it clear that log houses were being built for McCartney and Horr somewhere in the area of today's Clematis Gulch "to the right of . . . a huge monument [today's Liberty Cap]." Because this account was written two weeks before the Hayden party visited the site, it is likely that bathhouses were constructed by that time. Peale's several journal entries frequently refer to "the ranche," suggesting that buildings were available at the hot springs.

16. The peak was named for Truman Everts (1816–1901), a member of the Washburn expedition who achieved notoriety by being lost for thirty-seven days in the Yellowstone wilderness. Subsisting on thistle roots (now known as Everts Thistle) that he cooked in hot springs, he was found not near the mountain named after him but some seven miles east of Mammoth on the open slope of present-day Crescent Hill. In November 1871 he published his story, "Thirty Seven Days of Peril," in *Scribner's* 3, no.1, 1–17. Whittlesey 1988a, 100–103; see esp. Whittlesey 1995; Haines 1996, 83.

17. Possibly Sepulcher Mountain. Barlow named this 9,652-foot mountain "on account of its low black appearance." Whittlesey 1988b, 137.

18. Orange Spring Mound has received several names. It shows up on Hayden's first Yellowstone map as "Upper Geyser." On his 1878 map it appears as "Glenn Grotto." The "bath tubs" Peale describes are probably the numerous sediment-walled basins on the face of today's Jupiter Terrace, where one can choose the desired temperature at many places. I am grateful to Aubrey Haines for his identification of this area.

19. At this point in his journal Peale includes the temperatures of a number of springs found in this area. For the complete list, see Hayden 1872a, 175–76.

20. Barlow writes of this incident in his published report: the men killed "a large brown bear and three cubs. The latter were brought in and served our mess with delicious steaks for several meals." Barlow and Heap 1872, 11.

21. Nebraska Bill was one of the invalids staying at the ranch.

22. According to Barlow, the group had explored "the high red topped mountain to the south west of the Springs [Bunsen Peak] climbing over rocks and through thickets, and crossing mountain torrents . . . we felt repaid for our labor in observing the grand scenery upon our route." It was a fatiguing trip that included some climbing when "the ascent was so steep that we were compelled to cling to projecting rocks in many places to prevent sliding back to the bottom." Barlow erroneously reported that it was in this area that Truman Everts had been found the previous summer. Barlow and Heap 1872, 10.

23. Peale's *Press* account of Mammoth Hot Springs became the first widely read

description of this area. The Washburn expedition missed the area in 1870, as had the Cook, Folsom, and Peterson expedition in 1869. Hayden's party may have learned about the hot springs from the Bottler brothers or from Joe Clark and José, who also seemed familiar with the area. As early as 1867 a company of Montana's Territorial Militia followed the Yellowstone River as far as these hot springs. By 1871 the hot springs were becoming well known for their healing powers by people living in the area. In fact, Hayden's party missed (by only two days) a group of men who, according the July 24 *Gazette* account, were "met with a hearty reception from the denizens of that impromptu village — Chestnutville." This short-lived tent "city" was named for a Colonel J. D. Chestnut of Bozeman. Area residents were clearly anticipating the arrival of more visitors to the springs. By early August 1871 Chestnutville was being developed by Matthew McGuirk, who had erected a cabin, built bathing pools, and put in a garden. A year later, when Peale returned with another Hayden survey, he reported that McGuirk had added two new bath houses, three new log houses, and a number of tents, accommodating twenty to thirty people who were there "for the benefit of their health." One of the men bathing at Chestnutville in 1871 was Yellowstone prospector A. Bart Henderson, who, when he left (on July 24), headed straight for Bottler's Ranch and in August began preparing a road to "run from Bozeman to the Yellowstone Lake, by the Mammoth Hot Springs." Henderson wanted the road built "for the benefit of the travel to & from Wonderland, & to be a toll road." Haines 1974, 105–6; Haines 1977, 1:144, 349 n.128; Haines 1996, 63, 221; Peale Journal, July 28, 1872.

6. TO TOWER FALLS

1. The mountain Peale refers to is present-day Mt. Everts. Its cap is composed of rhyolite, not basalt.

2. The name of this plateau derives from the small creek, Blacktail Deer Creek, that runs through it. Prospectors named this creek before 1870, and its name first appeared in print on Barlow's 1871 map. Whittlesey 1988b, 26.

3. After Tyler's unsuccessful search, Barlow himself began searching for his party. He discovered "that they had obeyed their instructions, deviated from the direction taken by the doctor's party, and followed the course of Blacktail Deer Creek to the eastward and had struck across the valley of the Yellowstone." Finally reunited at dusk with his party at its campsite, about a mile and a half from the Yellowstone River, Barlow reported that he "had ridden thirty miles though the train had marched but seventeen." Barlow and Heap 1872, 11–22.

4. The bridge was Baronett's Bridge. See chap. 9, n.12.

5. Peale's *Press* account, written at Yellowstone Lake on July 30, summarized his journal entries from July 24 through July 30. It appeared in print on Aug. 29.

6. In 1869 the Cook-Folsom party described "the smell of sulphur, the delicate frost-like sulphur crystals, and the rising steam" and discovered that the hardened black liquid was pure enough sulfur to burn when ignited. Researchers in the 1930s found the park's highest percentage of hydrogen sulfide gas at Calcite Springs. Whittlesey 1988b, 30.

7. For his *Press* article, Peale adjusted this elevation to 10,000 feet. Identified as Elephant Back Mountain on the 1859–60 Raynolds expedition map, it is probably the best-known Yellowstone mountain. Its main peak is measured today at an elevation of 10,243 feet. It was named for General Henry Dana Washburn by members of his party after he made the first recorded climb of the mountain, on Aug. 28, 1870. Whittlesey 1988b, 107.

8. This "small range of snow covered mountains" was probably the Teton Range. Hayden confirms this in his account of the same view from Mt. Washburn. The Absaroka Range (forming the eastern boundary of what is now Yellowstone National Park) had been called the Yellowstone Mountains or the Snowy Range by trappers and explorers in the 1860s and 1870s. Hayden 1872a, 80; Whittlesey 1988b, 13.

9. The falls are measured today at 308 feet, and thus Peale's calculation of their height was off by nearly 100 feet. Robert Adams described this descent for the *Inquirer* but neglected to acknowledge Peale's role in the adventure: "Mr. Elliot[t], our artist, performed the daring and hazardous feat of descending the canyon, wishing to gain the best position for his sketch. This he accomplished by means of lariats tied together. . . . It is to his energy we owe the measurement of the depth of the valley by barometrical reading." The photographers also took risks to obtain their photos of Lower Falls, descending several times into the canyon with their cameras strapped to their backs. Jackson identified present Grand View as the site where Moran sketched details for his famous painting, *The Grand Cañon of the Yellowstone* (completed in 1872). Art historian and Moran scholar Joni Kinsey disagrees with Jackson's recollection and argues that Moran's vantage point for this painting was based on a compilation of a series of points of view from around the canyon. Kinsey believes Moran relied on Jackson's canyon photos and his own on-site drawings made from several widely separated vantage points. Kinsey 1992, 54, 55; Moran Sketchbooks, YRL.

10. Peale's explanation for the yellow colors in the canyon is incorrect. Hydrothermically altered rhyolite (called limonite) is responsible for the yellow coloration.

11. Hayden determined correctly that this valley was "once the bed of a great lake," of which the present Yellowstone Lake "is only a remnant." There is disagreement, however, over who named the valley for Hayden and when. S. P. Panton, a railroad surveyor, wrote that the earl of Dunraven named the valley for Hayden when he

toured Yellowstone in 1874, but William H. Holmes (1846–1933), artist and geologist on Hayden surveys from 1872 to 1878, claimed that he named the valley for Hayden. Haines 1977, 1:146; Whittlesey 1988b, 70.

12. Today Crater Hills contains five individually named features: Sulphur Spring, Locomotive Jet, Turbid Blue Mud Spring, Blue Mud Pot, and Foam Spring. In 1867 prospectors visited this area and named it Hell. Descriptions of the area became exaggerated over time as stories circulated about the Yellowstone country before its recorded discoveries in the 1869, 1870, and 1871 expeditions. Whittlesey 1988b, 345.

13. This camp was located near the outlet of the Yellowstone River on the northwest shore of the lake, "in a beautiful grassy meadow or opening among the dense pines." The name "Lake View" has since been given to a different view. Hayden 1872a, 96.

14. The name of the boat first appeared as *Annie*, but in later woodcut engravings done after the survey the name became *Anna*. The engraving (used as an illustration in Hayden's published report) was based on Jackson's photograph of the boat, on which the name *Annie* appears to have been added later by hand. In his report Hayden claimed that Stevenson named the boat for Anna Dawes, daughter of the "Hon. H. L. Dawes . . . [*who*] had contributed so much toward securing the appropriation which allowed [us] to explore this marvelous region." Not mentioned was the fact that Anna Dawes was also the sister of survey member Chester Dawes, who is pictured with Stevenson in the boat (see photo 34). Robert Adams, however, wrote a report to the *Philadelphia Inquirer* at the time of the boat's launching, saying that the boat was named "*Annie*" and that "no one knew for whom it was named." Thus, perhaps *Annie* was initially named in fun for Chester Dawes's sister (the party bestowed other place-names for sisters and sweethearts; for instance, "Mary Bay") and Hayden only later recognized the political potential of formally honoring Henry Dawes's daughter. The change to *Anna* may have come about because *Annie* seemed too familiar a name for a prominent congressman's daughter. Hayden 1872a, 96; Adams, *Philadelphia Inquirer*, Sept. 8, 1871.

15. The lake is currently measured at an elevation of 7,731 feet.

16. Stevenson reported that one of the first things that he and Elliott spotted was "the track of a bear." He claimed that its dimensions "indicated one of the largest of his kind. On alighting from the boat and looking around, numerous tracks were observed of the same animal; also those of wolf, elk, deer, rabbit, and evidence of a variety of smaller quadrupeds, such as mice, moles, etc." Stevenson and Elliott intended to explore the island, "but the great number of dangerous animals that appeared to infest it, and the difficulty of penetrating the dense jungle which overspread it, deterred us from making an attempt." Instead, they circled the island by

boat and landed on the western shore, where they discovered a spearhead of white flint and concluded that "Indians had once been present." Norton 1873, 37–38.

17. This attack took place in the Gallatin Valley. Two (not three) men were killed and two to three hundred head of cattle and horses run off. Two companies of cavalry from Fort Ellis and some five hundred people from the valley started in pursuit. The *Philadelphia Inquirer* reported: "The Indians are supposed to belong to a band of Sioux under Sitting Bull, the main body of which camped below Yellowstone and Powder Rivers. They are not treaty Indians, belong to no reservation. . . . Further trouble is expected" (Aug. 5, 1871).

7. THE GEYSER BASINS

1. Hayden's small party was heading for the Firehole River and the geyser basins. In later published accounts of this trip Hayden rarely mentions Barlow's party as fellow explorers of this area. In these accounts Hayden identifies only himself, Schönborn, Elliott, and Peale as members of his party, and he claims they had no guide. Not only did José act as their hunter-guide, but the party was also piloted by two hunters (whom Hayden's men had met the previous day) who were journeying toward the geyser basins on a trapping expedition. Hayden's reliance on the trappers' shortcut (by way of today's Bridge Creek and Beach Lake to Spruce Creek) turned out to be a mistake. Barlow and his party fared far better by striking out immediately for the Hayden Valley and Mary Mountain, where the routes were less obstructed by fallen timber. Hayden 1872a, 101; Hayden 1872c, 394–95; Barlow and Heap 1872, 19–20; Haines 1977, 1:148.

2. The *Press* carried Peale's report on the geyser basins in its Oct. 19 issue. Peale wrote the report from Yellowstone Lake, although he did not date it. He undoubtedly completed it on Aug. 7, and it summarized the period from July 31 to Aug. 7.

3. In their published writings both Hayden and Barlow refer to present Nez Percé Creek as the "East fork of the Madison."

4. Now out of meat, the party was relying on game procured by José. They may not have realized that Yellowstone's hot daytime temperatures, as well as swarms of flies in the area's wet lowlands, drove large game into deeper shade as well to the cooler temperatures of higher elevations. Moreover, the presence of Hayden's and Barlow's large party undoubtedly frightened away animals.

5. This campsite is described in Hayden 1872a, 103–4, 182, and shown on Hayden's 1883 map of the Lower Geyser Basin (inserted after p. 178 in his Twelfth Report). The reports by Hayden and Barlow about the Lower Geyser Basin were the first detailed and scientific accounts of the thermal features of this area. Although the Washburn party had visited there briefly in September 1870, Doane provided only a

short, general description, concentrating instead on the more dramatic hydrothermal features of the Upper Geyser Basin. See Bonney and Bonney 1970, 367–68.

6. Peale was the first scientist to record the temperatures of Yellowstone's geysers and hot springs and to chemically analyze their deposits. He determined the temperatures of about three hundred thermal features in the Lower Basin alone and concluded that there were two kinds of deposits in the area's thermal features: calcareous and siliceous. Except for Mammoth Hot Springs, most of the material deposited in Yellowstone's thermal features is siliceous because the main rock type through which hot underground water passes is rhyolite, a rock rich in silica. At Mammoth, however, Peale found that deposited material was composed primarily of calcium carbonate because there the underground water passes through thick beds of limestone. Peale, *Press*, Oct. 19, 1871; Hayden 1872a, 175–88; Keefer 1976, 77.

7. The Washburn party had already given the name "Giant" to one of Yellowstone's more powerful geysers in the Upper Basin. Hayden undoubtedly later realized that his party had created a second "Giant," and he subsequently changed the name to "Architectural Fountain"; in 1872 he renamed it the "Great Fountain." Apparently, Hayden's party was unsure of its location, especially in relation to the Upper Geyser Basin described in Doane's journal. Barlow wrote on Aug. 2: "I was now satisfied that I had entered the Firehole Valley below or to the north of the great geysers, and decided to move to the south in search of them. [I left] directions for camp to move across the plain about 2.5 miles and locate near the geyser hill." Barlow and Heap 1872, 22; Whittlesey 1988b, 66–67.

8. That day, Hayden, Schönborn, and Barlow visited and named the Twin Buttes, about ten miles west of camp. They are almost identical in shape and about six hundred feet high. Barlow and Hayden climbed the southern butte to survey the surrounding valley and ascertain their location in relation to the Upper Geyser Basin. Barlow and Heap 1872, 22–23; Whittlesey 1988a.

9. In his published report Peale says these were the only sulfur springs in the region, "although the amount of sulphur present . . . was not great" (Hayden 1872a, 183). Hayden also reported that silica predominates in the Firehole Basin and that there "was very little, if any, lime. Sulphur occurs in very small quantities in the lower basin, although there were two or three springs the orifices of which were lined with it" (Hayden 1872b, 170).

10. "Hell" was often used by early trappers as a description of areas with numerous boiling hot springs. Hell Fire Stew was undoubtedly stew cooked over the hot springs adjacent to the Firehole River.

11. Part of the journal page is missing here. In an early transcription (presumably when the original page was intact) the words "mud springs" were supplied for this missing portion.

12. Fairy Falls is the fourth highest named waterfall in the park. Barlow and Hayden discovered it while observing the area from the Twin Buttes. After an arduous hike to the foot of the falls Barlow named it "Fairy Falls" because of "the graceful beauty with which the little stream dropped down a clear descent." Aubrey Haines adds, "Barlow's photographer, Thomas J. Hine, photographed the waterfall, marking the print (one of the sixteen that survived the great Chicago fire) 'Fall of the Fairies.' " Barlow and Heap 1872, 23; Whittlesey 1988b, 54; Haines, personal communication, Aug. 1998.

13. Located in what is now named the Midway Geyser Basin, Grand Prismatic Spring is Yellowstone's largest hot spring in diameter. Osborn Russell, a fur trapper, described it in his 1839 journal, making it the earliest described thermal feature in the park. Peale named it "Prismatic" in 1878, "on account of the brilliant coloring displayed in it." At that time Peale was making a point of checking the spring's colors to determine whether Moran's 1871 sketches of it were "a little too bright." His visit confirmed "the truthfulness of [Moran's] pictures . . . the colors cannot be exaggerated." Hayden 1883, 180–81; Whittlesey 1988b, 65–66.

14. The cascade is actually lined with colorful cyanobacteria, not sesquioxide of iron. Lee Whittlesey, personal communication, spring 1997.

15. For Doane's account of the Washburn party's time in the Upper Geyser Basin, see Bonney and Bonney 1970, 340–59. Peale (and probably Hayden) arrived in camp considerably *after* Elliott observed and sketched this powerful geyser eruption. The party named the geyser the Grand Geyser. Hayden and Peale observed it in action (by moonlight) the following night. Their later published reports incorrectly describe the Aug. 4 eruption on a firsthand basis. Hayden 1872a, 116; Peale, *Press*, Oct. 19, 1871; Hayden 1883, 2:212.

16. As mentioned in note 14, cyanobacteria creates the red color.

17. Hayden's party saw the Giant's crater but did not observe the geyser erupting — a disappointment since it was the highlight of the Washburn party's time in the Upper Basin. Barlow remained another day at the Upper Basin hoping to see more geyser action. His delay paid off, for the party observed both the Giant and Grotto geysers erupting, leading Barlow to conclude that "the wonders of this valley can only be obtained by long and patient investigation during the whole season, by a corps of observers stationed at several points in the basin . . . [who] record every phenomenon attending each spring." Today's geyser gazers would heartily agree. Barlow and Heap 1872, 25.

18. Today the elevation of this geyser area is calculated at 7,365 feet.

19. Barlow's party was encamped across from Hayden's on the south side of the Firehole River. Hayden 1872a, 116.

20. Barlow and his party stayed on, hoping to photograph the Comet Geyser in

eruption. They were unsuccessful, for the Comet erupted at night. His party did measure and successfully photograph Old Faithful and the Giant in eruption, neither of which Jackson was able to photograph during his visit there later. Hayden's party left the geyser basins on Aug. 6. Although Hayden featured both the Upper and Lower Basins in his official report as well as his later published articles, he and his small party observed thermal features only during the evening of Aug. 4, the day and evening of the 5th, and the morning of the 6th. They saw only two of the great geysers in action (the Grand and Old Faithful). Jackson's one day at the Upper Basin on the 8th resulted in only one photograph of an erupting geyser, the Grotto. The Washburn party had been luckier, for its members saw eruptions of the Giant, Beehive, Castle, Old Faithful, Fan, and Grotto. In fact, for their official reports of this area, Peale and Hayden had to rely on Doane's journal descriptions of hydrothermal displays. Nevertheless, Hayden's party did discover and name the Grand, as well as a number of smaller geysers and springs. Peale recorded the temperatures of 104 springs and geysers in the Upper Basin and collected, examined, and reported on their water chemistry and the makeup of their exterior deposits. Bonney and Bonney 1970, 358–62; Hayden 1872a, 185; Peale, *Press*, Oct. 19, 1871.

21. The party was crossing the continental divide somewhere in the vicinity of Norris Pass. The small lake was probably Scaup Lake.

22. Heart Lake is about nine miles southeast of Shoshone Lake. Later, in his report of the trip, Peale referred to the lake he visited this day as "Madison Lake" (one of Shoshone Lake's earlier names along with "DeLacy/deLacy Lake" and "Washburn Lake"). Doane's map (1870), as well as the 1871 Barlow and Hayden maps of the area, shows *two* large lakes between Yellowstone Lake and the Firehole Basin, when there is actually only one. The name "Madison Lake" designated a very small lake that was erroneously thought to be the head of the Madison River. The name "Shoshone" was attached to the far bigger lake. It is the park's second largest lake and is the source of the Lewis River, which flows to the Pacific Ocean by way of the Snake River. Bonney and Bonney 1970, 401; Whittlesey 1988b, 93, 138.

23. This small lake may have been the mysterious Lost Lake that has evaded discovery for decades, leading to a disagreement between park historians Aubrey Haines and Lee Whittlesey as to whether it ever existed at all. Whittlesey believes it did and, "like other glacier lakes, [since Hayden's visit] filled in with vegetation." Hayden observed that the lake had no outlet and was "simply a depression which receives the drainage of the surrounding hills." He calculated that the lake was about two miles long and one wide and further observed that the water was not clear and cold as in other mountain lakes. Named in 1885, Lost Lake appeared on park maps after 1871, placed on or near both sides of the continental divide in the vicinity of Norris Pass. Up until 1939, fishermen and rangers described the lake in documents

held now in the park archives. When Aubrey Haines served as assistant park engineer, however, he worked extensively in the area of the lake's reported location and found no evidence of its having existed. Furthermore, Haines contends that a 1956 aerial survey of the West Thumb area failed to disclose the existence of any such filled-in lake. Aerial photogrammetry, he argues, "is quite capable of differentiating a vegetation-choked pond from a meadow grass, a sage-brush flat, or a lodgepole forest." The identity of the small lake mentioned by Peale and described by Hayden remains unresolved. Whatever it was or is, it clearly existed at the time Hayden's small party camped on its shore. Hayden 1872a, 127; Whittlesey 1988b, 91; Haines 1996, 124–26, 244–45.

24. Peale continues to misidentify Shoshone Lake as Heart Lake in his journal text.

25. Base camp at Yellowstone Lake had been moved south by those in the party who had not accompanied Hayden and Barlow to the geyser basins. It was located on the West Thumb of Yellowstone Lake, south of the hot springs area. Hayden 1872a, 127.

26. Half of Hayden's military escort (including Lieutenant Grugan and Captain Tyler) was being sent back to protect a group of Northern Pacific engineers traveling through Sioux country near Bozeman (*Philadelphia Inquirer*, Aug. 5, 1871; Peale, *Press*, Oct. 19, 1871). Doane had been unable to join Hayden's party until Aug. 6 or 7 (because of an assignment in St. Paul MN; see Bonney and Bonney 1970, 30). Just when Jackson and Moran left for the geyser basin is unclear. Barlow's report places Doane at the Upper Geyser Basin on the morning of Aug. 8, when Barlow and his party were heading for base camp at the lake. Peale's statement that Jackson, Doane, and Smith had left base camp by the time he and the Hayden party returned there on Aug. 7 conflicts with Moran's journal entry for Aug. 8: "Set out with Jackson, Smith and the Escort across the country for the Geysers in Fire Hole River, led by Doane. Struck the river 9 miles below the Geysers & camped." The following day, Aug. 9, Moran records: "Went to the Geysers. Helped Jackson during the day & returned by myself to Camp." According to Peale's entry for Aug. 8, Jackson returned to base camp at the West Thumb of the lake that night. Years later a recollection by Jackson adds only more confusion to these events. He writes that from the "far end of the 'Thumb' of the Lake . . . I took a small party over to the Fire Hole. . . . We had but one day and confined our visit to the Upper basin only. My photographic work was limited to details of formations about the geyser cones and but one of them — the Grotto — was caught in eruption" (Jackson Recollection, n.d., 12–14, NYPL). Jackson's account omits any mention of Doane or Moran in his small party, let alone Doane's leading them. Furthermore, even with Doane's knowledge of the area from his experiences with the Washburn expedition the year before, it is doubtful

that Doane and Jackson could have made the trip, taken photographs, and returned to camp all in one day, as they would have had to do if they left, as Moran states, on Aug. 8.

Peale's journal account seems to supply the best timeline: Doane probably arrived at the West Thumb on the 6th and started for the Upper Geyser Basin on the morning of the 7th with Jackson, Moran, Smith, and most of the escort. They camped (as Moran describes) nine miles below the Fire Hole River, and the next day (Aug. 8) Jackson and Moran worked together at the geyser basin and, with Doane, met up with Barlow's small party, which was returning to base camp. Later in the afternoon Moran joined the escort at its campground and the next morning headed with it for Fort Ellis. Doane may have accompanied Barlow to base camp or joined Smith and Jackson later in the afternoon when they headed back to base camp at the West Thumb. Doane did not meet up with Hayden until the 9th, back at Yellowstone Lake.

27. Park archivist Lee Whittlesey notes that Winter Spring is the only lake spring where the top water is hot and lower water is cold.

28. Hayden overlooks the fact that Native Americans may have used some kind of boat on Yellowstone Lake. During the Washburn expedition Doane reported that on Sept. 4, 1870, "we built a raft for the purpose of attempting to visit [the islands of Yellowstone Lake], but the strong waves of the lake dashed it to pieces in an hour" (Bonney and Bonney 1970, 301).

29. Doane was probably depending on his hand-drawn map of the area, which was not published at the time of his official report (spring 1871). Orrin and Lorraine Bonney discovered Doane's map, buried for almost ninety years "in confidential army files" at the National Archives. They reproduced it for the first time in their book on Doane, *Battle Drums and Geysers*, along with an original tracing of Washburn's own map that they discovered at park headquarters in Mammoth Hot Springs. A published form of Washburn's map would have been available to Hayden, for it appeared in the May 1871 issue of *Scribner's Monthly*, accompanying Nathaniel Langford's article, "The Wonders of Yellowstone." Bonney and Bonney 1970, 399-400.

30. Hayden miscalculated the elevation of Yellowstone Lake. On his official map its elevation appears as 7,427 feet. It is now officially listed as 7,733 feet.

31. Today people who fish for cutthroat trout in Yellowstone Lake still find some infested with tapeworms (*Diprobothrium cordiseps*). Based on specimens sent him from the survey, naturalist Joseph Leidy described, illustrated, and named these tapeworms in a short piece written for Hayden's report: "Notice of Some Worms Collected during Professor Hayden's Expedition to the Yellowstone . . ." (Hayden 1872a, 381-82). Aubrey Haines points out that there are "no worms in the Yel-

lowstone River trout *below* the falls; the pelicans on Yellowstone Lake are responsible for the worms — an alternate host relationship" (personal communication, Aug. 1998).

32. The Raynolds party thought it had discovered a new species of snowshoe rabbit in the Wind River Mountains in June 1860 although the sex of the specimen could not be determined. Hayden was probably instrumental in naming the species *Lepus bairdii* after Spencer Baird. During Hayden's second survey to Yellowstone, C. Hart Merriam reported that he was fortunate to have secured five specimens of this "rare and remarkable rabbit." According to Merriam, "all the males have teats and take part in suckling their young." Because no females were found among the specimens, Merriam thought this species might be a "hermaphroditic form" but later discovered during dissection that although the males contained the usual genital organs, there were no uterus, ovaries, or other female organs. These "rare" rabbits turned out to be typical snowshoe hares that raise their young in a fairly normal manner. Hayden 1873b, 667–68; Bartlett 1962, 72. I am indebted to historian Bill Resor, of Jackson WY, for calling my attention to the Hayden reference.

33. This letter was stamped "received" on Aug. 26.

8. On and around Yellowstone Lake

1. This baseline was part of a rudimentary triangulation process the party would use to determine distances and elevations at different points beyond the lake. According to Hayden's later topographer, Henry Gannett, Hayden did not begin using more sophisticated triangulation methods until 1872. Hayden 1883, 1:458–59.

2. See chap. 7, n.26. Both groups were returning from the Upper Geyser Basin. Edward Osborn Dunning probably met up with one of these groups after leaving Fort Ellis with the latest mail for the survey party. Dunning's full name is found in Heitman 1903, 389.

3. Guns were fired as a way of indicating location.

4. Hayden wrote that "on the night of August 9, we camped at the main bay, west of Flat Mountain." Mt. Sheridan, situated farther to the southwest, had been named Yellow Mountain in 1870 by Doane, then Red Mountain by Hayden in 1871 (a name that was ultimately transferred to the whole range). Barlow changed the mountain's name to Sheridan (in honor of his superior, General Philip H. Sheridan, 1831–88) after climbing the peak on Aug. 10, 1871. Hayden 1872a, 131; Whittlesey 1988b, 107; Barlow and Heap 1872, 32.

5. Barlow and his party separated from the Hayden party on Aug. 10 and first explored the area of Heart Lake, then followed a course fifteen or twenty miles southeast to the valley of the upper Yellowstone River. During this time they named three mountains: Sheridan, Hancock, and Humphreys (the last-named is now Turret

Mountain; the name "Mt. Humphreys" was transferred in 1878 by Hayden to a peak east of Yellowstone Lake in the Absaroka Range). Barlow wished to explore the headwaters and tributaries of the Snake River and the valley of the upper Yellowstone River. He also wanted to assess the feasibility of a road, or railroad, "to connect Yellowstone Lake south to [the] Snake River [in] the direction of the Tetons." Barlow and Heap 1872, 33–37; Whittlesey 1988b, 105.

6. Camped near Heart Lake, both Peale and Hayden mistakenly believed they had found the head of the Snake River. Later, in his official report, Peale revised this opinion and stated that the party was camped "on one of the small streams that contributes to form the Snake River." The source of the Snake was debated for many years. The difficulty was to single out the longest branch in Two Ocean Plateau, an area thoroughly interlaced with streams. Today's maps show the head of the Snake to be about three miles north of Phelps Pass, inside present Yellowstone Park boundaries. Peale, "Yellowstone Lake, Showing the Watershed of the Snake, Madison, and Yellowstone Rivers" (map), 1871; Hayden 1872a, 189; Whittlesey 1988b, 142.

7. Peale's *Press* report was written Sept. 2, 1871, at Fort Ellis and appeared in print Oct. 25, 1871.

8. Bridger's Lake and Bridger's River first appeared on Father Pierre Jean DeSmet's 1851 map of the Yellowstone region with information supplied by Bridger himself. Hayden's campsite appeared so-named in his official report's Meteorological Table (except it appears as "Bridger," p. 514). The river was also sometimes referred to as "Bridger's Creek." Hayden, however, labeled it on his map "the Upper Yellowstone River." The USGS later dropped this name because it did not recognize this portion of the stream as separate from the river north of the lake. Haines 1977, 1:85; Haines 1996, 30–31.

9. Hayden and this small party, guided by Doane, were starting up the valley of the Yellowstone "for the purpose of making a careful geological as well as topographical survey of the district bordering the great divide" (Two Ocean Pass). They would follow the upper Yellowstone River as far south as today's Bridger Lake (although later Hayden, curiously, denied the lake's existence). Bridger Lake is outside today's park boundary. Like Barlow, Hayden believed there were "many points on the south rim of the basin where a [rail]road could be made with ease into the valley of [the] Snake River." Hayden mistakenly noted in his official report that he left on this excursion on Aug. 12; according to other reports, he left on Aug. 13. Hayden 1872a, 132–36; Bonney and Bonney 1970, 36, 521.

10. The soldier was Private Daniel Starr, who would later accompany Doane on his 1876–77 Snake River exploration. Doane described Starr as "a man of powerful voice and massive form . . . of infinite jest and humor, and reckless beyond all descrip-

tion" (Bonney and Bonney 1970, 455). The fire was built to signal Elliott and Carrington, on the lake, to the party's new campground.

11. Peale, in his official report, described Camp Hovey as located "in one of the small prairies so numerous on this side of the lake." It was probably located near today's Signal Point. Hayden 1872a, 189.

12. The survey's observation record cites "hazy," "smoky," or "very smoky" skies from Aug. 15 to Sept. 27. Hayden 1872a, 514–17.

13. Steve Hovey was alerting the pack train (returning from Bottler's Ranch) to the party's new campsite on the east shore of the lake.

14. This is Brimstone Basin, on Alluvium Creek, first named by Doane in 1870. Whittlesey 1988b, 29.

15. Located just south of present Mt. Doane, this mountain was named by Hayden for his assistant, James Stevenson. Its elevation is 10,352 feet. Whittlesey 1988b, 107.

16. Here Peale has written in the margin: "Mt. Stevenson is 11,100 ft. high." He later changed this estimate to 12,650 feet for his *Press* report. Apparently, neither Doane nor Hayden knew that the Washburn party had already named a mountain after Doane, and it appears on today's park maps as an unnamed peak (elevation 10,149 feet), just north of Colter Peak. Hayden's Mt. Doane (elevation 10,656 feet) retains its official name and is at the head of Rocky Creek, east of Yellowstone Lake. Whittlesey 1988b, 103, 106; Peale, *Press*, Oct. 25, 1871; Washburn's 1870 map is reproduced in Bonney and Bonney 1970.

17. The "Mary Bay" that Peale describes was east and south of Steamboat Point. In 1878 the Hayden Survey transferred the name to the bay north of Steamboat Point. It was named after Mary Force, a friend of Elliott's. Whittlesey 1988b, 95.

18. Hayden believed Yellowstone's hot springs and geysers are the closing stages (in effect, the escape valves) of earlier volcanic eruptions. He reported that the earthquake felt on July 20 was also felt by two other groups, "fifteen to twenty-five miles distant, on different sides of the lake." Such earthquake activity, he noted, was not uncommon and could be very severe at some seasons of the year, according to what he had heard from mountain men of the area. Hayden also reported that Indians cited the frequency of earthquakes in the region "as the reason why they seldom or never visit this portion of the country." Hayden 1872b, 162.

19. By the time Peale wrote up this experience for the *Press*, he was better able to organize the episode. He identifies the two men who searched for the mule as Jack Baronett and one of the soldiers. Barlow does not mention that Baronett had joined his party or that Baronett and the soldier had actually seen Indians prowling about their former camp. Barlow and Heap 1872, 38.

20. Some anthropologists claim that Sheepeaters were much better off than other

Shoshones; that even without horses, they were highly skilled hunters who used dogs as pack animals for hunting bighorn sheep and other large game. Many Sheepeaters left Yellowstone in 1871 when Shoshone chief Washakie invited them to settle on Wyoming's Wind River Indian Reservation. Janetski 1987, 39–55; Schullery 1997, 24–26; Whittlesey 1988b, 138.

21. This was one of the mud springs at Camellia Mudpots. Whittlesey 1988b, 31.

9. PELICAN VALLEY

1. Inserted material is from Peale's report to the *Press*, written at Fort Ellis on Sept. 2 and published Oct. 25. Although Peale refers in his journal to writing a later report for the *Press*, it does not show up in later issues.

2. Hayden's men were probably the first white people to discover this small lake on the high divide (Mirror Plateau) between the present Lamar River and the Yellowstone River. Whittlesey 1988b, 99.

3. Two species of pine tree in Yellowstone produce pinenuts: white bark pine and limber pine.

4. Late summer fires are frequent in Yellowstone. The devastating Yellowstone fires of 1988 were the greatest in recorded history.

5. This mountain is most likely the Thunderer, elevation 10,554 feet. Hayden later reported the elevation as 10,950 feet. Hayden 1872a, 138; Peale, *Press*, Sept. 2, 1871.

6. Petrified wood abounds in this area, especially at higher elevations in and around the fossil forest located on Specimen Ridge. Here twenty-seven different forest layers are buried in breccia, ash, and dust from nearby volcanoes that erupted fifty million years ago. Peale was probably finding silicified wood in conglomerate rocks near and in the creek. Hayden believed the wood became embedded "in volcanic cement . . . thrown out of the active craters with the fragments of basalt." Keefer 1976, 28; Hayden 1872a, 138.

7. Peale described this campground in greater detail for Hayden's official report, saying it was located in a wide open valley a few miles above the junction of the north and south branches of the east fork. The campground was probably north of the confluence of Cache Creek (Peale's "south fork") with today's Lamar River at the plateau where Soda Butte Creek (Peale's "north fork") also joins the Lamar. Peale also reported that he obtained in an area stream "good specimens of agate, quartz, and chalcedony. Some were in the form of geodes, and contained opal in the center." Hayden 1872a, 190.

8. Named by prospector A. Bart Henderson in July 1870, Soda Butte is an extinct hot spring of travertine, resembling the Liberty Cap at Mammoth Hot Springs. Today it measures closer to 30 feet high. Hayden described the cone as "a curious mammiform mound . . . a complete ruin . . . [and] a fine example of the tendency

of the cone to close up its summit in its dying stages." Hayden 1872a, 138; Haines 1996, 57–58.

9. Hayden 1872a, 138. A later visitor to the spring likened its "horrible" taste of "acid, sulphur, and saline" to a "diabolic julep of lucifer matches, bad eggs, vinegar, and magnesia" (Whittlesey 1988b, 143).

10. Barlow and his group had left the Hayden party at Steamboat Springs on Aug. 22. They followed the east bank of the Yellowstone as far as the Lower Falls (where Barlow descended the canyon "immediately below the great fall"). On the 24th they struck across to the northeast toward the valley of the Lamar River. Here Barlow expected to meet Hayden's party but continued to move on, heading toward Baronett's bridge and "keeping along the foot of the hills on the southern side of the river." Barlow and Heap 1872, 39–41.

11. Some of the oldest rock in Yellowstone, these boulders (in present Lamar Canyon) are Precambrian gneiss and are more than 2.5 million years old. Keefer 1976, 13; Lageson and Spearing 1988, 245.

12. This bridge (claimed to be the first across the Yellowstone River) was built early that summer from heavy pine timbers by John ("Jack") Baronett (1829–1906). Born in Scotland, Baronett had traveled in the South Pacific and the American West before serving as an officer in the First Texas Cavalry before the Civil War. He came to the Yellowstone area in 1864 to prospect for gold. His two-span toll bridge was located just above the mouth of the Lamar River (then referred to as the "East Fork of the Yellowstone") at its confluence with the Yellowstone River. Barlow noted that the banks of the river at the bridge site were one hundred feet apart and that the bridge was constructed primarily for the accommodation of parties and their pack trains visiting new mines about forty miles east of this point, on the headwaters of Clark's Fork. Hayden named "Barronette" Peak (10,404 feet) in the northeast corner of the park for Jack Baronett in 1878, a place-name that was officially approved in misspelled form. Haines 1996, 136, 108–9; Peale Journal, July 30, 1872; Barlow and Heap 1872, 12; Whittlesey 1988a, 57; Whittlesey 1988b, 19.

13. According to Aubrey Haines, this camp was 1.7 miles west of Baronett's Bridge. "The road, which is still visible (though not used since 1915), . . . passed directly over the ridge that parallels the river and dropped into Paradise Valley, midway along it." Haines 1996, 162, 221, and personal communication, Aug. 26, 1998 (quotation).

14. Peale, Jackson, and José were following the Bannock Indian Trail instead of the "Turkey Pen" route behind Mt. Everts, which the main party had used. Peale's party then passed McGuirk's Medicine (later Medicinal) Springs, located in the vicinity of Hot River (also called Boiling River) where the subterranean runoff from Mammoth Hot Springs empties into the Gardner River. Haines 1996, 162, 221, and personal communication, Aug. 1998.

15. This campsite was probably on today's Stephen's Creek, known in the 1870s as Henderson Creek. Whittlesey 1988a, 1763.

16. Barlow agreed that the trip had been hard on the animals. Two of his horses had given out from exhaustion (one on Aug. 24, the other on Aug. 28). The mules, he declared, "endured the march much better, and, had they not suffered from sore backs caused by too narrow saddles, would have returned in as fine condition as when they started." Barlow concluded that horses were too large for such service and that ponies would have endured the hardships much better. In later Hayden surveys mules were "almost exclusively used both for pack and riding animals." Barlow and Heap 1872, 41; Peale 1876, 412.

17. Hayden's report lists the elevation of Emigrant Peak as 10,629 feet. It is measured today at 10,960 feet.

18. Yellowstone Lake has today approximately 110 miles of shoreline. Elliott's hand-drawn map of Yellowstone Lake is deposited at the map division of the National Archives. The published map of the lake that later appeared in Hayden's report was drawn by E. Hergesheimer, who was in charge of the engraving division of the U.S. Coast Survey. Hergesheimer based his map on Elliott's work and Schönborn's recovered field notes. Schönborn's valuable field notebooks have remained unidentified in government records despite several attempts to locate them.

19. Hayden had discovered these fossil remains on June 29 or 30 while the party was in the area of Junction Station, Montana Territory. The fossil was from an equid (belonging to the family of horses, zebras, mules) that developed in lower Tertiary North America and crossed the Bering Strait from North America to Asia at the beginning of the Miocene period. Leidy (who discovered the existence of the early horse in America) named the beast *Anchitherium bairdii* after Spencer Baird, who "from the first fully appreciated the importance of a complete examination of the Mauvaises Terres [of Nebraska] and their animal remains." Hayden 1871, 33; Grzimek 1975, 3:541; see also Leidy 1853, 13, 67–71, plates X, XI; Goetzmann 1966, 494.

20. Titian Ramsey Peale (1800–1885), A. C. Peale's great-uncle, was a painter, explorer, and naturalist. He accompanied Major S. A. Long's expedition in 1819–20 to explore country between the Mississippi and the Rocky Mountains and was a member of the first white party to climb Pike's Peak. Later he painted many large canvases of Rocky Mountain sheep, bison, and other animals that he had observed and sketched on the expedition. Still later he explored South America and the South Seas and prepared reports and illustrations from these expeditions. For several years, he was in charge of the Peale (later the Philadelphia) Museum. See *DAB*.

21. See chap 5, n.7.

22. Doane joined this NPRR survey's military escort on Sept. 16. Composed of

two companies of the Second Cavalry from Fort Ellis, it undertook a survey of the Powder River. Burlingame 1942, 216.

23. As officers' wives, Amelia Link Doane and Mrs. Wright were permitted to live with their husbands in officers' quarters at the fort.

10. TO THE JEFFERSON VALLEY

1. Barlow and most of his party would leave the next day, taking stagecoaches to Corinne, where they would board the Union Pacific railcars for Chicago—arriving there Sept. 15. Franklin Kneass was a civil engineer and served as chief engineer for a number of railroads. He undoubtedly was part of the team that would survey the Powder River area (see chap. 9, n.22). Barlow and Heap 1872, 42.

2. Located northwest of Bozeman in Gallatin County, Hamilton's post office was established in 1868. In 1883 (when the NPRR had completed its line across Montana) a station in Ravalli County was also given the name Hamilton. To eliminate confusion, the name of the earlier Hamilton was changed to Moreland. In 1891 the town's name was changed again, this time to Manhattan, the name by which it is known today. Cheney 1984, 128.

3. Curiously, neither Peale nor Hayden says much about the Missouri River in Hayden's report. Peale reports only that the party forded both the Gallatin and Madison Rivers and "passed the junction of the three forks of the Missouri." Hayden describes the canyon that the Missouri passes through below the Three Forks and surmises that it was "evidently the outlet of [a] lake, that had its deepest portion around the Three Forks." Hayden 1872a, 140, 191.

4. The owner of this ranch may have been Stephen Allen, who left Wisconsin in April 1864 with his family as part of a wagon train heading for gold fields in Idaho. Somehow he wound up ranching in an area west of Gallatin City. Besides ranching, he taught school and became the town's first school superintendent. Three Forks Area Historical Society 1983, 181–82.

5. A ferrotype (also called a tintype) is a positive photograph made directly on an iron plate varnished with a thin sensitized film. Peale wrote to his mother that the party enjoyed "an abundance of milk, cream and fresh butter," and that "the old gentleman" was very pleased with the tintype and said "we were the nicest set of fellows he had ever come across." A. C. Peale to Mrs. C. W. Peale, Sept. 8, 1871, RG B/P 31.m, APS.

6. The little settlement of Fish Creek (in Madison County), formerly known as Jefferson Bridge, was located at Parson's Bridge, which crossed the Jefferson River. Fish Creek's post office was established in 1870 and discontinued in 1896 after much of the settlement had departed for the richer strikes at Last Chance Gulch. Cheney 1984, 88–89.

7. Twin Bridges has had a post office since 1869. It was named either for the two bridges that spanned the Jefferson River close by or for the two bridges built in 1865 over the Beaverhead and Big Hole Rivers. The town is close to the three tributaries of the Jefferson River, named in 1805 by Lewis and Clark to commemorate the "three cardinal virtues" of Thomas Jefferson: Philosophy, Wisdom, and Philanthropy. These tributaries were later renamed, respectively, the Beaverhead, Big Hole, and Ruby Rivers. Cheney 1984, 271.

8. Peale was mistaken. He has clearly written "1847." Lewis and Clark camped in this area on Aug. 8, 1805.

9. Beaver Head Rock stage stop and post office (1869–71) was located twelve miles south of Twin Bridges. Captain Meriweather Lewis wrote in his diary (Aug. 8, 1805) that their expedition's Shoshone guide, Sacagawea, recognized Beaver Head Rock, "which, she informed us, was not very distant from the summer retreat of her nation. . . . This hill, she says, her nation calls the beaver's head from a conceived resemblance to the head of that animal." Cheney 1984, 16–17.

10. Located near present Dillon, Ryan's Station was a tollgate for the Great Beaver Head Wagon Road, built in 1866 by James M. Ryan. The road ran from the Idaho border down Red Rock Creek, across Black Tail Creek, through Beaverhead Canyon, to a point on the Stinking Water River about ten miles northeast of Virginia City. This road greatly shortened the distance between the Overland Trail and the mining camps at Helena and Butte. Madsen and Madsen 1980, 143–44.

11. This campsite was south of Bannack, in the area of the early settlement of Watson and on a branch line of the Great Beaverhead Wagon Road. Hayden noted that both the Horse Plain and Beaverhead valleys were "broad [and] fertile, and now occupied by settlers." Cheney 1984, 284; Hayden 1872a, 145.

12. Jackson succeeded in producing a fine photograph of this Bannock family (see photo 46), perhaps returning there the next morning when it was lighter.

13. Frustratingly, Frazier Ford Curtin remains unidentified.

14. Hayden, in his published report, attested to the still unknown character of the Rocky Mountain divide: "None of our published maps convey any idea of the almost innumerable ranges. . . . From longitude 100° to 118°, a distance of over five hundred miles, there is a range of mountains, on an average, every ten to twenty miles." He also reported that "a large portion of Idaho and Montana [reveals] that the surface is literally crumbled or rolled up in one continuous series of mountain ranges, fold after fold." Hayden 1871, 146–48.

15. A singletree is a crossbar on a horse-drawn wagon that pivots at the middle and thus gives more freedom of movement to the horses' shoulders.

16. Desert Wells Stage Station (also called Sand Hole) was part of a small Mormon farming community dependent on irrigation from artesian wells in the area. The

settlement is currently named Hamer. Boone 1988, 169; Madsen and Madsen 1980, 260.

17. It is unlikely that Peale is referring to the Young Men's Christian Association. The "Y.M.C.A." probably refers, in jest, to a group of tentmates who had received a humorous name from other members of the party.

18. Albert Peale's uncle, J. Burd Peale (1834–81), received his medical degree in 1856 and had been Albert's preceptor in the Medical Department of the University of Pennsylvania. Mark Frazier Lloyd, University of Pennsylvania archivist, letter to editor, Nov. 24, 1992. According to several newspaper accounts, Charles Willson Peale died at his "residence" in Norristown on Sept. 30. It is unclear why he was living in Norristown at the time of his death. In a September letter to his mother Albert expressed the hope that it was only indigestion that bothered his father and warned that "he ought to be very particular about his diet." Charles Peale's funeral took place in Norristown but was reported to be delayed until Oct. 9, perhaps in the hope that Albert might attend. *Press*, Oct. 9, 1871; Norristown *Herald*, Oct. 5, 1871; Philadelphia city directories for 1864–72; A. C. Peale to Mrs. C. W. Peale, Sept. 8, 1871, RG B/P 31.m, APS.

19. The phrase "alligator mess" may refer to eating like hungry alligators. No letter of Peale's was located in the *Chicago Tribune* during this period, probably because nearly all of that paper's news coverage was about the fire that devastated the city, Oct. 8–10.

20. Peale reported that there were remains of old hot springs at Twin Springs (sometimes called Three Springs). He also described the campsite as near "two extinct craters" and noted that "the whole valley [Lincoln Valley] was overflowed with lava." Hayden 1872a, 192.

21. Hayden noted in his report that the "limestones were charged with fossils. . . . In no portion of the Rocky Mountain Range have I seen [fossils] of greater abundance and variety. Quite thick layers of a compact, bluish limestone were entirely composed of corals and crinoidal stems." Hayden 1872a, 150.

22. Soda Springs, first settled in 1863, is an area of many mineral springs and unusual rock formations, occupying about six square miles. At the time of the expedition both a Mormon and a non-Mormon village were developing there. Soda Springs is now the county seat of Caribou County. Boone 1988, 350.

23. Vichy water is a naturally effervescent mineral water from springs at Vichy, France.

24. W. H. Hooper, Salt Lake City's leading banker and president of Zion's Cooperative Mercantile Institution, had his summer home in Soda Springs. Today there is still a Hooper Springs Pavilion. It is located two miles northeast of town. Hooper did a great deal to promote Soda Springs and its soda water industry while serving

as Utah's delegate to Congress. After 1882, when the railroad serviced the area, soda water from here was marketed nationally. Sign observed by editor in Soda Springs Park, June 26, 1991.

25. According to Peale, settlers called this area "petrifying springs," from the abundance of calcareous tufa that exists in and around the basins. Anticipating specimen hunters of even a later day, Hayden wrote that the calcified leaves and stems, "beautiful decorations," were all destroyed by people who sold them to travelers and curiosity seekers. He reported, "When I visited these springs . . . I found them a mass of ruins, and the specimens that I obtained for the museum of the Smithsonian Institution were those that had been rejected by these traders." Hayden 1872a, 153, 294.

26. These dates are based on information in Hayden's report (Hayden 1872a, 4, 196) and in a letter of Hayden's to Joseph Leidy, dated Sept. 29, 1871. Leidy Papers, ANS.

27. Evidence of Hayden's and Peale's activities during the remainder of the time the two men were together is found in several sources. Ever since his work with Meek in the 1850s, Hayden had collected western fossils to support his theory that western lakebeds were (in part) of Tertiary age (not solely Cretaceous, as was generally believed). Because this theory was controversial among geologists and related to the Great Lignite Controversy, as well as to the existence of a Tertiary land connection joining Greenland, Spitzbergen, and the U.S. continent, Hayden was eager to support his position by extending his Tertiary fossil collection westward. Earlier in the summer he had received word from Joseph Leidy of exciting and diverse fossil discoveries in southwest Wyoming Territory, near Fort Bridger, an area known for its coalbeds and mines. Hayden concluded his 1871 report by indicating his interest in them as well, writing: "At Evanston we have the great coal mines. . . . [I wish] to collect the facts which shall establish the age of the different formations of this portion of the West; more especially to ascertain the relation the coal beds sustain to the Cretaceous and Tertiary periods." In the same report Hayden remarked that after the survey disbanded he spent "a portion of the month of October . . . in reviewing points of geological interest along the railroad." Because the exposed strata in roadbeds and mines provide easily accessible geological information and specimens, it is very likely that Hayden and Peale were looking for Tertiary fossils. Paleontologist Leo Lesquereux examined the fossil plants collected by Hayden and his party in 1871 and reported that Hayden had obtained many hundred specimens (from twenty different localities) representing more than eighty species of Tertiary fossil plants. The following year both Lesquereux and Meek examined the same area Hayden and Peale examined in 1871 — from Evanston to Weber City (east of Ogden) — for more evidence relating to the Great Lignite issue. They did this at Hayden's expense, thereby testifying to the importance of this particular area to

Hayden's Tertiary theories. Hayden 1872a, 4, 159, 305, 317; Leidy to Hayden, July 19, 1871, RG 1638, Box 43, AHC; Foster 1994, 210. On Hayden's role in the Great Lignite Controversy, see Foster 1994, 184–92.

AFTERWORD

1. Jackson 1929, 121–22.

2. Hayden to Leidy, Sept. 20, 1871, Leidy Papers, CPS; *Annual Report of the Board of Regents of the Smithsonian Institution . . . for the year 1871*, Washington DC: Government Printing Office, 1873, 28, 46; Hayden 1872a, 165.

3. Jackson reports in *Pioneer Photographer*, 122, that the survey headquarters were located in a building on Pennsylvania Avenue, where photographic workrooms were fitted up for his use.

4. On Nov. 9 Hayden married Emma C. Woodruff, the daughter of a Philadelphia merchant.

5. No paintings of geysers or hot springs by Elliott have been located.

6. Peale to Allen, Nov. 27, 1871, Allen Papers, OCA.

7. *Omaha Daily Herald*, Oct. 15, 1871; *Philadelphia Inquirer*, Oct. 24, 1871.

8. Hayden 1872a, 5.

9. Barlow to Hayden, Dec. 4, 1871; Jan. 13, Feb. 2, 1872. Scattered correspondence relating to the Barlow-Heap party's need for further records can be found in letters to Hayden on the dates above as well as on Oct. 27, Nov. 7, Nov. 9, Jan. 17, and Jan. 19. Hayden Survey Papers, RG 57, microfilm 623, reel 2, NA.

10. Barlow and Heap 1872, 11.

11. Hayden 1883, 1:459.

12. Hayden 1872a, 143–44, 146–48.

13. Goetzmann 1966, 511 n.1.

14. Goetzmann 1966, 509.

15. Haines 1977, 1:155.

16. Yellowstone scholars have looked in vain for evidence to support claims that Hayden bestowed gold-embossed, bound folio albums containing the best of his Yellowstone photos to congressmen before the park bill was passed. Jackson contended that Moran's watercolors were also available for congressmen to view. This latter claim may be true. Joni Kinsey's discovery of an article in *Harper's Weekly* ("The Geysers of the Yellowstone," Mar. 30, 1872, 243) confirms that these watercolors were indeed among Hayden's exhibited material in Washington and that they "played an important role in the passage of the Yellowstone Park Bill." Haines 1977, 1:166; Kinsey 1989, 154; Milstein 1996, 144.

17. The issue of who first thought of preserving the Yellowstone area as a national park has occupied historians for more than a century. It appears that Northern Pacific

interests precipitated the actual move toward congressional action. But Hayden's and Langford's firsthand knowledge of Yellowstone, and especially Hayden's political savvy, led to the creation of the park bill as well as its later passage. The belief that the idea of preserving Yellowstone originated at a fireside discussion during the Washburn expedition is rejected by many, including former park historian Aubrey Haines, present park archivist Lee Whittlesey, and historian Paul Schullery. See Schullery and Whittlesey, "The Madison Campfire Story: Yellowstone's Creation Myth and Its Legacy," paper presented at the Fourth Biennial Scientific Conference on the Greater Yellowstone Ecosystem, "People and Place: The Human Experience in Greater Yellowstone," Mammoth Hot Springs WY, Oct. 12–15, 1997. For a detailed account of how the park bill was navigated through Congress, see Haines 1977, 1:164–73.

18. Hayden's Report to COPL, appendix 4.

19. Hayden's Report to COPL, appendix 4.

20. Kinsey 1989, 160; see also Runte 1979.

21. Moran to Hayden, May 26, 1872, NA, microfilm 623, reel 2. In the summer of 1892 Moran went to Yellowstone and revisited the Grand Canyon. He wrote his daughter that the canyon "is as glorious as ever and I was completely carried away by its magnificence. I think I can paint a better picture of it than the old one after I have made my sketches. I will not attempt to say anything about it as no words can express the faintest notion of it." This second painting of the Grand Canyon of the Yellowstone (8 by 14 feet) was exhibited at the Chicago World's Fair in 1893, as well as in San Francisco and other cities. Moran's early canyon painting (after being "all but ruined by attempts at cleaning and restoring," according to William Henry Jackson) was moved from the Capitol to the Interior Department Building in about 1950. It is now on loan to the National Museum of American Art at the Smithsonian. Moran's later painting of the canyon was given to the Smithsonian in 1928. Bassford 1967, 148–52; Kinsey 1992, 87, 91; Jackson 1940, 200.

22. Watson Gilden to Hayden, May 27, 1872, NA, microfilm 623, reel 2; Kinsey 1992, 64; Kinsey 1989, 200.

23. Moran to Hayden, Mar. 3 1872, NA, microfilm 623, reel 2.

24. Gilden to Hayden, May 23, 1872 NA, microfilm 623, reel 2.

25. Foster 1994, 235.

26. Langford made only two visits to Yellowstone during his term as superintendent (1872–77). Haines 1977, 1:180, 212.

27. Schullery 1997, 201–2.

28. Hayden 1873b, 92–95.

29. Hayden, Report to COPL, appendix 4.

30. Haines 1996, 221.

Glossary of
Geological Terms and
Fossil Shells

Several sources were consulted in order to define the geological terms found in the Allen and Peale journals in a readily accessible manner: *The American Heritage Dictionary* (Boston, 1976, 1985, 1992); *The Concise Oxford Dictionary of Earth Sciences*, edited by Ailsa Allaby and Michael Allaby (Oxford: Oxford University Press, 1991); and *The Dictionary of Geological Terms*, edited by Robert L. Bates and Julia A. Jackson (New York: Doubleday, 1984). The geologic table is adapted from the Bates and Jackson dictionary.

GEOLOGICAL TERMS

agate: a fine-grained, fibrous variety of chalcedony with colored bands or irregular clouding.

alluvium: sediment deposited by flowing water, as in a riverbed, floodplain, or delta.

anticline: a fold, generally convex and upward, whose core contains stratigraphically older rocks.

amygdaloidal spaces: spheroidal, ellipsoidal, or almond-shaped cavities in a lava flow.

auriferous: containing gold.

basalt: a hard, dense, dark volcanic rock, often having a glossy appearance.

breccia: literally, "rubble"; a rock composed of sharp-angled fragments cemented in a fine matrix.

calcareous: composed of calcium carbonate, calcite, or limestone; chalky.

chalcedony: a translucent to transparent milky or grayish quartz with distinctive microscopic crystals arranged in slender fibers in parallel bands.

chlorite: a generally green or black secondary mineral often formed by metamorphic alteration of primary dark minerals.

conglomerate: a rock consisting of pebbles and gravel, generally embedded in a sandy matrix; one variety is called "pudding stone."

crinoid: any of various marine invertebrates of the class Crinoidea, the most primitive living class of echinoderms.

dike (European spelling is *dyke*): a tabular mass of igneous rock (trap) that cuts across the structure of adjacent rock.

drift: rock debris transported by glaciers and deposited directly from the ice or through the agency of meltwater; generally applied to Pleistocene deposits in large regions that no longer contain glaciers.

feldspar: an important group of rock-forming silicate minerals that are the major constituents of most igneous rocks.

fluvial: of, pertaining to, or inhabiting a river or stream; formed or produced by the action of flowing river water, as in a channel or floodplain.

gneiss: a banded or foliated metamorphic rock, usually of the same composition as granite.

granite: a common, coarse-grained, light-colored, hard igneous rock consisting chiefly of orthoclase (or microcline) and quartz.

hornblende: a common, green or bluish green to black amphibole mineral formed in the late stages of cooling in igneous rock. It is also a common metamorphic mineral.

lacustrine: pertaining to, produced by, or inhabiting a lake or lakes.

limestone: a common sedimentary rock, consisting mostly of calcium carbonate ($CaCO_3$), used as a building stone and in the manufacture of lime, carbon dioxide, and Portland cement.

lode: a mineral deposit in solid rock as opposed to a placer deposit (made up of sand or gravel containing eroded particles of minerals).

loess: a buff to gray windblown deposit of fine-grained, calcareous silt or clay. Much of it is windblown rock flour of glacial origin or fine granite dust blown out of desert areas.

marl: a crumbly mixture of clays, calcium, and magnesium carbonates, and remnants of shells; used as fertilizer for lime-deficient soil.

metamorphic rock: an aggregate of minerals formed by the recrystallization of preexisting rocks in response to changes of pressure, temperature, and/or volatile content.

mica: any of a group of chemically and physically related aluminum silicate minerals, common in igneous and metamorphic rocks; the most common of these sheet silicates are muscovite and biotite.

monocline: a local steepening in an otherwise uniform gentle dip.

obsidian: a usually black or banded, hard volcanic glass that displays shiny, curved surfaces when fractured and is formed by the rapid cooling of granitic lava.

orthoclase: a common rock-forming mineral; a feldspar, essentially potassium aluminum silicate, commonly found in granitic igneous rocks.

phenocryst: a conspicuous, usually large, crystal embedded in finer-grained matrix of an igneous rock (porphyritic texture).

phonolite: a volcanic rock composed principally of orthoclase and nepheline; also called "clinkstone."

porphyry: rock containing relatively large conspicuous crystals, especially feldspar, in a fine-grained igneous matrix.

quartz: a very hard mineral composed of silica, SiO_2, found worldwide in many different types of rocks, including sandstone and granite. Varieties of quartz include agate, chalcedony, chert, flint, opal, and rock crystal.

sandstone: a sedimentary rock formed by the consolidation and compacting of sand and held together by a natural cement such as silica, calcite, or iron oxide.

schist: any of various medium-grained to coarse-grained metamorphic rocks composed of laminated, often flaky parallel layers of chiefly micaceous minerals.

scoria: rough, dark-colored fragments of burnt, crustlike lava, basaltic or andesitic; also called "cinder" or "slag." Contains a high proportion of large vesicles.

sedimentary: of or relating to rocks formed by the deposition of sediment.

selenite: gypsum in the form of colorless clear crystals.

silica: a white or colorless crystalline compound, SiO_2, occurring abundantly as quartz, sand, flint, agate, and many other minerals and used to manufacture a wide variety of materials, notably glass and concrete.

siliceous sinter: the lightweight porous opaline variety of silica, white or nearly white, deposited as an incrustation by precipitation from the waters of geysers and hot springs; also called "geyserite."

syenite: a coarse-grained igneous rock composed primarily of alkali feldspar mixed with other minerals such as hornblende.

trachyte: a light-colored, volcanic, igneous rock consisting essentially of alkali feldspar.

trap: any dark, fine-grained igneous rock, such as basalt. Often formed in a steplike configuration, for example, as successive lava flows.

travertine: a light-colored, banded $CaCO_3$. Formed by the evaporation of river and spring waters, it is a variety of limestone that takes a good polish and is the most common cave deposit.

tufa: a chemical sedimentary rock composed of calcium carbonate formed by evaporation as an encrustation around the mouth of a spring or along a stream.

vesicle: a small, bladder-like cell or cavity formed as a bubble in a lava flow.

FOSSIL SHELLS

George Allen made numerous references in his journal to shells that he collected on the expedition. All were freshwater shells and Tertiary or early Cretaceous in age.

F. B. Meek, in his "Preliminary List of the Fossils Collected by Dr. Hayden's Exploring Expedition of 1871, in Utah and Wyoming Territories, with Descriptions of a Few New Species," published in Hayden's Fifth Report, remarks: "The condition of most of the fossils . . . is such that from a mere preliminary examination, it is scarcely possible, in a majority of cases, to do more than refer them to their proper genera. The Carboniferous forms are especially difficult to make out, the specimens being generally in a fragmentary condition, and imbedded in a very hard matrix that renders it almost impossible to work them out" (Hayden 1872a, 376).

Anodons: an alternate name for the genus *Anodonta*, of the bivalve (clam). Family: Anodontinae. First appearing in freshwater environments during the Cretaceous period.

Cyclas: an alternate name for the genus *Eupera*, of the bivalve (clam). Family: Pisidiidae. First appearing in freshwater environments in the Cretaceous period.

H. arborea, *H. cooper*[i], *H. solitaria*, and *H. striatella* are all species of the genus *Helices*.

Lymnea: a genus of freshwater gastropod (snail) of the order Basommatophora, first appearing in freshwater environments in the Jurassic period.

Paludina: a genus of freshwater gastropod of the family Viviparidae, first present in the Carboniferous period.

Physa: a genus of freshwater gastropod of the order Basommatophora.

Planorbis: a genus of freshwater gastropod of the order Basommatophora.

Unio arcuata: a species of freshwater bivalve of the family Unionidae, first appearing in the Triassic period.

Geologic Time Scale

ERAS	YEARS AGO	PERIODS	EPOCH	DOMINANT ANIMAL LIFE
Cenozoic	10,000 2 million 10 23 40 55 63	Quaternary Tertiary	Recent Pleistocene Pliocene Miocene Oligocene Eocene Paleocene	Modern humans Mammals
Mesozoic	140 190 230	Cretaceous Jurassic Triassic		Dinosaurs Primitive Reptiles
Paleozoic	280 310 345 405 425 500 570	Permian Pennsylvanian Mississippian Devonian Silurian Ordovician Cambrian		Amphibians Fishes Intervertebrates
Precambrian	2.5 billion 5 billion	Proterozoic Archeozoic		Beginnings of Life

References

MANUSCRIPT SOURCES

Academy of Natural Sciences, Philadelphia. Leidy Papers. Hayden correspondence.

American Heritage Center, Laramie WY. Fryxell Collection. RG 1638.

American Philosophical Society Library, Philadelphia. Peale Papers. RG B/P 31.m.

College of Physicians and Surgeons, Philadelphia. Joseph Leidy Papers. Sec. 1.1. Hayden letters.

Library of Congress, Washington DC. Department of the Interior. RG 48. Hayden letters to Delano.

National Archives, Washington DC. Records of the Geological and Geographical Survey of the Territories ("Hayden Survey Papers"), 1867–70. RG 57. Microfilm 623.

———. Records of the Office of the Chief of Engineers, Chief of Topographical Engineers, and Bureau of Explorations and Surveys. RG 77.

———. Records of the Office of the Interior, 1869–80. RG 48.

New York City Public Library, New York City. William Henry Jackson Journal (typescript of recollections of the 1871 expedition). n.d.

Oberlin College Archives, Oberlin OH. Alumni Records (Necrology Files). RG 28/2.

———. George Allen Papers. RG 30/67. George Allen Field Notes, 1871. George Allen Journal, 1871. Letters from F. V. Hayden.

———. James Monroe Papers, RG 30/22. Letters from F. V. Hayden. Letters from George Allen.

Smithsonian Institution Archives, Washington DC. Office of the Assistant Secretary (Spencer Baird). Incoming Papers. RG 52.

———. Office of the Secretary (Joseph Henry and Spencer Baird). Incoming Papers. RG 26.

United States Geological Survey, Field Records Library, Federal Center, Denver. Peale Journal, June 2–July 3, July 20–Sept. 3, 1871.

Yellowstone Research Library, Park Headquarters, Mammoth Hot Springs WY. A. C. Peale Journal, May 21, July 4–19, Sept. 4–24, Oct. 5, 6, 1871.

———. A. C. Peale Journal, July 21–Oct. 24, 1872.

———. Thomas Moran Journal and Sketchbooks.

PRINTED SOURCES

Adams, Robert. 1871. "The U.S. Geological Survey." *Philadelphia Inquirer*, June 14, July 25, Sept. 8, Sept. 15, Sept. 26.

Anderson, Nancy K. 1997. *Thomas Moran*. Washington DC: National Gallery of Art; New Haven: Yale University Press.

Arrington, Leonard J. 1985. *Brigham Young: American Moses*. New York: Alfred A. Knopf.

Arrington, Leonard J., and Davis Britton. 1979. *The Mormon Experience: A History of the Latter-day Saints*. New York: Alfred A. Knopf.

Barlow, J. W., and David P. Heap. 1872. *Report of a Reconnaissance of the Upper Yellowstone in 1871*. 42d Cong., 2d sess., Senate Exec. Doc. 66, SN-1479, vol.E. Washington DC: Government Printing Office.

Bartlett, Richard. 1962. *Great Surveys of the American West*. Norman: University of Oklahoma Press.

———. 1974a. *Nature's Yellowstone*. Tucson: University of Arizona Press.

———. 1974b. *The New Country: A Social History of the American Frontier*. New York: Oxford University Press.

———. 1985. *A Wilderness Besieged*. Tucson: University of Arizona Press.

Bassford, Amy O., ed. 1967. *Home Thoughts from Afar: Letters of Thomas Moran to Mary Nimmo Moran*. Introduction and notes by Fritiof Fryxell. East Hampton NY: East Hampton Free Library.

Beck, Warren A., and Ynez D. Haase. 1989. *Historical Atlas of the American West*. Norman: University of Oklahoma Press.

Berrett, William E. 1985. *The Latter Day Saints: A Contemporary History of the Church of Jesus Christ*. Salt Lake City: Deseret Book Co.

Bigglestone, William E. "George Nelson Allen: Teacher in Spite of Himself." *Northwest Ohio Quarterly*. Winter, 1975–76.

———. 1983. *Oberlin: From War to Jubilee*. Oberlin OH: Grady Press.

Bonney, Orrin H., and Lorraine Bonney. 1970. *Battle Drums and Geysers: The Life and Journals of Lt. Gustavus Cheyney Doane*. Chicago: Swallow Press. Reprint, 3 vols. Houston: n.p.

Boone, Lalia. 1988. *Idaho Place Names: A Geographical Dictionary*. Moscow: University of Idaho Press.

Bragg, Bill. 1976. *Wyoming's Wealth: A History of Wyoming*. Basin WY: Big Horn Book Co.

Brown, Mark H. 1961. *Plainsmen of the Yellowstone: A History of the Yellowstone Basin*. Lincoln: University of Nebraska Press.

Burlingame, Merrill G. 1980. *The Montana Frontier*. Bozeman MT: Big Sky Books.

Burt, Nathaniel. 1991. *Wyoming*. Oakland CA: Compass American Guides.

Busch, Briton Cooper. 1985. *The War against the Seals: A History of the North American Seal Fishery*. Montreal: McGill-Queen's University Press.

Cassidy, Gerald James. 1991. "Ferdinand V. Hayden: Federal Entrepreneur of Science." Ph.D. dissertation, University of Pennsylvania.

Chambers, Frank. 1988. *Hayden and His Men: Being a Selection of 108 Photographs by William Henry Jackson of the U.S. Geological and Geographical Survey of the Territories for the Years 1870–78*. Hoosick NY: Francis Paul.

Cheney, Roberta Carteek. 1984. *Names on the Face of Montana*. Missoula MT: Mountain Press.

Chenoweth, William L. 1987. "Albert C. Peale, M.D. – Pioneer Rocky Mountain Geologist." In *Four Corners Geological Society Guidebook*, 10th Field Conference, Cataract Canyon. Durango CO. 25–27.

Chittenden, Hiram Martin. 1895. *The Yellowstone National Park*. Reprint, ed. Richard A. Bartlett. Norman: University of Oklahoma Press, 1964.

Clark, Carol. 1980. *Thomas Moran: Watercolors of the American West*. Published for the Amon Carter Museum. Austin: University of Texas Press.

Conaway, James. 1995. *The Smithsonian: One Hundred Fifty Years of Adventure, Discovery, and Wonder*. New York: Alfred A. Knopf.

Cramton, Louis C. 1932. *Early History of Yellowstone Park and Its Relation to National Park Policies*. Washington DC: Government Printing Office.

Cronin, Janet, and Dorothy Vick. 1992. *Montana's Gallatin Canyon*. Missoula MT: Mountain Press.

Delo, David. 1998. *The Yellowstone Forever!* Helena MT: Kingfisher Books.

Dunraven, Windham T. W. Q. 1876. *The Great Divide: Travels in the Upper Yellowstone in the Summer of 1874*. Reprint, Lincoln: University of Nebraska Press, 1967.

Elliott, Henry Wood. 1871a. "The Hayden Geological Survey." *Omaha Daily Herald*, Sept. 28.

———. 1871b. "The New Wonderland." *Cincinnati Daily Gazette*, Oct. 18, 1871.

———. 1872. *Profiles, Sections, and Other Illustrations: Designed to Accompany the Final Report of the Chief Geologist of the Survey and Sketched under His Direction*. New York: Julius Bien.

Faulk, Odie B. 1976. *The U.S. Camel Corps: An Army Experiment*. New York: Oxford University Press.

Foster, Mike. 1984. *Summits to Reach: An Annotated Edition of Franklin Rhoda's "Report on the Topography of the San Juan Country."* Boulder CO: Pruett.

———. 1989. "The Permian Controversy of 1858: An Affair of the Heart." *Proceedings of the American Philosophical Society* 133, no.3, 370–90.

———. 1994. *Strange Genius: The Life of Ferdinand Vandeveer Hayden*. Niwot CO: Roberts Rinehart.

Frazer, Robert W. 1965. *Forts of the West*. Norman: University of Oklahoma Press.

Fritz, William J. 1985. *Roadside Geology of the Yellowstone Country*. Missoula MT: Mountain Press.

Fryxell, Fritiof M. 1962. "Albert Charles Peale: Pioneer Geologist of the Hayden Survey." *Annals of Wyoming* 34 (Oct.), 175–92.

———, ed. 1958. *Thomas Moran: Explorer in Search of Beauty*. East Hampton NY: East Hampton Free Library.

Gates, Paul W. 1968. *History of Public Land Development*. Washington DC: Government Printing Office.

Gillett, Jane Brown. 1993. "Restaking the Claim: Preservationists Struggle to Rescue Virginia City, Montana's Miraculous Survivor of the 1863 Gold Rush." *Historic Preservation* (Jan.–Feb.), 35–41, 89–92.

Goetzmann, William H. 1966. *Exploration and Empire: The Explorer and the Scientist in the Winning of the American West*. New York: W. W. Norton.

———. 1982. "Explorer, Mountain Man, and Scientist." In *Exploring the American West, 1803–1879*, produced by the National Park Service, 17–95. Washington DC: U.S. Department of the Interior.

Goetzmann, William H., and William N. Goetzmann. 1986. *The West of the Imagination*. New York: W. W. Norton.

Grzimek, h. c. Bernard. 1975. *Grzimek's Animal Life Encyclopedia*. 5 vols. New York: McGraw-Hill.

Hafen, LeRoy R., and Ann W. Hafen, eds. 1959. *The Diaries of William Henry Jackson, Frontier Photographer*. Glendale CA: Arthur H. Clark.

Haines, Aubrey. 1964. *The Bannock Indian Trail*. Reprint, Washington DC: National Park Service and Yellowstone Library and Museum Association, 1980.

———. 1974. *Yellowstone National Park: Its Explorations and Establishment*. Washington DC: Government Printing Office.

———. 1977. *The Yellowstone Story: A History of Our First National Park*. 2 vols. Yellowstone National Park WY: Yellowstone Library and Museum Association.

———. 1996. *Yellowstone Place Names: Mirrors of History*. Niwot: University Press of Colorado.

———, ed. 1965. *The Valley of the Upper Yellowstone: An Exploration of the Headwaters of the Yellowstone River in the Year 1869*. Norman: University of Oklahoma Press.

Hales, Peter B. 1988. *William Henry Jackson and the Transformation of the American Landscape*. Philadelphia: Temple University Press.

Hardwick, Bonnie Skell. 1977. "Science and Art: The Travel Writings of the Great Surveys of the American West after the Civil War." Ph.D. dissertation, University of Pennsylvania.

Hayden, F. V. 1870. *Sun Pictures of Rocky Mountain Scenery*. New York: Julius Bien.

———. 1871. Excerpts from Hayden's letters to Spencer Baird. *Harper's Weekly*. June 17, July 18, Sept. 2, Sept. 9, Sept. 16, Oct. 7, Nov. 4.

———. 1872a. Fifth Report: *Preliminary Report of the United States Geological Survey of Montana and Portions of Adjacent Territories; Being a Fifth Annual Report of Progress*. Washington DC: Government Printing Office.

———. 1872b. "The Hot Springs and Geysers of the Yellowstone and Firehole Rivers." *American Journal of Science and Arts* 3, nos. 14 and 15 (Jan.–June).

———. 1872c. "The Wonders of the West – II: More about the Yellowstone." *Scribner's Monthly* 3 (Feb.), 388–96.

———. 1873a. Introduction to *First, Second, and Third Annual Reports of the U.S. Geological Survey of the Territories for the Years 1867, 1868, and 1869*. Washington DC: Government Printing Office.

———. 1873b. Sixth Report: *Sixth Annual Report of the United Geological Survey of the Territories, Embracing Portions of Montana, Idaho, Wyoming, and Utah*. Washington DC: Government Printing Office.

———. 1876. *The Yellowstone National Park and the Mountain Regions of Portions of Idaho, Nevada, Colorado, and Utah*. Portfolio of chromolithographic reproductions of watercolor sketches by Thomas Moran. Boston: Louis Prang.

———. 1877. *Sketch of the Origin and Progress of the United States Geological and Geographical Survey of the Territories*. Washington DC: Darby and Duvall.

———. 1883. Twelfth Report: *A Report of Progress of the Exploration in Wyoming and Idaho for the Year 1878*. 2 vols. Washington DC: Government Printing Office.

Heitman, Francis B. 1903. *A Historical Register and Dictionary of the U.S. Army, 1789–1903*. Washington DC: Government Printing Office. Microfiche.

Holmes, William H. 1916. "In Memoriam, Matilda Coxe Stevenson and James Stevenson." *American Anthropologist* 18, 552–59.

Idaho Water Resources. n.d. *The Snake River Plain Aquifer*. Moscow: Research Institute, University of Idaho.

Jackson, William Henry (with Howard R. Driggs). 1929. *The Pioneer Photographer: Rocky Mountain Adventures with a Camera*. New York: World.

——— (with Karl Brown). 1940. *Time Exposure*. New York: Van Ress Press. Reprint, Albuquerque: University of New Mexico Press, 1986.

———. n.d. "1871 The Yellowstone." Unpublished typescript recollection. New York Public Library. Manuscript collection.

Janetski, Joel C. 1987. *Indians of Yellowstone Park*. Salt Lake City: University of Utah Press.

Johnson, Allen, ed. 1956. *Dictionary of American Biography*. New York: Charles Scribner's Sons.

Johnson, Everett F. 1987. "Early Stage Stations and Stage Routes in Beaverhead County, Montana." Unpublished manuscript. Dillon MT: Beaverhead County Museum.

Keefer, William R. 1976. *The Geologic Story of Yellowstone National Park*. Reprinted from *Geological Survey Bulletin 1347* by Yellowstone Library and Museum Association in cooperation with the U.S. Geological Survey.

Kinsey, Joni Louise. 1989. "Creating a Sense of Place: Thomas Moran and the Surveying of the American West." Ph.D. dissertation, Washington University.

———. 1992. *Thomas Moran and the Surveying of the American West*. Washington DC: Smithsonian Institution Press.

Lageson, David K., and Darwin R. Spearing. 1988. *Roadside Geology of Wyoming*. Missoula MT: Mountain Press.

Lamar, Howard R., ed. 1977. *Reader's Encyclopedia of the American West*. New York: Harper and Row.

Langford, Nathaniel. 1871. "The Wonders of Yellowstone." Parts 1 and 2. *Scribner's Monthly* 2 (May), 1–17; (June), 113–29.

———. 1906. *The Discovery of Yellowstone Park, 1870*. Reprint, Lincoln: University of Nebraska Press, 1972.

Leidy, Joseph. 1853. *The Ancient Fauna of Nebraska*. Washington DC: Smithsonian Institution.

Limerik, Patricia. 1987. *The Legacy of Conquest: The Unbroken Past of the American West*. New York: W. W. Norton.

Logan, Mrs. John A. 1913. *Reminiscences of a Soldier's Wife*. New York: Charles Scribner's Sons.

Loohse, E. S., and Richard N. Holmer. 1990. *Fort Hall and the Shoshone-Bannock*. Pocatello: Idaho State University Press.

Love, J. David, leader. 1989. *Yellowstone and Grand Teton National Parks and the Middle Rocky Mountains*. Field trip guidebook. Washington DC: American Geophysical Union.

Love, J. David, and John C. Reed Jr. 1976. *Creation of the Teton Landscape*. Rev. ed. Moose WY: Grand Teton Natural History Association.

Lutz, Dennis J., and Montana Chapter No.1, National Association of Postmasters of the United States. 1986. *Montana Post Offices and Postmasters*. Rochester MN: Johnson Printing Co.

McPhee, John. 1986. *Rising from the Plains*. New York: Farrar, Straus, Giroux.

Madison County History Association. 1982. *The History of Madison County: The Progressive Years, 1920–1950*. Vol. 2. Madison County History Association MT.

Madsen, Betty M., and Brigham D. Madsen. 1980. *North to Montana! Jehus, Bull-whackers, and Mule Skinners on the Montana Trail*. Salt Lake City: University of Utah Press.

Manning, Thomas G. 1967. *Government in Science: The U.S. Geological Survey, 1867–1894*. Lexington: University Press of Kentucky.

Marker, Joe L. 1980. *Eagle Rock, U.S.A. (Now Idaho Falls, Idaho)*. 2d ed. Idaho Falls: Robco Printing.

Merrill, George P. 1924. *The First One Hundred Years of American Geology*. New Haven: Yale University Press.

Meschter, Daniel Y. 1989. *The Postal History of Montana through June 30, 1870*. La Posta Monograph Series, vol. 4. Lake Oswego OR.

Meyer, Judith L. 1996. *The Spirit of Yellowstone: The Cultural Evolution of a National Park*. Boulder CO: Rowman and Littlefield.

Miller, Lillian. 1996. *The Peale Family: Creation of a Legacy, 1770–1870*. Washington DC: Abbeville Press in association with the Trust for Museum Exhibitions and the National Portrait Gallery, Smithsonian Institution.

Mills, Ada Black. 1966. "Madison Toll Bridge." *Bozeman Chronicle*, June 5. In *Progressive Years: Madison County*, vol. 2, 1920–1950, compiled by the Madison County History Association MT, 1982.

Milstein, Michael. 1996. *Yellowstone: One Hundred Twenty-Five Years of America's Best Idea*. Bozeman MT: Billings Gazette.

Muir, John. 1898. "The Yellowstone National Park." *Atlantic Monthly*. Reprint, Golden CO: Outbooks, 1986.

National Park Service. 1982. *Exploring the American West, 1803–1879*. Washington DC: National Park Service.

Nelson, Clifford M., and Fritiof M. Fryxell. 1979. "The Antebellum Collaboration of Meek and Hayden in Stratigraphy." In *Two Hundred Years of Geology in America*, ed. Cecil J. Schneer, 187–200. Hanover NH: University Press of New England.

Nelson, Clifford M., and Mary C. Rabbitt. 1982. "The Role of Clarence King in the Advancement of Geology in the Public Service, 1867–1881." In *Frontiers of Geological Exploration of Western North America*, ed. Alan E. Leviton, Peter U.

Rodda, Ellis L. Yochelson, and Michele L. Aldrich. San Francisco: American Association for the Advancement of Science, Pacific Division.

Nelson, Clifford M., Mary C. Rabbitt, and Fritiof M. Fryxell. 1981. "Ferdinand Vandeveer Hayden: The U.S. Geological Survey Years, 1879–1886." *Proceedings of the American Philosophical Society* 125, 238–43.

New York Times. 1871. "The Yellowstone Expedition," Sept. 18. "The New Wonderland," Oct. 23.

Norell, Mark A., Eugene S. Gaffney, and Lowell Dingus. 1995. *Discovering Dinosaurs: In the American Museum of Natural History.* New York: Alfred A. Knopf.

Norton, Harry J. 1873. *Wonder-land Illustrated; or, Horseback Rides through the Yellowstone National Park.* Reprint, Virginia City MT, 1997.

Oliver, Sandra Ireland. 1978. "Ferdinand V. Hayden: Scientist or Charlatan? The Wyoming Years." Master's thesis, University of Wyoming.

Parezo, Nancy J. 1993. *Hidden Scholars: Women Anthropologists and the Native American Southwest.* Albuquerque: University of New Mexico Press.

Paul, Rodman W. 1988. *The Far West and the Great Plains in Transition, 1859–1900.* New York: Harper and Row.

Peale, A. C. 1871. "The Yellowstone" [various titles]. *Philadelphia Press*, June 15, June 29, July 14, July 29, Aug. 8, Aug. 29, Oct. 19, Oct. 25.

———. 1876. "The Hayden Exploring Expedition." *Illustrated Christian Weekly*, June 10, Aug. 12, Aug. 26, Sept. 23.

———. 1891. "Biographical Sketch of F. V. Hayden, M.D., with Bibliography." Peale Papers, RG 7208, Smithsonian Institution Archives, Washington DC.

———. 1892. "Ferdinand Vandiveer Hayden." *Bulletin of the Philosophic Society of Washington* 11, 476–78.

———. 1896. *Explanation and Description Accompanying the Three Forks Folio. Geologic Atlas of the United States.* Charles D. Walcott, director. Washington DC: U.S. Geological Survey.

Pierce, Steve. 1987. *The Lakes of Yellowstone: A Guide for Hiking, Fishing, and Exploring.* Seattle: The Mountaineers.

Rabbitt, Mary C. 1979. *Minerals, Lands, and Geology for the Common Defense and General Welfare.* Vol. 1 [Before 1879]. Washington DC: Government Printing Office.

———. 1989. *The United States Geological Survey, 1879–1989.* U.S. Geological Survey Circular 1050. Washington DC: Government Printing Office.

Raynolds, William F. 1868. *The Report of Brevet Brigadier General W. F. Raynolds on the Expedition of the Yellowstone and the Country Drained by that River.* 40th Cong., 1st sess., Senate Exec. Doc. 77. Washington DC: Government Printing Office.

Rivinus, E. F., and E. M. Youssef. 1992. *Spencer Baird of the Smithsonian.* Washington DC: Smithsonian Institution Press.

Runte, Alfred. 1979. *National Parks: The American Experience*. Lincoln: University of Nebraska Press.

————. 1990. *Trains of Discovery*. Niwot CO: Roberts Rinehart.

Schreier, Carl. 1987. *A Field Guide to Yellowstone Geysers, Hot Springs, and Fumaroles*. Moose WY: Homestead.

Schullery, Paul. 1997. *Searching for Yellowstone: Ecology and Wonder in the Last Wilderness*. Boston: Houghton Mifflin.

Sears, John F. 1989. *Sacred Places: American Tourist Attractions in the Nineteenth Century*. New York: Oxford University Press.

Sellers, Charles Coleman. 1947. *The Peale Family*. Philadelphia: American Philosophical Society.

Selmeier, Lewis. 1972. "William Henry Jackson: First Camera on the Yellowstone." *Montana: The Magazine of Western History* 22, no.3, 43–53.

Shalkop, Robert L. 1982. Introduction to *Henry Wood Elliott – A Retrospective Exhibition*. Anchorage: Anchorage Historical and Fine Arts Museum.

Sloan, Edward L. 1874. *Salt Lake City Directory*. Salt Lake City: Salt Lake *Herald*.

Smith, Phyllis. 1997. *Bozeman and the Gallatin Valley: A History*. Helena MT: A Twodot Book.

Smithsonian Board of Regents. 1873. *Annual Report*. Washington DC: The Institution and the Government Printing Office.

Smithsonian Institution. 1873. *Annual Report of the Board of Regents . . . for the Year 1871*. Washington DC: Government Printing Office.

Stegner, Wallace. 1953. *Beyond the Hundredth Meridian: John Wesley Powell and the Second Opening of the West*. Lincoln: University of Nebraska Press, 1982.

Stenzel, Franz. n.d. *Anton Schönborn: Western Forts*. Fort Worth: Amon Carter Museum.

Sterling, Keir B., Richard P. Harmond, George A. Cevasco, and Lorne F. Hammond, eds. 1997. *Biographical Dictionary of American and Canadian Naturalists and Environmentalists*. Westport CT: Greenwood Press.

Stucker, Gilbert F. 1967. "Hayden in the Badlands." *American West* 2.

Three Forks Area Historical Society. 1983. *Headwaters Heritage History*. Butte MT: Artcraft Printers. [Articles on Stephen Allen, 181–84, and Gallatin City, 41–43.]

Topping, Eugene Sayre. 1883. *The Chronicles of the Yellowstone: An Accurate, Comprehensive History of the Country Drained by the Yellowstone*. Reprint, Minneapolis: Ross and Haines, 1968.

Trenton, Patricia, and Peter H. Hassrick. 1983. *The Rocky Mountains: A Vision for Artists in the Nineteenth Century*. Norman: University of Oklahoma Press.

U.S. Department of the Interior, Geological Survey. 1973. "Ferdinand Vandiveer

Hayden and the Founding of Yellowstone National Park." Washington DC: Government Printing Office.

Urbanek, Mae. 1988. *Wyoming Place Names*. Missoula MT: Mountain Press.

Van Cott, John W. 1990. *Utah Place Names*. Salt Lake City: University of Utah Press.

Van West, Carroll. 1986. *A Travelers Guide to Montana History*. Helena: Montana Historical Society.

Viola, Herman J. 1987. *Exploring the West*. Washington DC: Smithsonian Institution Press.

Waldman, Carl. 1985. *Atlas of the North American Indian*. New York: Facts on File.

Wharton, Tom, and Gaylen Wharton. 1993. *Utah*. Oakland CA: Compass American Guides.

Wheat, Carl I. 1963. *Mapping the Transmississippi West*. Vol. 5, pt.2. San Francisco: Institute of Historical Cartography.

White, Richard. 1991. *"It's Your Misfortune and None of My Own": A History of the American West*. Norman: University of Oklahoma Press.

Whittlesey, Lee H. 1988a. *Wonderland Nomenclature: A History of the Place Names of Yellowstone National Park*. Helena: Montana Historical Society. Microfiche.

————. 1988b. *Yellowstone Place Names*. Helena: Montana Historical Society Press.

————. 1995. *Lost in Yellowstone: Truman Evert's "Thirty-Seven Days of Peril."* Salt Lake City: University of Utah Press.

————. In press. *Yellowstone's Horse and Buggy Tour Guides: Interpreting the Grand Old Park, 1872–1920*. Washington DC: National Park Service.

————. n.d. "Proper Presentation of the Park." Manuscript.

Wilkins, Thurman. 1966. *Thomas Moran: Artist of the Mountains*. Norman: University of Oklahoma Press.

Wilkins, Thurman, and Caroline Hinkley. 1988. *Clarence King: A Biography*. 2d ed. Albuquerque: University of New Mexico Press.

Worster, Donald. 1985. *Rivers of Empire: Water, Aridity, and the Growth of the American West*. New York: Pantheon Books.

MAPS

Barlow, J. W. 1871. "Sketch of the Yellowstone Lake and the Valley of the Upper Yellowstone River." RG 77–b (Office of the Chief of Engineers), US 490–47, NA.

DeLacy, W. W. 1870. "Map of the Territory of Montana, with Portions of the Adjoining Territories." New York: G. W. and C. B. Colton and Co. [See Wheat 1963 for reproductions of this and other maps from the period.]

Hayden, F. V. 1871. "Parts of Idaho, Montana, and Wyoming Territories." RG 77 (Office of the Chief of Engineers), Q 392–2, NA.

Metlin, George. 1932. "Map of Beaverhead County, Montana." Montana Historical Society, Helena.

Peale, A. C. 1871. "Yellowstone Lake: Showing the Watershed of the Snake, Madison, and Yellowstone Rivers." Records of the General Land Office, RG 49, Montana State Office, 2–1, NA.

Index

Modern names for locations are used in the index

Earthquake Camp, 166–67, 273 n.18; at East Fork camp, 170; 1871 field journal, xvi; with exploration team, 131; exploration team tent for, 126; exploring with Schönborn, 97; at Fairy Falls, 146, 266 n.12; fishing at Medicine Lodge Creek, 191; to Flat Mountain, 157; at Fort Ellis, 111, 115, 179; at Fort Hall, 84; to Fort Hall, 193; government survey philosophy of, 5–6, 235 n.3; to Grand Canyon of the Yellowstone, 164; Grand Teton and, 209; on "Great West," 6, 235 n.4; at Horse Plain Creek Valley, 187; on igneous rock at Port Neuf River, 247 n.14; Indians' nickname for, 25, 240 n.2; Langford and, 13; on Lost Lake, 268 n.2; on earlier maps' inaccuracies, 249 n.21; mentoring Peale, 189, 190; misplaces barometer, 155; on monoclinal mountains, 79; mountain-climbing of, 169; at Mud Geyser, 139; names Locomotive Jet, 138; names Pope's Nose, 120; names Yellowstone Range, 136, 263 n.8; to Nez Percé Creek, 143–44, 265 n.3; north of Gardner River, 174; official reports of, xv; in Ogden, 63, 70; Old Faithful and, 149; and Peale explore railroad cuts, 200–202; as Peale's professor, 6; recruiting hunters/trappers, 92, 252 n.34; post-survey scientific work, 203–7; at Red Rock Creek, 189; reputation of, 5–6; role in park bill, 207–8; side-trip away from Yellowstone Lake by, 159, 272 n.9; on Snake River source, 271 n.6; at Soda Springs, 200; study with Allen by, 6; at Sulphur Spring, 140; Survey appointments of, 18; on Tetons origin, 249 n.26; on Three Tetons, 86; to Tower Falls, 132; at Twin Buttes, 266 n.8; at Twin Springs, 197; Upper Geyser Basin, 146–47; USGS and, 236 n.8; vision of, 7–8; wedding of, 204; at Yellowstone Lake camp, 150, 151, 152–54, 270 n.30; Yellowstone National Park and, 207–8, 210–11, 231–33, 281–82 n.17
Hayden, Mount, 209
Hayden Survey, 241 n.5; budget allocation objectives for, 14–15. See also 1871 Yellowstone Survey
Hayden Valley, 138, 143, 217, 263 n.11
Heap, David Porter, 18, 257 n.40; Chicago

fire and, 205; at Earthquake Camp, 166; Peale's description of, 121–22. See also Barlow, John
Heart Lake, 150, 157, 268 n.22, 271 n.5
Hedges, Cornelius, 237 n.24
hell fire stew, 146, 266 n.10
Henderson, A. Bart, 11–12, 236 n.22, 262 n.23, 274 n.8
Henry, Joseph, 21, 215
Henselbecker, Henry, 258 n.5, 261 n.23
Hergesheimer, E., 176
Highland (quartz) mine, 185
Hine, Thomas J., 247 n.40, 266 n.12
Holmes, Mount, 250 n.28
Holmes, William Henry, xx, 206, 250 n.28, 263 n.11
Hooper, W. H., 279 n.24
Hooper's Spring, 199
Horn, George Henry, 63, 238 n.38, 245 n.16
Horr, Harry R., 128, 260 n.15
Horse Plain Creek Valley, 187, 278 n.11
Hot Spring Creek, 104–5
hot springs, Yellowstone, Firehole Basin, 131, 224, 232
Hot Spring Station, 73
Hot Spring Valley, 230
Hovey, Stephen D., 19, 132, 140; biography of, 217; at Camp Hovey, 160, 161–62, 272 n.13; at Dry Creek, 191; at Earthquake Camp, 19; missing horses and, 72, 73, 170; trades for pony, 100; at Trail Creek, 120; at Yellowstone Lake, 156, 157, 159
Hubely, Ed, Peale letters to, 189, 190
Hudson's Bay Company's trading post, 248 n.18
Humphreys, Mount, 271 n.5
hunters, Survey, 19. See also Clark, Joe; food; José
Huse, Frederick J., 18, 20, 115, 179, 181; arrives at Camp Hovey, 162; Hayden's evaluation of, 177, 180; north of Gardner River, 174; ornithology study of, 45, 63, 70; on passenger train to Ogden, 46; at permanent camp, 125; at Spring Creek, 119
Hyde, William, 246 n.7
Hyde Park, Utah Territory, 75, 246 n.7
Hyrum (Hiram), Utah Territory, 75

Made in the USA
Middletown, DE
21 December 2022

19498759R00208